To Bob, Tom, and the entire CIRCE crowd—
A moment in time, fixed, transformed,
but never transcended

PROFESSIONAL EVALUATION

Social Impact and Political Consequences

Ernest R. House

SAGE Publications
International Educational and Professional Publisher
Newbury Park   London   New Delhi

For information address:

SAGE Publications, Inc.
2455 Teller Road
Newbury Park, California 91320

SAGE Publications Ltd.
6 Bonhill Street
London EC2A 4PU
United Kingdom

SAGE Publications India Pvt. Ltd.
M-32 Market
Greater Kailash I
New Delhi 110 048 India

Printed in the United States of America

Library of Congress Cataloging-in-Publication Data

House, Ernest R.
    Professional evaluation: social impact and political consequences
/ Ernest R. House.
      p.   cm.
    Includes bibliographical references and index.
    ISBN 0-8039-4995-2 (cloth).—ISBN 0-8039-4996-0 (pbk.)
    1. Evaluation research (Social action programs) 2. Evaluation—
Methodology. I. Title.
H62.H643 1993
361.6'1'068—dc20   92-39718

94 95 96 10 9 8 7 6 5 4 3 2

Sage Production Editor: Diane S. Foster

ૐ

Contents

ঈ

Introduction: Evaluation in Advanced Capitalist Society

Over the past three decades, evaluation has emerged as a formal field of practice, transformed from a sideline activity conducted by part-time academics into a minor profession. It has its own books, journals, awards, conferences, and standards. In North America alone, there are approximately 3,000 members in the American Evaluation Association and 1,500 in the Canadian Evaluation Society. Evaluation is expanding in many other countries as well. One can envision a time 50 years from now when evaluation of programs, policies, personnel, and products will be a much larger enterprise around the globe, playing a central role in decision making in many countries.

The major impetus to development in the United States was the evaluation mandate attached to the Great Society education legislation in 1965, a mandate that spread to other social programs and beyond. During this period of rapid development, evaluation also changed character (Chapter 1). Both the structural basis and conceptual underpinnings of the field have changed dramatically. Structurally, evaluation has become more integrated into organizational operations. Conceptually, it has moved from monolithic to pluralist notions, to multiple methods, criteria, measures, perspectives, audiences, and interests. The field became multidisciplinary, with separate traditions emerging from different disciplines. It also became too important to be left to the evaluators: Large bureaucracies developed their own internal evaluation offices.

Philosophically, evaluators ceased believing that their discipline was value-free. Politically, they saw that evaluation had political effects. Their early attempts to find definitive solutions to social problems proved to be a disappointing venture. Rather, the concepts of evaluation that evolved reflected the change from consensus to pluralism that was occurring in the larger society during this period. How to synthesize and resolve all these multiple multiples remained a formidable question for evaluation, and for the larger society as well.

The emergence of evaluation as a formal practice is a result of advanced capitalism (Chapter 2). Advanced capitalism breaks down the traditional institutions of society—the church, the family, and the local community. Traditional frameworks that always served as the basis for personal and public decisions become weakened. People migrate across vast distances in search of jobs, encounter others from different regions and backgrounds, and live in cities far removed from their family and friends. In this engulfing, confusing cultural mix, old values and traditions disappear. Yet there is still a need for decisions as to what to buy, what to do, how to live.

Governments face serious problems in governing such an amorphous mass of people. No longer bolstered by traditional institutions, governments must find new ways of legitimizing their actions. The main legitimation is to provide increasing material abundance for the population, but science is another basis for legitimizing and informing government actions. Evaluation is scientific authority applied to practical decisions and actions, particularly public decisions and actions. Governments, increasingly large, centralized, and removed from contact with citizens, often appeal to scientific authority, and answering this appeal is a role that formal evaluation plays. It is no accident that formal evaluation began in the most advanced capitalist countries.

Although governments are capable of making decisions based on their own political authority, it is easier to govern based on voluntary acceptance by the populace attained through persuasion, particularly when the populace is pluralistic and nontraditional. Formal evaluation, then, is a new form of cultural authority, cultural authority being manifested in the probability that descriptions of reality and judgments of value will prevail as valid, an increasingly difficult accomplishment in societies with disparate value systems. In practical terms, the government can say to antagonistic parties, "Look, we have subjected the situation to a fair determination of the facts and arrived at this decision objectively. What more can you ask?"

Given that there is a social need for evaluation, what shape has evaluation taken as a profession? Legitimation of professional authority involves three claims: that the knowledge and competence of the professional have been validated by a community of peers, that this consensually validated knowledge rests on scientific or scholarly grounds, and that professional judgment and advice are oriented toward important social values. In other words, a modern profession rests on collegial, cognitive, and moral authority. Evaluation has established itself as a profession in ways similar to those of the other professions—through university training, professional associations and journals, and official recognition.

Evaluation operates in a highly professionalized society formed by the increasing specialization of labor. Professional career hierarchies compete with each other for resources, with the state acting as mediator. The professional career is based on selection by merit and trained expertise and on human capital created by education and exclusion of the unqualified. University teaching itself has become a specialized profession that limits access, offers training, and conducts research for the other professions. One profession after another has transferred its training from apprenticeship to the university. In fact, the university has become the gatekeeper to the professional career hierarchies.

One important task of evaluators has been to help mediate the claims of the different professions, claims often embodied in social programs. In a sense, evaluators help governments determine resource allocations to professional groups by evaluating programs, although the goals of the programs are phrased in terms of benefits to clients or stakeholders. Evaluations are cast in social scientific arguments that other professionals recognize, including esoteric jargon and research terminology. The widening split between public professionals, who advocate more public expenditures on social programs, and private professionals, who advocate reduced government spending, is reflected in the evaluation community itself.

How evaluation develops in the future depends on how modern market societies develop. If these societies become more authoritarian—a distinct possibility in reaction to managing turbulent societies with sluggish economies—evaluation could be used for repressive purposes. On the other hand, if market societies become less ideological, then evaluation could become more useful. Whichever scenario occurs, it seems likely that central state power will increase substantially. Either governments must implement and legitimize unpopular programs and/or governments must make industries more competitive internationally, which means national industrial policies. In either case, the future for evaluators will be busy.

The relationship between government and evaluation is one in which evaluation is used to legitimize, inform, and sometimes control government activities (Chapter 3). Evaluation is an acceptable means of achieving guidance and compliance with government policies. Government, in turn, legitimizes evaluations by making them official. Set in a position between government and the professions, and itself a profession, evaluation often finds itself caught in conflicting demands. The "professional ideal" for evaluation, as for other professions, is one of service plus efficiency, but service and efficiency are not always compatible.

There are at least four different accountability/evaluation situations. On the one hand, professionals may be accountable to their own profession or to the public, either at the central or local levels. Different types of information produced by different forms of evaluation are suited to these different demands. Professional evaluation, such as that of doctors to other doctors or that of professors within their disciplines, is not the same as evaluation for the central government ministry. In fact, information from one type of evaluation often is misused at other levels of the state and the profession. Evaluation information for consumers is different yet again.

Evaluation takes place within particular authority structures and cultures. What works in one place may not work in another. In the United States, evaluation in government has been a blending of applied social science and economic decision making. Hundreds of evaluations are being conducted in the federal government at a cost of more than $100 million a year. Typically, federal evaluations are focused on the narrow goals of the program, rather than on broader issues and structures. Independent, critical evaluations are the exception. Not surprisingly, evaluations are relevant to the careers of high-level bureaucrats, who need to make their programs look good.

In Britain, government departments have commissioned studies for their own purposes, asserted ownership of the data, and controlled publication by requiring prior approval. The government has tried to install a culture of management modeled on the corporate sector in order to curtail the spending of local governments and the demands of professionals and unions. Professional authority is subsumed under managerial authority. Managerial evaluation, focused on efficiency and productivity under direct government control, has been attempted in many departments.

In Canada, each federal government department has its own evaluation unit, and evaluation is tied directly to the budget. The process for organizing evaluations is defined in detail by policies spelled out in government guides, and personnel inside the department ordinarily conduct the studies. The primary clients are deputy-heads of departments, who focus on program change and accountability. Relevance and practicality are critical concerns, and the timeline for studies is short. Evaluation is not conceived as something done by a questioning third party.

In recent years, evaluation has been tied to managerialism in many countries, in attempts to improve economic productivity and management, and to control sectors of society. As economies falter and governments lose legitimacy, evaluation has been a tool for informing and legitimizing the actions that governments must take, particularly budget cutting. In performing this role, evaluation has taken different forms in different countries. Underlying these events are fundamental conflicts between professionals and managers.

These conflicts are increasingly manifested in the higher education system, the stronghold of professional knowledge and legitimation (Chapter 4). In many countries, governments have curtailed funding for and increased control over university functions, even research. The research university, first established at the University of Berlin in 1810, has the unusual task of producing research as well as educating people for the professions. Knowledge production requires a very particular culture that provides the basis for the disciplines themselves, a culture not well understood by the outside world.

The university protects this research culture by employing professional review procedures. A typical departmental evaluation consists of a committee internal to the unit under review, another committee of peers from outside the unit, and yet a third committee composed of disciplinary colleagues from outside the university, who provide the judgment of the discipline. These committees embody balancing perspectives and criteria. However, such procedures do not provide information that higher education governing boards want. Such boards are interested in comparative statistics and are driven toward quantitative indicators as means of judging quality and cutting costs. There is a conflict between managerial and professional concerns.

The peculiar culture and structure of the scholarly disciplines raises the question as to whether evaluation itself is a discipline

(Chapter 5). Some contend that real disciplines, such as physics, have agreed-upon sets of ideals against which work in the field may be compared by those in the disciplinary community. Intellectual and factional disputes are settled by reference to these established ideals. Using this criterion, evaluation is not a discipline, nor are the social sciences. However, this criterion of total agreement on ideals within the field is somewhat extreme.

Other criteria for a discipline might include the degree to which the basic concepts in the field are "joined" and the degree to which the social structure of the discipline promotes internal critical review. There is a contrast among physics, evaluation, and policy studies. Policy science is not a discipline, by these criteria, because internal criticism is factional or haphazard, compared to physics or psychology. Evaluation is a discipline, or nearly a discipline, because it is possible to have correct and incorrect evaluations. There is enough agreement in the field to make such judgments about most evaluations. However, the most important feature is not whether people agree on ideals but whether issues can be productively discussed and debated. The successful critique of studies is an important indicator of the joining of issues that characterizes a discipline.

Evaluation also has, or is close to having, a social structure that supports internal critique and dialogue. A discipline is composed of groups and subgroups of scholars linked together through common communication: journals, meetings, associations, informal contacts, e-mail. The boundaries overlap with other disciplines, so that some scholars are in two different disciplines. At the center are the leading authorities, who act as gatekeepers for new ideas. The discipline changes as people in the field argue and debate ideas.

This authority is not democratic. People do not vote on whether something is valid. Nor is the system authoritarian, even though the leading authorities carry on the debate. Rather, the process of decision is one of deliberation and argumentation until a consensus is reached. All concepts are subject to change over a period of time, so there is no certain foundation of knowledge, just the continual debate, dialogue, and argument, the disciplinary discourse. The discourse itself is the center of the discipline. And if it is disciplinary, it must be a discourse in which the issues can be joined.

U.S. evaluation inherited many key ideas from the social sciences, which developed in the United States in the late 19th and early 20th centuries (Chapter 6). U.S. social science was shaped by a deep-seated belief in U.S. exceptionality. From the beginning of colonization, America represented something exceptional, and this idea of exceptionality was woven into the national identity, so that most Americans still think their country is not subject to the same social and historical forces as other countries. Rather, the United States is destined to have a greater, happier future. The explanation for this optimism has been that the lack of a hereditary aristocracy, the establishment of a republican form of government, and endless economic opportunities made the United States exceptional. In particular, the United States would not have the mass poverty and social classes so characteristic of other countries.

A major intellectual task of the founding social scientists was to reconcile their exceptionalist beliefs about the United States with the enormous historical changes taking place in the country as a result of industrialism, a monumental transformation from agrarian, yeoman society. To accommodate the exceptionalist ideology and make sense of the actual U.S. experience that was unfolding, the social sciences came to be based on a model of the natural sciences, which evolved into a form of scientism—the view that the inductive methods of the natural sciences are the only source of factual knowledge and that only such methods can yield knowledge about nature and society.

In this view, the main purpose of the social sciences was the technocratic manipulation of nature and society for the betterment of humankind. Each social science discipline developed differently, but radical ideas were expunged so that each conformed to mainstream ideology. Economics and sociology were particularly hard hit by charges of radicalism in the early years. This scientism eventually contributed to ideologies in evaluation—separatism, positivism, managerialism, and relativism—that the field is freeing itself from only now.

After World War II, the liberal ideological consensus in the United States included beliefs that economic productivity could be improved forever, that an inherent harmony of interests existed among social groups, and that there was no need for poverty or social classes (Chapter 7). Poverty and social classes had ceased to exist, or would soon. Social problems could be solved, like engineering problems, by the application of resources and intelligence. Evaluation could determine which programs maximized the desired outcomes.

By the 1960s, this national ideological consensus began fragmenting. Different groups asserted different interests. Many groups protested, and civil disobedience became routine. This social discord led political scientists to develop the pluralist-elitist-equilibrium model of democracy, in which group leaders bargain with other leaders for their constituencies, with the government acting as referee. Similarly, evaluators developed the stakeholder model of evaluation, in which the negotiated interests, perspectives, and criteria of stakeholder groups are included in the evaluation. Although the stakeholder model was a substantial improvement over the previous technocratic model, which had assumed there were no conflicts of interests, problems still exist with the stakeholder model itself. The interests of the poor and powerless usually are not represented in the evaluation.

Nor does precision of research method guarantee the fairness and justice of evaluation studies (Chapter 8). For example, in the 19th-century field of craniometry, the leading scientists used careful, precise methods to prove that the brains of white males were larger than those of females and other races, thus confirming the obvious knowledge (to them) that white males were more intelligent. Craniometry was never able to overcome the pervasive ideology of its own era, in spite of the precision of its methods.

Twentieth-century evaluation methods are much more sophisticated, but the possibility remains that such methods may contain subtle biases that lead to injustices. In fact, the dominant theory of causation is a likely candidate for such distortion. The regularity theory of causation leads to expectations for social programs that these programs cannot meet and to evaluation designs that yield wrong answers. Because many programs are programs for the poor, powerless, and disadvantaged, injustice is sometimes the result.

One of the most difficult problems that any pluralist society faces is how to incorporate different cultural groups (Chapter 9). Ethnic and nationalist conflicts abound. Nationalism remains a potent force in the world, even as societies become multicultural. In fact, nationalism—the idea that political boundaries should coincide with ethnic boundaries and that one ethnic group should not be ruled by another—is a relatively recent phenomenon, first traceable to the North and South American colonial revolts. In these nationalist outbursts, led by the upper and middle classes, blocked access to careers and positions played a central role. Language as the medium of jobs and status was also an important concern. These problems of multicultural societies translate directly into problems for evaluation, such as what criteria to employ in evaluating programs, which stakeholders to include in the evaluation, and how to balance the various ethnic interests in drawing conclusions.

One resolution is to conceive cultural membership as a primary good, necessary for self-respect and personal identity. One's culture provides the context for individual choices and for exploring and evaluating life options. Hence, minority cultures have the right to maintain themselves, as long as they do not violate the individual liberties of their members. On the other hand, although individuals are entitled to their cultural identity, they should be able to opt out of their own culture if they choose. In circumstances in which the existence of the minority culture is threatened, the culture's interest may take priority over those of other groups.

What does this mean for evaluators? Evaluators should search for and define the views of minority groups if those groups are stakeholders in the program being evaluated. In most cases, these particular interests will not be at issue, but if they are, then the evaluator has an obligation to give them special consideration. In other words, not all group interests should be weighted equally in all circumstances. This position contrasts with that of the standard stakeholder evaluation, in which minority groups receive no more consideration than other groups. The standard stakeholder view results in the majority culture prevailing, even on issues that are vital to the minority culture.

Finally, evaluators face particular ethical problems (Chapter 10). They exercise special powers that can injure self-esteem, damage reputations, and stunt careers. On the other hand, evaluators are themselves vulnerable to people awarding future work. Some people are powerful within the evaluators' career realm. Also, evaluators come from the same social classes and educational backgrounds as the people who sponsor the evaluations and whose programs are being evaluated. These circumstances create ethical difficulties.

Codes of professional standards and ethics have been developed for evaluators, and in these codes, evaluators are urged to forge a written contract with the sponsor and adhere to that contract, being aware of how conflicts of interest may be involved. Openness, full disclosure, and release of information are ways of dealing with ethical problems. The rights of subjects are understood to limit full disclosure, and informed consent of subjects must be obtained. Mutual agreement among evaluators, sponsors, and subjects is emphasized. The fundamental notion is that of contractual ethics: the establishment of a voluntary contract as the basis for conduct.

General principles suggested for guiding ethical decisions in evaluation include beneficence, respect, and justice; also, mutual respect, non-coercion and non-manipulation, and support for democratic values and institutions. Even when evaluators endorse the same principles, however, there can be reasonable disagreement as to how principles are applied. Some of the most intractable ethical problems arise from conflicts among principles and the necessity of trading off one principle against another. The balancing of such principles in concrete situations is the ultimate ethical act.

Several ethical mistakes occur so frequently that they deserve the label of ethical fallacies. These include clientism (taking the client's interests as the ultimate consideration), contractualism (adhering inflexibly to the contract), managerialism (placing the interests of the managers above all else), methodologicalism (believing that proper methodology solves all ethical problems), pluralism/elitism (including only the powerful stakeholders' interests in the evaluation), and relativism (taking all viewpoints as having equal merit).

In conclusion, evaluation is a powerful social force that has emerged only recently in advanced capitalist societies, a new institution that promises to be a major influence over the long term. Its influence can be both good and bad. Society before formal evaluation is not the same as society afterward. Evaluation has been shaped and continues to be shaped by powerful and complex social forces. Exactly what shape the institution, profession, discipline, and practice will take in the future is impossible to predict. What is clear is that the fate of evaluation will be bound to the government and the economic structure and will be determined in part by its own history and traditions. Part of the destiny of evaluation lies within the control of evaluators themselves; part does not.

❧ *1* ❧

Trends

*W*hen I began a career in evaluation more than 25 years ago, I tossed all the papers I could find about the topic into a small cardboard box in the corner of my office and read them in one month. Since that time, evaluation has been transformed from a small sideline activity conducted by part-time academics into a professionalized minor industry, replete with its own journals, awards, conventions, organizations, and standards. Evaluation even has its own entry in the *Harper Dictionary of Modern Thought* (Bullock, Stallybrass, & Trombley, 1988). During this time both the structural basis and the conceptual underpinnings of the field have changed dramatically. Structurally, evaluation has become more integrated into organizational operations, and conceptually, evaluation has moved from monolithic to pluralist notions, to multiple methods, criteria, and interests.

Evaluation is usually defined as the determination of the worth or value of something—in this case, of educational and social programs, policies, and personnel—judged according to appropriate criteria, with those criteria explicated and justified (Scriven, 1991). At its best, the evaluation of educational and social programs aspires to be an institution for democratizing public decisions by making programs and policies more open to public scrutiny and deliberation. As such, evaluation should serve the interests not only of the sponsor but also of the larger society and of diverse groups within society. Of course, evaluation has not always lived up to its own noble aspirations.

Thanks to Steve Lapan and Ken Howe for comments on earlier drafts.

1

❧ Structural Changes

The strongest stimulus to development was Lyndon Johnson's Great Society legislation, which, though not capable of changing U.S. society as a whole, certainly transformed educational and social research. At Senator Robert Kennedy's insistence, the Elementary and Secondary Education Act of 1965 mandated evaluation of programs for disadvantaged students, and this mandate spread to all social programs and beyond (McLaughlin, 1975). Before 1965, evaluation in education meant testing or curriculum evaluation and a handful of measurement people struggling to come to grips with the import of the "new curricula." After 1965, the field resembled the early California gold camps, with large numbers of individuals from many disciplines straggling in to offer their ideas about how evaluation should be done. In addition to measurement specialists, there were psychologists, sociologists, economists, administrators, and even a few philosophers. Although the field was dominated initially by a psychometric view of research, a new brew of people, ideas, and problems simmered.

The field became multidisciplinary, with separate traditions and multiple histories of development. Educational evaluators usually start their historical accounts with Ralph Tyler; psychologists, with Donald Campbell; and sociologists, with Edward Suchman. Previous experience with testing and curriculum evaluation gave educational evaluators a head start, and they have been among the most influential theorists in the melded evaluation field, an unusual accomplishment for researchers in education, who rarely are accorded equal status with social scientists. However, all the constituent fields have contributed seminal work.

From this strange mélange, several major schools of evaluation emerged: Illinois, with its long experience in measurement and curriculum evaluation; Northwestern, with its strong experimental design; Western Michigan, with its focus on decision making; UCLA, with the federal research and development center; and Stanford, with a cross-disciplinary effort. Projects multiplied, evaluation models proliferated, and new organizations came into being. The evaluation field lived in intellectual and entrepreneurial ferment for more than a decade—until the cuts in social programs. The Reagan years brought fewer opportunities for evaluation, and the field of evaluation entered a more sober existence, distinct from the "gold rush" days.

During the quiet decade of the 1980s, other transformations became apparent as well. Evaluation had become too important to be left to the evaluators, and large bureaucracies developed their own internal evaluation offices. Not only large school districts and state departments of education but also organizations such as the Federal Bureau of Investigation (FBI), the Food and Drug Administration (FDA), and the General Accounting Office (GAO) hired internal evaluation staffs. These internal units posed novel questions of credibility and procedure, for evaluation theory had been constructed on the basis of contractual relationships between a sponsoring organization and external evaluators. To whom are the internal evaluators responsible? How public should their work be? What scientific controls are suitable? A new set of issues emerged as the structural base of the field shifted.

In addition, school reforms initiated by state governments brought a renewed emphasis on standardized achievement testing and performance indicators for purposes of centralized accountability. Increasingly, tests were employed as instruments of discipline rather than of diagnosis. William Bennett's "Wall Chart" became a report card for the nation's schools, without benefit of research design. Interpretation of test results became overtly political, with ideology supplying the putative causes for educational decline or resurgence. The curriculum itself began reflecting what the tests emphasized. Evaluators, who thought they had moved beyond test scores as the sole criterion of success, were faced with more testing than before. Similar trends became apparent with performance indicators in other social areas and in other countries (Henkel, 1991; see Chapter 3).

ᶻᵃ Conceptual Changes

Between 1965 and 1990 the methodology, philosophy, and politics of evaluation changed substantially, partly in response to the structural transformations. Evaluation moved from monolithic to pluralist conceptions, to multiple methods, multiple measures, multiple criteria, multiple perspectives, multiple audiences, and even multiple interests. Methodologically, evaluation moved from a primary emphasis on quantitative methods, in which the standardized achievement test employed in a randomized experimental control group design was most highly regarded, to a more permissive atmosphere in which qualitative research methods were acceptable. Mixed data collection methods are advocated routinely now in a spirit of methodological ecumenicalism. And having achieved legitimacy within the evaluation community, qualitative evaluators began quarreling among themselves.

Philosophically, evaluators ceased believing their discipline was value-free and realized their practice entailed promoting the values and interests of some groups over others, though evaluators were by no means clear what to do about this discovery. They struggled with the seemingly conflicting demands of being scientific on the one hand and being useful on the other. Politically, evaluators moved from a position in which they saw themselves as technical experts opposed to the evils of politics to a position in which they admitted evaluation itself had political effects. And these conceptual changes were stimulated by the rapidly evolving social context, as the United States itself changed character.

Following World War II, the United States achieved a preeminence in world affairs that rarely had been matched in history. In what Hodgson (1978) has called the "ideology of the liberal consensus," Americans believed that their free enterprise system had a revolutionary potential for social justice; that the economy could produce enough for everyone so that conflict between social classes, and indeed social classes themselves, could be eliminated; and that social problems could be solved like industrial problems. The problem would be identified, solutions would be generated by government (enlightened by social science), resources would be applied, and the problem would be solved. The key to this revolutionary system was ever-increasing economic productivity, which could provide enough for all.

In early formulations, evaluation was assigned the task of discovering which programs worked best, such as the Elementary and Secondary Education Act, Head Start, and Follow Through. Most evaluators thought social science would point to the clear causes of social problems and to interventions for overcoming these problems, that these interventions would be implemented and evaluated in ways that provided unambiguous answers, that these findings would be greeted enthusiastically by managers and policy makers, and that the problems would be solved. They were disappointed on all counts (Cook & Shadish, 1986).

The methodology for best accomplishing this task was deemed to be the experiment, lauded in seminal works: "This chapter is committed to the experiment: as the only means for settling disputes regarding educational practice, as the only way of verifying educational improvements" (Campbell & Stanley, 1963, p. 2). And this rationale for strong designs was carried forward in federal policy, leading to what Scriven (1983) has called the doctrines of managerialism and positivism. That is, studies were conducted for the benefit of managers of programs, and evaluators acted as value-neutral scientists who relied upon the methods of the social sciences to protect against biases. Evaluations were primarily experimental, quasi-experimental, or survey in methodology, utilizing quantitative outcome measures to meet the demand for surrogate measures of economic growth.

ᐓ Mixed Methods and the Unraveling of Consensus

Evaluators soon encountered many problems in these large-scale quantitative studies that were unexpected and not easily surmounted. Programs varied from one site to another, so that a program that performed well on one site did not do well on another, such as Follow Through. Statistical models overadjusted or underadjusted, such as analysis of covariance. Participants squabbled among themselves about the purposes of the program. Tests suited for measuring the outcomes of one program were not appropriate for another program. And, not least, most of the reform programs did not have powerful effects. The evaluations proved far more equivocal in providing definitive answers than anticipated. All in all, discovering solutions to social problems was considerably more difficult than originally envisioned.

Furthermore, the social consensus began unraveling. Martin Luther King, Jr., who began his civil rights crusade as a devout affirmation of the American dream, ended his life in disillusionment and assassination in 1968. Dissident groups marched in the streets, not only for civil rights and against the Vietnam War but also for feminism, black power, gay liberation, and ecology. The national economy staggered, with median family income reaching a peak in 1973, decreasing 6% by 1984, and becoming more unequal in distribution (Levy, 1987). Something was wrong, even with the economic pie. What had begun as an era of social consensus dissolved into an age of conflict and diversity.

This unraveling was reflected in evaluation. If diverse groups wanted different things, then collecting the views of people in and around the programs made sense. Qualitative methodology useful for obtaining the views of participants became popular. Qualitative methods had been employed in anthropology and sociology but had been deemed too subjective for use in program evaluation. Led by evaluators such as Robert Stake at Illinois and Barry MacDonald at East Anglia, qualitative methodology developed a following, a practice, and eventually research rationales. At the same time, many evaluators remained committed to quantitative methods as the methods of choice, and the battles between quantitative and qualitative advocates were hard fought (Boruch & Riecken, 1975; Eisner, 1979). After considerable dispute, a rapprochement ensued in which most theorists advocated mixed methods (Cronbach, 1982a).

So, the quantitative or qualitative distinction is still a major mark of identity for evaluators. In contrasting 14 evaluation theorists, Williams (1989) found that the major theoretical issue on which they were differentiated was "Qualitative versus Quantitative Methodology." The second dimension was "Accountability versus Policy Orientation," distinguished by whether evaluation should be used to judge programs and personnel to hold them accountable or should be used to inform stakeholders. The third dimension was "Client Participation versus Non-Participation," which referred to how and whether clients should participate in the evaluation.

The methodology debate, now 20 years old, eventually spread to issues other than legitimacy, such as whether different methods are commensurable. Some theorists saw quantitative and qualitative methods as different ways of viewing the world, whereas others saw the different methods as compatible (Guba & Lincoln, 1989; Smith, 1983). Most evaluators accepted the view that quantitative and qualitative methods are complementary, if not fully commensurable, though no one has shown how disparate methods can be melded. A related issue is what standards are appropriate for qualitative studies and whether standards can be general ones or must be derived from parent disciplines (Howe & Eisenhart, 1990).

Accompanying these disputes is conflict over the nature of causation itself. Cronbach (1982a) challenged the standard conception of causation, arguing that social phenomena are far less predictable than the standard formulation would imply and that traditional notions of internal and external validity must be redefined in such a way that people using evaluation findings should make their own judgments as to the utility of the information. In his view, external validity is partially dependent on the users' judgments in context and is more important than internal validity. House (1991c) extended the re-analysis of causation yet further, challenging some basic evaluation concepts. These ideas had yet to make their way through evaluation. Most textbooks, for example, were based on the old concepts.

ૐ Utilization, Values, and Politics

Another area of interest has been utilization of findings. The idea that program managers would readily accept the findings of evaluations and adjust or terminate their programs accordingly was not supported by the course of events. Debate has raged as to what extent findings are ever used, with Weiss (1988) contending that "instrumental" uses, which are revisions of programs as a direct result of the evaluation, rarely occur. She asserted that "enlightenment," in which results are incorporated gradually into the users' overall frame of reference, is the manner in which findings are used, if at all. On the other side, Patton (1988) argued strongly for the viability of instrumental use and that findings will be used if properly presented. Some of these differences may derive from the level of government at which attention is focused. Changes seem to come irregularly at the federal level, in line with political and ideological considerations, whereas utilization in local school districts seems to be more instrumental (Smith, 1989). One issue on which evaluators do agree is that if evaluations are to be useful, they must provide better descriptions of the programs and their context.

An emerging idea is that of misuse of findings. The original debate concerned use and non-use of evaluation results. However, results from poorly conceived studies frequently have been given wide publicity, and findings from good studies have been used improperly. Alkin (1990) introduced a taxonomy of misuse of evaluation results in which use and misuse lie on opposite ends of a scale, with non-use in the center. The fact that so much standardized achievement testing is reported to the public in general and its interpretation left to the media or government officials makes misuse particularly salient. In fact, the professional standards for evaluation, developed by a committee led by Stufflebeam, devoted considerable space to issues of misuse, but the context in which evaluation results are presented does not lend itself to the employment of such standards, even though the standards are widely accepted in the evaluation community itself (Joint Committee, 1981). How misuse can be curtailed is by no means clear.

Increasing social conflict also has pushed the problem of values into prominence. Where do the values come from in an evaluation? The act of public evaluation requires that criteria of merit be established and that these criteria be justified. Typically, stated program goals have served as the source of criteria, with the evaluator assessing whether the program has met its goals. Furthermore, by taking the program manager as the client for the evaluation, the evaluator could act on what was important to the manager. However, several theorists challenged this acceptance of managerial goals as the basis for evaluation, and Scriven (1980) in particular worked out the logic of evaluation in general terms, contending that "Is X good (bad, indifferent)?" and its variants ("How good is X?" "Is X better than Y?") are the prototypical evaluative questions and that answering these questions requires identifying and validating standards of merit for X in addition to discovering X's performance on dimensions that are merit-related. According to this reasoning, the program goals themselves must be assessed. For example, a responsible evaluator would not accept General Motors' goal that the best car is the one that earns the highest profit as the criterion for evaluating cars.

This general logic still leaves open the question of where the particular criteria of merit come from. One can say in general that criteria are derived from what is appropriate for things of its kind. For example, one would not say that an educational program that warped personality and retarded intellectual growth was a good educational program, regardless of whether the developers wanted these effects. Given a particular entity in a particular context, criteria of merit can be justified. The fruit of this reasoning is that evaluative judgments are not arbitrary, any more than is a descriptive statement that an elephant is large compared to other animals but small compared to an office building.

Of course, the social world is not simple. For complex entities such as educational and social programs, there are multiple and often conflicting criteria of merit. There is immediate retention versus long-term recall, knowledge of facts versus critical thinking, or more history versus more math. Furthermore, people do not always want the same things from public programs. People's values and, in fact, their interests differ. A program good for one group may not be good for another. And for the practicing evaluator there is no choice but to make a choice of criteria of merit.

Many choose the traditional measures of performance and achievement, believing that those best reflect overall interests. Others contend that clients and program participants should be enlisted in defining what is important for the evaluation, by soliciting opinions from them, by attending to them as audiences, or even by engaging them in the conduct of the study itself. Multiple criteria, multiple perspectives, multiple audiences, multiple interests—pluralist conceptions, reflecting the change from consensus to pluralism that occurred in the larger society.

Of course, having multiple criteria does not solve the problem of how to combine these multiplicities into overall judgments. How does one put together the results of different methodologies, for example? How does one combine several perspectives? How does one adjudicate conflicting group interests? On these issues there is little agreement. Some evaluators believe they themselves should make these judgments; others suggest that they should only present the findings and have the various audiences make their own judgments; and still others propose ways of resolving conflicting interests by invoking techniques such as cost-effectiveness analysis (Levin, 1983), by appealing to procedures such as negotiated agreements, or by employing explicit theories of justice (House, 1980).

Over the years evaluation has come to be seen as political. That is, it is influenced by political forces and, in turn, has political effects. Whose interests are served and how interests are represented in an evaluation are critical concerns. In the early days it was assumed that the interests of all parties were properly reflected in the traditional outcome measures, but this assumption came to be questioned, and it was recognized that different groups might have different interests and might be differentially affected by the program and its evaluation. "Stakeholders" (those who had a stake in the program under review) became a common concept, and representing stakeholder views in the evaluation became an accepted practice.

The stakeholder concept is based on the prevailing pluralist-elitist-equilibrium theory of democracy, which disclaims any normative judgments and which holds that the current system of competing parties and pressure groups performs the democratic function of equilibrating the diverse and shifting political demands (MacPherson, 1987). It is believed that describing what others value is the stance best suited to the political context in which evaluators operate, because decision making depends on the values held by relevant policy makers and stakeholders. Presumably, these parties will use the findings to make informed decisions. Neither the government nor the evaluator is supposed to intervene to support any particular interests but rather only to provide information that is value-neutral and interest-neutral. The interests of various groups somehow dissolve into the values of decision makers and stakeholders.

The stakeholder approach has definite limitations, however. For example, in two highly visible stakeholder evaluations funded by the federal government, those of Cities-in-Schools and Jesse Jackson's PUSH/Excel program, the evaluations worked against the interests of the program participants and the inner-city students the programs were supposed to serve, thus calling into question the justice of these evaluations (House, 1988; Stake, 1986). The results of the PUSH/ Excel evaluation were used not only to discredit the program but also to question Jackson's ability to manage large enterprises during ensuing presidential campaigns. In fact, stakeholders do not have equal power to influence and utilize the evaluation, nor do they have equal protection from the evaluation.

The problem of multiple interests and how they should be represented in the evaluation takes one into the realm of social justice. Although the reality of multiple stakeholders who have legitimate and sometimes conflicting interests is recognized, how these interests should be adjudicated remains unresolved. The practice of describing various interests in a neutral fashion seems inadequate, and the fact that much evaluation activity has moved inside the large organizations, subject to bureaucratic authority, adds new pressures. The critical political question remains: Whose interests does the evaluation serve?

ᔊ Summary

Evaluation originally developed as a strategy to find grand solutions to social problems, but this proved to be a disappointing and chastening venture. The initial ideological consensus was that solutions to educational problems could be discovered by using the proper methodology, which usually meant quantitative outcome measures employed in experimental, quasi-experimental, or survey designs. All group interests were assumed to be represented in the traditional measures of performance. It was also assumed that program managers and policy makers would enthusiastically accept the results of evaluations for the purposes of program revision and termination. None of these presumptions proved to be correct.

As the social consensus fragmented, evaluators turned to qualitative methods to record the views of participants and clients, the stakeholders. Gradually, evaluators recognized that there were different interests to be served in an evaluation and that some of these interests might conflict with one another. The result was pluralist conceptions of evaluation in which multiple methods, measures, criteria, perspectives, audiences, and interests were recognized. Conceptually, evaluation moved from monolithic to pluralist conceptions, reflecting the pluralism that had emerged in the larger society. How to synthesize, resolve, and adjudicate all these multiple multiples remains a formidable question, as indeed it does for the larger society. Evaluation, which was invented to solve social problems, was ultimately afflicted with many of the problems it was meant to solve.

2

Evaluation as an
Institution and Profession

*W*hy do we have formal evaluation? In this chapter, I discuss evaluation as an institution, as a set of social practices like banking or schooling, and I characterize it as a profession, compared to other professions. I explain evaluation as a development of advanced capitalist society, as an attempt to use the authority of science to legitimate and inform government actions in societies in which the traditional institutions have lost much of their legitimating power. Evaluation itself is a new profession that has followed a developmental pattern similar to that of the other professions, and it operates in highly professionalized societies. In fact, one of its functions is to help adjudicate the claims of the other professions. Finally, I suggest what the future might bring for evaluation, based on these considerations.

To analyze the broad institutional aspects of evaluation, one must think long-term, of patterns that occur over 10, 20, 50, or even 100 years. One group that excels at such long-range thinking is the Annales school of history, which has been extremely influential from its home base in France. Traditional history has rested on belief in the importance of individual actor-heroes and the influence of dramatic events. Annales historians, by contrast, have tried to uncover the impersonal forces that shape what humans do over longer,

This chapter is based on a speech presented to the Southeast Evaluation Association, Tallahassee, Florida, January 23, 1991. I want to thank Meredith Pappagiannis for posing questions as a basis for the original talk and Nigel Norris, Ove Karlsson, and Rob McBride for comments on earlier drafts.

slower rhythms of time (Clark, 1985; Lloyd, 1986). Fernand Braudel, one of the leading historians of the 20th century, divides historical time into three units of varying duration, according to the rate at which change occurs (Braudel, 1980).

First, there is the fast-moving time of individual actors engaged in events—"micro-history." Second, there is the time of broad movements of social structures, economies, and institutions—time spans of 5, 10, 20, or 50 years that Braudel calls "conjunctures." Finally, there is the time span of "the long duration," *la longue dureé*, which requires the perspective of centuries to detect any change at all. During these very long time periods, humans interact with the environment to produce patterns of human movement and settlement, and even changes in the environment itself. According to Annales historians, short-term events, the subject of traditional history, are constituted by the influence of many different long-term structural forces. These long-term structures strongly influence what individual actors do.[1]

In his masterpiece, *The Mediterranean and the Mediterranean World in the Age of Philip II*, Braudel (1972, 1974) begins with the geography and climate of the region, discussing the mountains, plains, and plateaus of the Mediterranean peninsulas, then the seas and coasts, then the natural boundaries of the Mediterranean region—the Sahara, Alps, and Atlantic—then the land and sea routes, and then the towns and cities within. Halfway though the first volume, he discusses the global economy of the region, trade, and transport. In the second volume Braudel analyzes the empires and the two great civilizations, the Christian and Moslem, followed by the technical nature of the warfare of the period.

Not until page 904 does he arrive at events, politics, and people in the traditional style of narrative history. In Braudel's view, he has traced the history of humans in relation to the environment; followed the "history of gentle rhythms, of groupings and regroupings" of economies, states, and societies in broad perspective; and, finally, arrived at the traditional history of individual humans in particular events—geographic time, social time, and individual time (Braudel, 1972, p. 20). The *longue dureé*, the "conjuncture," and the "event" fitted into one another. In Braudel's view, history is quite complex and must be conceived as composed of overlapping series, somewhat like overlapping transparencies merged to produce a composite picture, or separate patterns of ocean waves combining together to produce new patterns.

> Our problem now is to imagine and locate the correlations between the rhythms of material life and the other diverse fluctuations of

human existence. For there is no single conjuncture: we must visualize a series of overlapping histories, developing simultaneously. It would be too simple, too perfect, if this complex truth could be reduced to the rhythms of one dominant pattern. . . . If we propose to use the economy in order to locate the chain of causality stretching back into the past, we may be obliged to handle ten or twenty possible languages—and as many causal chains. (1972, pp. 892-893)

In his later work, *Civilization and Capitalism*, Braudel (1981, 1982, 1984) traces the development of capitalism from the 15th to the 18th centuries, not in terms of individual actors such as politicians or kings, but rather in terms of the development of capitalist institutions over centuries. He begins with the size and disposition of populations in the 15th century and their food, clothing, houses, weapons, money, and technology—in short, the material basis of everyday life. Next, he explores processes of exchange: fairs, markets, merchants, trade circuits, transport, colonialism, banking, companies, monopoly, social hierarchies, and the evolving state.

Finally, he shows how simple local markets, places where goods were exchanged, became linked with other marketplaces through improved transportation, which promoted the growth of large cities, which dominated their hinterlands, and from which gradually evolved credit and money systems, banking institutions, and, eventually, multinational corporations operating in a single world market, fueled by the transfer and infusion of capital motivated by profit. Braudel's history of capitalism covers 400 years.

Now this is a long journey, indeed: 3 volumes and 1992 pages. I will not pursue the development of evaluation quite so far, but I do want to use the longer time frame, especially the middle framework, as a guide for thinking about evaluation as an institution. I would like to portray evaluation as having a changing institutional structure, with the institution slowly evolving over long periods of time. The institution is influenced by a large number of causal forces, which shape it in various ways. In turn, evaluation has causal effects on other aspects of society.

A more typical approach is to study the development of evaluation as the evolution of the ideas of well-known theorists over short durations. That is certainly a worthwhile endeavor, but such a study is really evaluation theory. Evaluation itself is something much larger and more diffuse, the entire practice, institution, and profession of evaluation, and not simply what is written about it. Noting that evaluators have devoted little attention to the institutional structure of evaluation, and how difficult it is to examine such issues, Levitan (1992) commented:

> Institutional aspects relating to evaluation should not be ignored because the institutional arrangements for evaluations frequently drive substantive decisions and the methodology used. . . . The purpose that evaluation serves, the way it is done, and the manner in which evaluation findings are incorporated into policy are directly affected by the way the evaluation is structured. (p. 43)

❧ Emergence of Evaluation as an Institution

Prior to 1965, evaluation was a minor activity, a sideline engaged in by academics as extra consulting work. Then came the Great Society legislation in the United States. With the passage of the Elementary and Secondary Education Act of 1965, everything changed. Senator Robert Kennedy insisted that an evaluation amendment be attached to the education bill, and evaluation became a federal mandate that spread to other social programs (McLaughlin, 1975). In North America alone, there are two large national evaluation associations, one in the United States and one in Canada; six or so major journals; more books on evaluation than one could ever read; plus training curricula in many universities. The field has expanded in size, complexity, and diversity. In fact, sometimes it seems as though there is no end to evaluation. Furthermore, evaluation activities are increasing in many other countries as well.

Why? Why do we have so much formal evaluation where there used to be so little? Was this field simply the whim of a politician? Well, no. We live in the most advanced capitalist societies in the world. Advanced capitalism breaks down traditional social structures, traditional bases of legitimation, and traditional ways of making decisions. A political economist has said:

> characteristic of a market economy is a tendency to incorporate every aspect of society into the nexus of market relations. Through such "commercialization," the market generally brings all facets of traditional society into the orbit of the price mechanism. . . . everything has its price, and . . . its value is its price. As a consequence, markets have a profound and destabilizing impact on a society because they dissolve traditional structures and social relations. (Gilpin, 1987, p. 20)

Under capitalism, society becomes reordered into a dynamic economic core, which contains advanced levels of technology and intense economic development, and a dependent periphery, which employs less advanced technology. As the dynamic core expands and develops, new secondary cores arise in the periphery, and these developments have profound consequences for the organization of societies and the lives of the people who live in them (Gilpin, 1987). As new economic growth centers emerge, people move there to secure jobs, away from their origins, away from their families and communities, even away from their native countries, away from the traditional institutions that have provided unquestioned frameworks for their lives.

Great masses of people migrate, from farms to cities, from one region to another, from one country to another, across continents and oceans. New multicultural countries are formed. Countries that once were culturally homogeneous become multicultural, mixing races, ethnicities, religions, and ideas. Exhausted by trying to eke out a living on a dirt-poor farm in Missouri, or having lost one's job at the steel mill in Pennsylvania (both the farm and the mill marginalized by market forces), people pick up their possessions and move to Florida or California looking for work. There they encounter a different world and a cacophony of sights, sounds, and ideas dissimilar from their origins.

These migrants are far removed from the support structures of their upbringing. Dr. Spock's advice on how to raise children was not necessary when Grandma was around, living in the extra room and providing more advice and help than wanted. Self-help books, voluntary associations, religious cults, and even a highly developed culture of romance promising intimacy to isolated individuals (all commercialized for market distribution) promise security, comfort, and identity. Such are the difficulties of the individual in advanced capitalism removed from traditional communities.

The problems of governing such a teeming mass of individuals detached from their traditional moorings are immense. In the past, political decisions were justified by appeals to common beliefs, traditions, and procedures, which were supported by the traditional institutions. But institutions such as the family, church, and local community are less and less influential in market societies. It is difficult to imagine the U.S. government justifying an important decision by reference to the church, for example, although this still is done in more traditional societies. And the problems of governing the newly emergent European Community are likely to be staggering.

In such a society, there are likely to be more disputes than there used to be. But the very forces which produce the disputes will also make the protagonists less likely to take the credentials of those who are supposed to regulate them on trust. Authority—whether the public authority of governments, courts, or policemen, or the private authority of party whips, trade union leaders, or university senates—will have to justify itself . . . justification by precedent will not be likely to carry conviction. . . . Meanwhile, the ethics of equal rights . . . has spread more widely. Claimants are more conscious of what they see as their rights, and more determined to stand on them. Decisions are scrutinised more carefully for evidence of bias. The net effect is that authority has been de-mystified. (Marquand, 1988, pp. 199-200)

Into this authority vacuum, science emerges as a basis for making and justifying public and personal decisions. Should you punish your child? Ask Dr. Spock, the scientific authority. What should you eat? See what the latest research says about cholesterol and oat bran. The demand for eggs and whole grain cereal varies with reports in the *New England Journal of Medicine.* It used to be that people ate what their parents ate, pure and simple. But as the traditional institutions lose influence, society turns to alternative forms of authority, such as science. The need for legitimation is especially acute for government actions.

Consider the episode that led to mandatory evaluation in the United States. Senator Kennedy believed that the federal money provided for disadvantaged children would not be used to benefit those children, but would be spent by educators without producing significant educational improvement (McLaughlin, 1975). He delayed passage of the legislation until an evaluation clause was attached to the bill. His remedy was to force the schools to provide test scores (scientific information) to parents, in the belief that the parents then could monitor the performance of their schools and bring pressure on the schools to improve. Kennedy's motive lay in his distrust of traditional schooling and professional educators. His means lay in providing scientific evidence to parents.

Governments, increasingly large, centralized, and removed from direct contact with the populace, and shorn of traditional supports, have turned to appeals to scientific authority, and answering this appeal is a role that formal evaluation now plays. It is no accident that formal evaluation as a large-scale enterprise started in the most advanced capitalist country of the time; then spread to Canada, England, Australia, and northern Europe; and is being attempted now in Spain and the Latin countries, with interest in Latin America and Asia. This is a rough map of the advance of capitalism and the retreat of the traditional social institutions.

Although governments are capable of making decisions based on their own political authority, justified by elections and backed by force of arms, it is much easier to govern through voluntary acceptance of the populace attained by persuasion, particularly when the populace governed is highly pluralistic and nontraditional. "Enhanced order, stability, effectiveness—these are the typical advantages that accrue to a legitimate system of power as a result of the obligations upon subordinates that derive from its legitimacy" (Beetham, 1991, p. 33). Legitimacy should not be understood as those in power controlling or determining the thoughts of others. Rather, the evidence presented and the interests of the populace are structured so that the justifications advanced are plausible within the social context (Beetham, 1991). Legitimacy is not arbitrary, but follows certain accepted rules.

Formal evaluation, then, is a new form of cultural authority based on persuasion, cultural authority being manifested in the probability that descriptions of reality and judgments of value will prevail as valid, an increasingly difficult task in societies with disparate value systems (Starr, 1982). In practical terms, the government can say to antagonistic parties, "Look, we have subjected the situation to a fair determination of the facts and arrived at this decision objectively. What more can you ask?" It is important for governments to demonstrate their impartiality and ability to adjudicate among competing interests.

These are the social dynamics that have led to the emergence of formal evaluation as an institution. Certainly, evaluation activities have existed before in a number of forms, such as professional accrediting organizations and school surveys (Madaus, Stuffelbeam, & Scriven, 1983). Only in the last third of the 20th century, however, has evaluation emerged as a fully organized institution, including a profession and discipline. Whether evaluation is a better method for making and justifying public decisions in an increasingly pluralistic society than priests reading the entrails of chickens is an interesting question. Certainly, government officials think that it is, and evaluators like to think so, too. In any case, the emergence of evaluation is a function of modern market societies, and its future is dependent on how those societies develop. Because at the moment there are only market societies and those that wish to become market societies, it appears that the future for evaluators will be busy.

❧ Evaluation as a Profession

Given that there is a social need for evaluation, what shape has it taken as a profession? Legitimation of professional authority involves three distinct claims: that the knowledge and competence of the professional have been validated by a community of peers, that this consensually validated knowledge rests on scientific or scholarly grounds, and that professional judgment and advice are oriented toward important social values (Starr, 1982). In other words, a modern profession rests on collegial, cognitive, and moral authority. Profit is not a sufficient motive for professionals: a doctor who administered treatments solely because they were profitable personally would be condemned. Although professionals exist in markets, the market cannot be the primary consideration. Furthermore, professionals work to secure the favorable opinion of colleagues and not simply to please clients, another departure from the marketplace.

The original professions were divinity, law, and medicine (Larson, 1977). Divinity never entered the marketplace (television evangelists excepted) and has suffered by being deemed not vital to modern society (though the resurgence of religious fundamentalism and the role of religion in politics raise questions; see Wills, 1990). Law certainly did enter the marketplace, but although law developed formal training and scholarly expertise as the passage to professional practice, it never successfully appropriated science as the basis of its authority, in spite of attempts to do so. Rather, case law, taught in university law schools and sanctioned by licensure and examination, became the basis of legal expertise, in lieu of law office apprenticeships that served this function before.

Medicine is the leading exemplar of a profession, but it is an exceptional case. One hundred and fifty years ago, medicine was practiced mostly within the home by the family, using folk remedies, or by lay healers, ranging from midwives to faith healers, all of whom were about as effective as the physicians (Starr, 1982). People lived on farms, miles away from the doctor, so obtaining professional help was expensive as much because of transportation costs as because of the doctor's fees. With the development of modern transportation systems and cities, doctors became much more accessible and affordable. Patients could come to doctors in the city, and doctors could see many patients a day, dramatically increasing their productivity. The developing market system defined the parameters of medical practice.

Of course, the need for good medical treatment was always present, but the opportunity for and the quality of treatment were lacking, as well as the money to pay for that treatment. Remarkable technological and scientific advances in medicine in the 19th century, including advances in physiology, bacteriology, and anaesthesiology by experimental scientists such as Pasteur, Koch, Cohn, and many others, greatly enhanced the ability of physicians to treat patients. In the United States, the establishment of science-oriented Johns Hopkins Medical School by John Billings with its attached research hospital, inspired by German medical science, spread scientific medicine throughout the country (Haber, 1991).

But the other enabling conditions were important as well. As specialization increased, a function of the division of labor and market forces, doctors became more dependent on one another and more collegial. Around the turn of the 20th century, medical training in the United States became standardized in a few medical schools (an event in which the Flexner evaluation played a significant role; see Floden, 1983). Laws, such as those permitting only doctors to prescribe drugs, reinforced the doctor's cultural authority. Furthermore, the transformation of hospitals, once relegated to the insane, made patients more dependent on their physicians. These factors increased the authority of physicians, even to the point where physicians in the United States gained unprecedented control of their market (Starr, 1982).

What is unusual about medicine is that physicians in the United States turned their professional authority into very high income, extreme professional autonomy, and considerable political power. After the transformation of medical care from a household endeavor to a market commodity, medical doctors succeeded in capturing the market itself. Physicians became highly organized, while simultaneously winning the battle to deal with patients as unorganized individuals, which meant physicians could establish fees and conditions of treatment without restriction or bargaining. They fought off popular movements to restrict their authority, ranging from consumer pay-in-advance arrangements that would require doctors to negotiate fees, to government health-care programs that would reduce costs.

While other professionals increasingly came under control of bureaucracies and corporations, often working for the organizations, doctors became small capitalists. However, this anomaly may be ending, due to escalating health-care costs and the extension of private enterprises into the health-care business, which means that doctors will be employees of the corporation, too. It seems likely that the government or corporations or consumer organizations will negotiate physicians' fees and working conditions in the future, thus reducing the physicians' autonomy, income, and influence.

In contrast to medicine, the evaluation profession was never in a position to capture its own market. Quite the contrary, evaluation was in part a creation of the government from the beginning, and even though evaluation may have been an idea whose time had come, the government always has been a senior partner in the enterprise. Although evaluation has spread to private enterprise, government still provides the major funding and remains the primary sponsor. In fact, the market situation is one in which there are a few large buyers, the governments, and many suppliers, the evaluators. This leads to a market in which the buyers are in control, a buyer's market, which is the opposite of medicine. The nature of this market presents certain ethical problems. Presumably, the role of evaluation is not to make government officials happy, any more than it is the purpose of medicine to make clients happy. The avowed purpose of evaluation is to serve the public interest, which includes the interests of more than government officials.

Like physicians, evaluators, too, claim to serve a higher purpose than profit and to have practices based on scientific authority, albeit a scientific authority much weaker than that of medical science. The degree to which evaluation is scientific is the subject of dispute within the evaluation community itself, but there is little question that much of evaluation's cultural authority rests in such perceptions by outsiders. Evaluation also has established recognized training programs in universities, a crucial step for professional recognition. It has evolved a community of peers who consensually validate professional knowledge through journals and internal critique (albeit peer critique is more acclaimed than acted on, as with physicians). Contending schools of practice, such as the qualitative and quantitative methodologists, have healed their differences, more or less, which parallels the healing of similar rifts among physicians, as different medical factions reconciled schisms and presented a united front to the public, a move necessary to secure cultural authority.

Furthermore, to a greater degree than in medicine, evaluation is being brought within the bureaucracies. Evaluation has become too important to be left as an independent external service. Large organizations have developed internal evaluation units, where professional autonomy is more difficult to maintain. In Canada, for example, evaluation has developed primarily within the government.

Internal evaluators who conduct evaluations inside organizations where their own careers are enacted face a situation significantly different from that of external evaluators, although both may be subjected to improper pressures.

Adequate professional controls to balance internal pressures do not exist currently. Ideas that have been proposed include having external advisory committees, auditing/accounting arrangements in which evaluators work for the organization and evaluation auditors examine the evaluations periodically, and arrangements in which senior internal evaluators provide oversight functions as specially assigned roles, and making internal evaluations subject to criticism by making them public. Of course, nothing can prevent abuses, but professional controls are necessary to maintain the credibility and authority of evaluators. Independence is vital for evaluator credibility in a way that it is not for public relations specialists.

As all the professions developed over the past 150 years, formal education became the basis of professional subcultures, and universities became the central institutions for training professionals, as well as for producing professional knowledge (Larson, 1977). As professional knowledge became standardized, and professional fields became unified internally and less subject to contentious disputes among competing factions, professional knowledge separated into the theoretical and the practical. This separation meant that the practitioner learns one thing in school, often referred to as theory, and then learns how to do the job on the job. In the "old days," one learned practical knowledge through apprenticeship and forgot about theory. So the split between theory and practice becomes more pronounced as a professional field develops. The field also becomes more specialized as theorists focus on topics of interest and opportunity, a function of university research and academic careers.

In reviewing the sociology of professionalization literature, Morell and Flaherty (1978) contend that a profession must have a monopoly over an esoteric body of knowledge that is important for the functioning of society, that the body of knowledge must be composed of abstract principles rather than practical experience, that strict control over entry must be exercised by the profession itself, that any included member of the professional group must be competent to practice, and that the profession must have altruistic motives that emphasize service to the client. They conclude that evaluation has almost achieved these things.

Morell and Flaherty (1978) suggest that there are certain generic problems of professionalization. There are likely to be intense debates internally about the purpose of evaluation, particularly among the contending factions, with the public image of the profession depending on which faction is dominant at a particular time. The profession is likely to develop an excessive sense of exclusivity concerning who is qualified. Also, there are likely to be training programs with inappropriate curricula that do not prepare students to do the job.

Morell (1990) also characterizes evaluation as a secondary discipline. Only 6% of the evaluators listed in the 1989 American Evaluation Association (AEA) membership directory declared evaluation their primary discipline. An AEA 1990 membership survey found 24% declaring evaluation their primary affiliation and 26% declaring it their secondary discipline (American Evaluation Association, 1990). Whatever the exact percentage, primary affiliation is low. I believe this is due to the recency of the field and the disciplinary organization of the universities. Morell's analysis found 40% of the membership located in universities, 12% in state or local governments, 9% in the federal government, 5% in school systems, 11% in nonprofit organizations, and 10% in private businesses.

Over time, I would expect the proportion of members in universities to decrease and the percentage of members in other locations to increase. As the number of practitioners grows, more will see evaluation as their primary discipline. It is difficult for university faculty to declare evaluation their primary discipline, because they work within disciplinary departments. Morell sees evaluation remaining a secondary job indefinitely, but I expect it to become more primary, although evaluators will perform other tasks as well. I expect more practitioners and fewer theorists, which will change the nature of the field. For example, on the AEA survey, 52% of the respondents indicated they wanted more journal articles on practice.

Morell (1990) views the evaluation profession as a loose coalition held together by personal contacts, media, intellectual history, and markets for the services of evaluators. Of course, evaluators also are held apart by factionalism, different histories, and competition over markets. The expansion and changing character of the evaluation market will result in more full-time employment and commitment. Another possible change may be the extension of evaluation into business enterprises, if corporations need legitimation for their activities, as seems likely (Morell, 1991).

There is also the matter of gender. When I entered evaluation in 1967, the field was overwhelmingly male. Now, judging by evaluation classes and professional meetings, the field is predominantly female.

This follows a general trend in the professions that could have important consequences. Gender composition of an occupation has far-reaching effects (Bergmann, 1986). "Female" occupations traditionally exert less power and command less money than "male" occupations. The central decision positions in both private and public organizations currently are held by men. Evaluators must be on guard against female evaluators becoming handmaidens to male decision makers. More than gender equity is at stake. The autonomy of the field is at issue.

In their personal lives, professionals of all types are concerned about their careers (Larson, 1977). The professional career is not simply a way of making a living but also a way of organizing one's entire life, of developing a life plan that provides stability and advancement. After all, in market societies, not much remains stable because market forces transform social relationships. Having a stable career is a privilege, a refuge, compared to the unpredictable market forces with which most workers must contend. Historically, professionals have enjoyed the privilege of security and stability in their jobs, though that may be changing. The philosopher John Rawls (1971) has said that happiness is having a life plan and feeling that one is making progress in achieving that plan (a distinctly professional way of regarding the problem). For the professional, the life plan is tied up intimately with career, which may be as important and demanding as family, as many career women discover as they balance career and family (Gerson, 1985).

Another central concern of professionals is status, comparing themselves to others in terms of how they are faring (Larson, 1977). "How are others progressing in their careers compared to how I am doing? Am I where I should be?" In market societies, social worth commonly is conceived as the self standing out individually from the masses and being differentiated from them. Comparison with one's peers is a preoccupation; envy, a familiar emotion.

ᨮ Among Other Professions

Evaluation does not exist alone as a profession but is instead part of a larger professional society, one profession among many. To a considerable degree, mass professional society has replaced 19th-century industrial society, which in turn replaced traditional agricultural society (Perkin, 1989). Professionals are a dominant part of contemporary society, whether as public professionals, such as employees of governments, or as private professionals, such as managers of corporations. In past eras, landed aristocrats dominated agricultural society, basing their position on control of land, and self-made entrepreneurs dominated industrial society, basing their position on control of capital.

In contemporary society, professionals base their position on possession of human capital. Possession of human capital, in the form of a professional career, gives professionals income, independence, security, self-confidence, the right to criticize without fear of consequences, the right to defend their place in society, and even authority to change society in their particular domains. The premium paid professionals for their human capital investment is roughly the difference between professional salaries and common wages. On the other hand, professionals must persuade society of the worth of their services. Or, "To put it more concretely, the object of the professionals manning the system is to justify the highest status and rewards they can attain by the social necessity and efficiency they claim for the service they perform" (Perkin, 1989, p. 360).

Through the continuing specialization of labor, a large number of occupations have become professionalized. These vertical career hierarchies compete with each other for resources, with the state acting as mediator. The professional career is based on selection by merit and trained expertise, on human capital created by education and enhanced by strategies of exclusion of the unqualified. Specialized training alone is not enough—access to the market is restricted, so as to create a scarcity of expertise, or at least not an oversupply. This is one task of professional associations, which have multiplied manifold. For example, in Britain, 20 professional associations were formed by 1900, 27 more by 1918, 46 between the world wars, and another 46 by 1970 (Perkin, 1989).

University teaching itself has been transformed into a highly specialized profession that limits access, conducts training, and does research for the other professions. One profession after another has transferred its training from apprenticeship to the university. In fact, the university has become the gatekeeper to the professional career hierarchies. University-based disciplines employ control of entry, esoteric jargon, knowledge of research, possession of a Ph.D., and scholarly reputation to separate themselves and their trainees from the laity. Professionalism has created opportunities for many people to advance themselves socially through the number of professional jobs available. Access to these jobs through education has been a major factor in upward social mobility.

Even politics has become professionalized, with politicians holding office for long periods of time and incumbents rarely being defeated. Politicians rely on professional pollsters, advertising, and media experts. Organized interest groups rely on professional lobbyists, who spend their careers working for one group and then for another, and the leaders of these groups also are professionals. Organized groups represent the collective self-interest of their particular hierarchies, with the leaders bargaining both with each other and with government leaders to set policy and pass legislation.

These interest groups compete for income, power, and status, three aspects of society viewed from the economic, political, and cultural perspectives, and these aspects are convertible into each other. That is, professionals who can persuade the public of the need for their services can convert their cultural authority into economic and political benefits, just as private professionals who manage corporations can convert their economic authority into power and status (Perkin, 1989).

There has always been a question as to where professionals fit into the traditional social-economic class structure of landowners, capitalists, and workers. Professionals exist only by convincing the rest of society to acknowledge and reward their expert services. They regard themselves as being outside the regular class structure, as being benevolent observers unallied with the other social classes, yet socially necessary and willing to provide services to all. They have a stake in playing down class conflict and in emphasizing efficient use of resources. Historically, they have been theorists and apologists for the other classes, leaving their own class position undefined.

Early on, in the 18th century, the traditional professions of the clergy and the upper ranks of law and medicine were occupations of gentlemen, who received a classical education. Their ethical code was that of their social class, which emphasized honor and authority (Haber, 1991). However, these social ranks became blurred in the United States, because men of lower social classes took up the professions. More important, the shift in the basis of the professions to scientific expertise led professionals to claim an impartial understanding of society, so that professionals placed themselves outside the social class structure. Nonetheless, many earlier notions of honor and authority persisted in modern professional ethics (Haber, 1991). In some ways the professional's ideal of existing outside the market harkened back to an earlier time.

Of course, all social classes and interest groups claim to be morally superior to the others and to provide invaluable contributions to society's well-being. The professional classes justify themselves on the basis of their expertise, efficiency, and service. From the professional perspective, social problems should be recognized out of humanitarian concerns, as well as because social problems waste resources. Professionals, such as educators and social workers, often articulate the needs of other social groups in such a way that more services are provided to these deserving groups, while at the same time opportunities are increased for the professionals themselves. Hence, professionals have been instrumental in expanding government services. Over the past many decades, there has been a huge expansion of state expenditure and employment, an expansion congruent with the interests of public sector professionals. Half of society's resources now are managed by governments.

On the other hand, private sector professionals, such as managers of corporations, are challenging expansion of the public sector, which reduces their own private domain and places demands on private resources. Hence, there are two versions of the "professional ideal." One version stresses government intervention to ensure equality of outcome, whereas the other stresses individual initiative to promote equality of opportunity. In general these positions are held respectively by public professionals, who work for public or quasi-public organizations, and professionals who work for private organizations, consistent with the material interests of each group. Arguments for and against government intervention are exacerbated by international competition and increasing scarcity of resources.

In the past few decades public professionals—bureaucrats, teachers, professors, social workers—have come under heavy attack, for example, in critical books, unfriendly newspaper reports, relaxation of rules for entering professional employment, and accountability schemes for scrutinizing professional behavior. These attacks have come from private sector professionals, such as journalists, doctors, and corporate managers. Private interests have even established institutes and foundations to promote the free market ideology, such as the American Enterprise Institute and the Heritage Foundation in the United States and the Institute of Economic Affairs in Britain. These foundations are staffed by professionals in the employ of the private sector.

One important task of evaluators has been to help mediate the claims of different professions, claims that often are embodied in social programs. Programs typically are professionally staffed, and, in a sense, evaluators help governments determine resource allocations to professional groups by evaluating programs. Evaluations are cast in social scientific arguments that other professionals recognize, including research terminology in which most professionals have been trained. Evaluations must withstand the scrutiny of other professionals. The split between public sector and private sector professionals sometimes is apparent within the evaluation community itself. Evaluation in the United States expanded greatly with the Great Society programs of the 1960s, only to cease expansion when the Reagan administration cut social programs and evaluation in the 1980s. Most evaluators have been allied with public sector activities. However, some have worked for the private sector and have launched attacks on government programs, such as Murray (1984).

Although evaluators are reluctant to define their own socioeconomic class, they clearly operate from an upper-middle-class position, while claiming to be outside the class structure (as do other professionals). Evaluators see themselves as neutral toward social classes and interest groups and espouse a rationale of expertise, service, and efficiency—the professional ideal. Their political position is that they should be neutral toward social interests and/or represent the relevant interests within the evaluation. A perennial concern is to persuade politicians and government officials of the usefulness of evaluation services.

⅔ Evaluation's Future

Evaluation as an institution and profession emerged in part as a result of the weakening of traditional social structures by advanced capitalism. It provides scientific authority to governments, which must deal with pluralistic, secular, professional societies that are difficult to govern. Because of this difficulty, there will be a continuing demand for evaluation services for some time to come. The main competitors to evaluation are policy research, which currently lacks the authority, scientific basis, and credibility of evaluation, and basic research, which lacks the relevance of evaluation. It seems likely that evaluation will have a more important role in society 50 years from now. On the other hand, there are those who question the utility of evaluations and whether they have "paid off" (Levitan, 1992).

Exactly in what form evaluation develops depends on how modern market societies develop. If these societies become more authoritarian, a distinct possibility in reaction to managing turbulent societies and sluggish economies, evaluation could be used for repressive purposes. On the other hand, if modern market societies become less ideological and more willing to consider new social possibilities, then evaluation could become more useful. For example, evaluation might provide less ideological studies of social trends, such as increases or decreases in test scores or infant mortality rates or labor force participation rates. Being involved with government programs means that evaluation is always connected to ideological and political issues.

The United States itself is at a crossroads of advanced capitalism. Through circumstance, the normal progress of capitalist development, and its own mismanagement, the United States has lost its global economic superiority, which placed it at the center of world capitalism (Gilpin, 1987). Japan, once a periphery of capitalist development, now threatens to become the new center, just as the United States replaced Britain, Britain replaced the Netherlands, and the Netherlands replaced Spain (Kennedy, 1987). Domestically, the United States either faces a decline in living standards, similar to Britain's, or must reverse its economic decline by repaying its enormous national debt, reversing its deindustrialization, and withstanding internal protectionist pressures while doing so (Gilpin, 1987). Difficult choices have to be made among consumption, investment, and defense. So far the loser has been investment. It also is possible that the declining standard of living will undermine political stability and that there will be a redistribution of power.

Another likelihood is the collapse of the liberal world trading order, as maintained since the Breton Woods agreement of 1944, and a resort to mercantilist competition. Mercantilist policy, first propounded by Alexander Hamilton in the 18th century and developed by German theorists later, subordinates economics to the political interests of the nation-state. Instead of continuing free trade and the low tariffs characteristic of a liberal trading order, the world may organize into three major trading blocs—North America, Europe, and East Asia, under the dominance of Japan. Each bloc would be organized to protect its own economy. What would ensue is a struggle for world markets and an increase in state power, which would be necessary to sustain successful competition. To prevent a turn to mercantilism, Americans must tolerate a declining standard of living and foreigners purchasing U.S. properties while reinvestment occurs. Mercantilist competition seems likely.

The role of evaluation depends significantly on the future of economic development. Whichever economic scenario occurs, it seems that state power will increase substantially. Either the government must implement and legitimize unpopular programs and/or the government must make industries more competitive internationally, which means a national industrialization policy. Currently, this productivity concern translates into government policies aimed at disciplining the workforce. For example, most new reforms in U.S. education in the 1980s have consisted of raising educational standards, such as entrance and graduation requirements, and establishing testing programs in the expectation that disciplining students will make the country more competitive economically (House, 1991a). Evaluation plays a major role in enforcing these standards. Ultimately, I expect these policies to fail because worker discipline is not the primary cause of national economic decline.

Evaluation will continue to move inside bureaucratic organizations, under the control of administrators, because it is necessary for bureaucracies to legitimize their activities, and this shift will threaten the autonomy of evaluators. Increasingly, evaluators will face conflicts familiar to other professionals in large bureaucracies. This internal shift will lead to new attempts to strengthen professional objectivity, which may or may not be successful. Because evaluation is valued for its scientific authority, methods of evaluation that claim to be nonobjective and unscientific will be marginalized. Society expects evaluation to be based on scientific authority. However, I expect the notion of what is scientific to be substantially redefined. The concepts of objectivity, validity, and scientific method will be recast to accommodate different evaluation approaches.

As evaluators conduct evaluations, they will come into conflict with political authorities, who rely on ideological explanations. In other words, the more objective and less ideological evaluation becomes, the more useful it is and the more it threatens established authority. A useful practice would provide sound evaluations that are not ideological. Theory-based evaluation may become more common. The evaluation theory developed so far is too ideological.

In reflecting on evaluation theory and its relationship to society, one might remember what the economist Thorstein Veblen (1918) said about university theorizing more than 75 years ago: "this esoteric knowledge is taken to embody a systematization of fundamental and eternal truth; although it is evident to any outsider that it will take its character and its scope and method from the habits of life of the group, from the institutions with which it is bound in a web of give and take" (p. 1).

Note

1. "By structure, observers of social questions mean an organization, a coherent and fairly fixed series of relationships between realities and social masses. For us historians, a structure is of course a construct, an architecture, but over and above that it is a reality which time uses and abuses over long periods. Some structures, because of their long life, become stable elements for an infinite number of generations: they get in the way of history, hinder its flow, and in hindering it shape it. Others wear themselves out more quickly. . . . Whether you take 1558 or this year of grace 1958, the problem of anyone tackling the world scene is to define a hierarchy of forces, of currents, of particular movements, and then tackle them as an entire constellation" (Braudel, 1958/1980, pp. 31, 34).

ᢊ 3 ᢊ

Government and Evaluation

*W*hat is the relationship between government and evaluation? Governments use evaluation to legitimate, inform, and control. Government legitimizes evaluation, and evaluation legitimizes government. Government also uses evaluation to inform its own activities and to control various sectors of society. As advanced capitalism breaks down the traditional social structures, governing becomes a much more difficult task. Job locations change, millions of people migrate to foreign places, detached individuals leave their defining social structures, and a certain amount of social chaos becomes the norm.

Government, which has depended on these traditional social structures for support, decreases in legitimacy, and legitimacy becomes a problem in new ways. In market societies, key functions, such as many economic activities, are outside direct government control, and governments seek new ways of legitimizing their authority and establishing control. Control by force and coercion are not as acceptable in individualistic, capitalist democracies as in more traditional societies. Liberal democracies have an ideological commitment to voluntarism and limited government intrusion. Evaluation is an alternative means of achieving guidance and compliance.

Governments can legitimize themselves and their activities in several ways. The primary way is to increase the material well-being of their citizens. As an anthropologist has written, sardonically:

> Industrial society is the only society ever to live by and rely on sustained and perpetual growth, on an expected and continuous

improvement. Its favoured mode of social control is universal Dane-geld, buying off social aggression with material enhancement; its greatest weakness is its inability to survive any temporary reduction of the social bribery fund, and to weather the loss of legitimacy which befalls it if the cornucopia becomes temporarily jammed and the flow falters. (Gellner, 1983, p. 22)

The modern liberal state depends on material well-being. In fact, no government in liberal democracies can long survive without increasing material productivity, or at least the appearance of such (Edelman, 1964, 1988). Image management has become a way of legitimating government actions, often by invoking national and cultural symbols. Another path to legitimacy is to solve problems or manage conflicts that arise from the continual breakdown of societal structures (or, again, to maintain the appearance of doing so). Both a poor economy and the perceived inability of the government to manage crises undermine government legitimacy. (The political legitimacy literature is vast. For recent interpretations, see Beetham, 1991; Habermas, 1975; and Held, 1984.)

Another source of authority in modern society is science. In the past few hundred years, science has emerged not only as a form of knowledge production but also as a popular belief system undergirding the operations of the economy. Governments sometimes substitute scientific authority for lapsed traditional authority. Organized science has achieved an unparalleled cultural authority, cultural authority being the ability to have definitions of reality and value judgments prevail as valid in the larger society. At this historical juncture in capitalism, the organized practice of evaluation emerges as a means of scientifically informing, legitimizing, and controlling.

Evaluation receives its authority not only from its presumed scientific method but also from government endorsement itself. That is, an evaluation is more authoritative when it is officially sponsored. Without such endorsement, evaluations have far less force. For example, parents evaluating a school have less legitimacy than government-sanctioned evaluators performing the same task. Governments are the main sponsors of evaluations, an indication of evaluation's importance to them. In short, government and evaluation legitimize each other, a complex relationship because evaluation can discredit particular government programs and policies.

Another feature of modern industrial society is the rise of professionalism. Beginning in the 19th century, the professions multiplied and expanded enormously, complicating the existing social class structure by creating new middle classes. These professions base their authority on claims of expert competence validated by peers, on knowledge based on scientific or scholarly research, and on value commitments to the public interest. Knowledge and expertise are produced by higher education, which expanded enormously during the rise of professionalism, largely as a result of training professional cadres. Knowledge is produced, validated, and legitimized by disciplinary structures, located mainly in the universities.

In the past few decades, however, professionalism itself has come under attack. Of course, there have always been critics—Molière, George Bernard Shaw, Ivan Illich—but criticism of professionals has reached a new intensity. Public professionals in particular—teachers, professors, social workers, bureaucrats—have come under increasing attack for being ineffective and inefficient, for forming guilds that impede rather than promote progress. Many of these attacks have come from private professionals—corporate executives, business managers, journalists, lawyers—who have been trained in professional programs themselves, but whose interests lie in the private sector and are opposed to public spending. The content of these attacks is supplied by the "free market" ideology.

A major role of public professionals has been to address the ills and deficiencies of advanced capitalism by treating the poor and sick, counseling fragmented families, administering to the unemployed, and educating children for the workforce. Many large-scale social programs employing professionals have arisen as reactions to social dysfunctions attributable to the economic structure, including evaluation, which began in the United States as an attempt to make educators more accountable for educating disadvantaged children. Many early applied social science studies, such as the London Statistical Society's and Charles Booth's studies of the London poor in Victorian England, also addressed social ills. However, concerted attacks on both the public professions and higher education may indicate a fundamental shift in direction.

Evaluation frequently deals with professionals who work in government-sponsored programs, and evaluation helps adjudicate the claims of various professional groups concerning the efficacy of their particular programs. Set in a role between government and the professions, itself a profession, evaluation often finds itself caught in conflicting and ambivalent circumstances. The "professional ideal" for evaluation, as for the other professions, is one of service plus efficiency, but service and efficiency are not always in harmony.

⋆ Accountability and Evaluation

Kogan (1986) contends that there are three models of educational accountability, and I believe these models apply to other social institutions as well: (a) state or public control, which entails elected representatives and politically appointed officials managing institutions such as schools; (b) professional control, which entails control by teachers, professors, and administrators or other professionals working within the institution; and (c) consumer control, which operates through direct participation of the public or market mechanisms derived from the private sector. Market mechanisms, such as voucher plans in which students attend schools of their choice, are central features of current British and U.S. policies, which are strongly free-market in orientation.

Combining political and professional accountability, Lundgren (1990) has represented the governing of education along two dimensions, the central/local dimension and the political/professional dimension, which creates four possibilities for accountability and evaluation, as shown in Figure 3.1. An institution can be accountable to the political center or to the professional center, to the local political group or to the local professional group, or to some combination of these. Each of these groups requires different evaluation information for purposes of accountability, and many dysfunctions in evaluation emerge from mismatches in information needs and demands among these levels. That is, the wrong information is supplied to the wrong group, or a group tries to use information to make decisions that are inappropriate for its level.

For example, in U.S. elementary and secondary schools, local political governance is exercised through local school boards for each school district. This board of laypeople is elected and supervises the operations of the schools. The board approves personnel appointments, budgets, and operating procedures, usually without interfering in internal processes, which are left to the professionals. The information used by local governing boards is local financial and personnel information.

At the central political level, schools are administered by government ministries or departments of education. Central political bodies formulate and enforce rules, regulations, and policies. They collect financial and personnel data throughout their governing region. In decentralized systems, such as those in the United States, Canada, Germany, and Australia, control is exercised by intermediate units

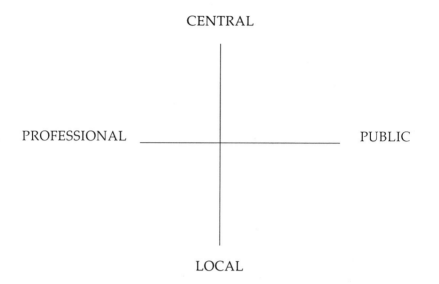

Figure 3.1. Dimensions of Accountability and Evaluation

such as states or provinces, which have state ministries of education. Again, these are public entities, even though they may employ professional administrative staffs.

By contrast, professional authority at the central level is manifested in individual disciplines and organized interest groups, such as teachers' unions. Faculty members belong to teachers' unions and to recognized professional disciplines, such as physics or psychology or the science teacher association. Members communicate through professional publications and meetings. At the local professional level, accountability is exercised through reviews by administrators and department heads and through such devices as accreditation evaluations, conducted by the professionals themselves. The manner in which the disciplines function is discussed later (Chapter 5). In general, the disciplinary structures of elementary and secondary education are weak compared to those in higher education.

Although I have not included consumers in this scheme, information for consumers may be quite different from information that professional and political groups find useful. Consumers want information about the comparative merits of products, programs, personnel, or institutions so they know which to patronize. A complete conceptual scheme would include a separate dimension for consumer accountability, represented in Figure 3.1 by a line designated "consumers" rising from the page perpendicular to the chart. Such a dimension would represent the market as a means of regulation and accountability.

Consumer control is becoming increasingly important in market societies. Students and their parents want information about the schools that is different from what governments and professionals want. I have not included the consumer dimension in this overall scheme for reasons of simplicity: A third dimension would increase the total number of cells in the scheme to eight, which creates a rather complex diagram. But the market dimension will be much more important in the future. These three dimensions of accountability—the public, the professionals, and the consumers—represent three major modes of social regulation: the state, the civil society, and the market (Wolfe, 1989).

Each of these modes of accountability requires different evaluation information. Mixing different types of evaluation, or using the same data for each, frequently leads to inappropriate evaluations and misuse of results. For example, central government officials sometimes try to use quantitative indicators to ascertain and mandate what strategies and tactics professionals at the local level should employ, to "micro-manage" the institution, almost always a mistake. Some evaluation schemes, such as MacDonald's (1977), which differentiates bureaucratic, autocratic, and democratic evaluation, are concerned with the power relationships among these levels of accountability and evaluation.

Central state authority typically is exercised in two ways: through regulating behavior and through allocating resources (Weiler, 1990). In education, for example, the principal rationale for centralized state regulation is the need for standardization of curricula, qualifications, and examinations to facilitate mobility and exchanges of personnel. Centralized allocation is justified in the name of equity of resources and increased efficiency. State demands for information reflect these concerns.

In addition to the political authority of the state, there is also the disciplinary authority of the professions, exemplified in the give-and-take discourse within academic disciplines. Disciplinary authority is not democratic—people do not vote on issues. Nor is it authoritarian—one or two people within the field do not decide issues, although the leading authorities in the field are engaged in key debates. Rather, issues are resolved more or less by consensus based on evidence, deliberation, and persuasion of members of the discipline. This authority is cultural, rather than based on power or money. Disciplinary authority is difficult for the government and public to understand, and it sometimes is in conflict with political authority.

In summary, there are at least three mechanisms for regulating society: the state, the civil society, and the market. These are reflected in political (public) authority, cultural (professional) authority, and economic (consumer) authority—power, status, and money. To some degree these forms of authority are convertible into one another. However, they serve different purposes and operate in different ways. Different information is needed to provide accountability and evaluation in each situation. So evaluation schemes may differ according to what is being emphasized, and changes from one type of authority system to another are reflected in changes in the evaluations themselves.

Although this basic authority structure characterizes all advanced capitalist societies with highly developed professions, each society is unique in having its own history and culture. For example, some countries, such as Spain, do not have as fully developed and autonomous a civil society. There, even the professions depend heavily on the state, are more recently developed, and are relatively lacking in cultural authority.[1] Evaluation always takes place in a particular authority structure within a particular culture, which significantly affects its operation. What works in one country may fail in another. Each advanced capitalist country will have evaluation because of the ways in which market societies are similar, but each country will have it differently.

❧ Government Evaluation in the United States

In both the United States and Britain, certain basic ideas underlay the early development of evaluation (Norris, 1990). In both countries, "The belief that the structure of society is not immutable, that the inherited order is not preordained, that social systems can be rationally managed and are amenable to research and development—these are the beliefs that sustained evaluation in the common experience of industrialization, with its associated demographic and social upheavals" (Norris, 1990, p. 15). Early evaluation in the United States dates back at least to the progressive movement of the early 20th century, which shifted control of urban education and other social services from politicians to professionals, with the social disorder created by industrialization and heavy immigration from Europe as background and stimuli.

In both countries, management of individuals emerged as a priority. "Educational evaluation is about social planning and control, and the key value is that of order" (Norris, 1990, p. 16). Taylor's "scientific management" in industry was a primary influence on educational evaluation (Callahan, 1962; House, 1978). By 1930 the 8-Year Study had emerged as a product of these early ideas, and Ralph Tyler developed his objectives-based evaluation model and coined the phrase *educational evaluation*. Tyler's evaluation model focused on specification and evaluation of individual student behaviors, and this approach dominated evaluation in the United States until the *Sputnik*-generated curriculum projects of the 1960s.

McLaughlin (1975) has traced the beginnings of federal government involvement in evaluation to the Great Society programs of 1965, beginning with the Senator Robert Kennedy episode and progressing to heavy influence by government economists. Rist (1990) has contended that government evaluation in the United States has been a blending of two traditions—applied social science and economic decision making. In recent times the Office of Management and Budget (OMB) has acted as a major proponent of evaluation within the executive branch of government, as revealed in a 1979 circular:

> All agencies of the Executive Branch of the Federal Government will assess the effectiveness of their programs and the efficiency with which they are conducted and seek improvement on a continuing basis so that Federal management will reflect the most progressive practices of both public and business management and result in service to the public. (OMB Circular A-117, quoted in Rist, 1990, p. 73)

The Reagan administration reduced evaluation activity in the 1980s, and this circular was suspended by OMB director David Stockman in 1983, so that there is now no overall executive directive, even though there are many evaluation activities. From 1980 to 1984, the number of evaluation units in nondefense departments decreased from 206 to 141, and the number of evaluation personnel was reduced from 1,507 to 1,179. Funding for these evaluation units declined from $177.4 million to $110.9 million. Whereas overall federal funding declined 4%, funding for evaluation declined 37% (Rist, 1990). Apparently, the Reagan administration had little appetite for evaluation. Much evaluation activity continued, however, far more than in any other country.

In 1984, 1,689 evaluations were conducted in the executive branch (Rist, 1990). Most requests for evaluation came from top agency officials (54%), followed by program personnel (18%), self-initiation (14%), and legislative request (9%). In executive departments, money for evaluation came from internal budgets (52%) and legislative "set-asides" (47%), whereas in independent agencies, all funding came from inside. About 73% of the evaluations were internal and 27% external. Of the external, 399 were bid competitively versus 94 that were contracted sole source. In general, the larger the evaluation, the more likely it was to be conducted externally. Only 15% of department and 5% of agency evaluation reports were distributed outside the organizations (Rist, 1990). Rist (1990) comments, "more studies are in-house, nontechnical, smaller, and aimed at the internal management and operations of the programs, not at the broader policy questions of overall program utility and impact" (p. 84).

The division of powers within the federal government allowed Congress to create its own evaluation unit in 1980, so that it could have independent evaluations to challenge executive policies. The main purpose was congressional oversight and direction. Eleanor Chelimsky, who pioneered the establishment of the General Accounting Office's (GAO) Division of Program Evaluation and Methodology, discerned big differences between evaluations in executive agencies and those for legislative bodies (Chelimsky 1987, 1990, 1991). The GAO works directly for Congress, conducting studies suggested by individual members, and its evaluators come from education, public assistance, health, and criminal justice. They evaluate programs in defense, environment, transportation, agriculture, community development, and immigration, as well as in their areas of expertise.

The GAO contains about 100 social scientists and 4,000 auditors, the auditors reflecting the original mission of GAO, financial auditing. This mix of personnel has resulted in procedural crossovers between evaluation and auditing. Auditing techniques call for statements of objectives, with success determined by comparisons between objectives and outcomes. According to Chelimsky, evaluation methods have broadened the auditors' analysis possibilities. On the other hand, auditors have been helpful in showing how to protect the independence of evaluation work from intrusions. The GAO conducts about 1,050 studies a year, of which about 50 are evaluations. These studies are in the public domain, except for national defense studies.

There are four major types of studies: assessing a program or policy still in the design stage, measuring program or policy implementation, establishing the effects of programs and policies, and critiquing the soundness of evidence reported to the Congress by others. To be used, the studies must address questions of interest to the intended users, and the evaluation must answer the questions posed for the study. Of critical importance is the credibility of the study, which includes the responsiveness of the study to the specific policy questions, as well as whether the study employed appropriate methodology.

Timeliness is most critical, because studies that do not fit the legislative time schedule are not used. However, use of results is the rule, rather than the exception, according to Chelimsky. The studies most frequently requested are effectiveness studies, followed by methodological critiques. The evaluators first reach a precise understanding with the congressional sponsor of a study as to information needs and later inform the sponsor as to the progress of the work. The length of studies varies from 3 months to 3 years. Multiple research methods often are employed.

Sometimes "mismatches" limit contributions to decision making (Chelimsky, 1991). Political demands may be so strong that information is neither sought nor attended to when available. For example, policy makers had plenty of information available to them to indicate the likely disastrous effects of the Vietnam War, but they chose not to heed it. Policies and programs may be so politicized that evaluation is not possible or is ineffective if conducted. Furthermore, contextual or resource constraints or an inadequate research base may prevent evaluators from providing good information. For example, the Bureau of Labor Statistics failed to predict the entry of millions of women into the workforce between 1970 and 1980. A mature research base is necessary to conduct certain studies. Or there may not be enough time or money to conduct the evaluation that the policy or program demands.

According to Weiss (1991), who has studied the use of evaluation in several government agencies, politics intrudes on government evaluation in three ways: (a) Programs are created and maintained by political forces, (b) higher-level decision makers are embedded in politics, and (c) the very act of evaluating has political consequences. Program personnel have high psychological and career stakes in their programs. Furthermore, the very process of garnering political support for a program leads to constructing unrealistic goals that can win support from many factions. Higher-level decision makers are susceptible to the partisan politics necessary to sustain their agencies, and unfavorable evaluations are viewed as threats. On the other hand, the very act of evaluating indicates that the program is worthy of study and attention.

When a program is evaluated, the evaluation typically is limited to the few effects the program hopes to achieve and neglects the larger, underlying social and institutional structures. Evaluation sponsors are almost always the agencies that fund the program. Hence, evaluations tend to be "establishment" oriented, according to Weiss, who believes that qualitative studies of program processes give superordinate groups greater control over program staff, while at the same time making legitimation of the evaluation more difficult. In her view, independent critical evaluation is more necessary and difficult to do than it used to be, now that evaluation itself has become more politicized.

The range and variety of evaluation activities in the United States are so extensive that they are difficult to characterize fully. Even within the federal government, each department and agency is different, and this brief review does not treat state and local activities at all. Evaluation is constrained by political considerations in several ways, wherever it is conducted, and the high proportion of evaluations that are conducted internally and not distributed to external audiences raises issues of independence and credibility. On the other hand, evaluation in the United States has the support of a strong professional evaluation community.

ꝯ Government Evaluation in Britain

In Britain applied social research extends back to the Royal Commission on the Poor Laws in 1832-1834; Charles Booth's survey of the London poor in the 1890s; and the eugenics movement led by Galton, Pearson, Spearman, and Burt (Norris, 1990). After World War II, there were evaluations of the initial teaching alphabet and curriculum development efforts, especially in science and technology, both as a basis for manpower planning and as a remedy for the persistence of poverty. In the early 1960s the Nuffield Foundation funded science curriculum projects, and the Schools Council, a professional education group funded by the government, sponsored a team approach to curriculum innovation, with evaluators attached to the teams as independent observers. Evaluation was closely related to curriculum development (Norris, 1990). At least one major evaluation group, the Centre for Applied Research in Education at the University of East Anglia, emerged from these projects.

In the 1970s, however, this orientation changed. Local projects run by professionals gave way to centrally administered projects run by bureaucrats, with important consequences for evaluation (Norris, 1990). When Margaret Thatcher was secretary of state for education and science in 1972, she launched the National Development Programme in Computer Assisted Learning, the purpose of which was to stimulate the British computer industry. Educational and financial evaluations were integral parts of the project, and the evaluators ran into difficulty with the program's governing board because the evaluators insisted on evaluating all parts of the program, including management, rather than simply reporting on individual projects to the management committee. Tensions between local and central governments and between professionals and bureaucrats increased sharply from the 1970s onward.

Historically, British governments have nurtured secrecy in their operations, and this tendency affected evaluation. "This general reluctance to open policies to public scrutiny is not confined to the British government, but the operating styles of successive British administrations, aided and abetted by the structures of the Official Secrets and Public Records Acts, make public evaluations of the policy programs of central departments problematic" (Jenkins & Gray, 1990, p. 63). During the 1980s, control of research shifted substantially from the universities to the central political authorities.

Government departments became autonomous sponsors for evaluations and considered studies to be departmental property, conducted for the departments rather than for the general interest. This attitude was manifested in the language and management of government research grants and contracts. Increasingly, British bureaucracies commissioned studies for their own purposes, asserted ownership of the data, and controlled publication by requiring prior approval. Prior to this, publication and handling of data had followed the rules of academia (Norris, 1990). Parliament itself has only weak capabilities for oversight, so that government departments are very much in control.

In one of the most extensive studies conducted anywhere on the interaction of government and evaluation, Henkel (1991) studied British government evaluation across several departments in the 1980s. The Thatcher government

> was faced with incompatible demands to keep inflation in check, to maintain full employment and to control the balance of payments. The

problems were seen as an inevitable outcome of the development of democracy and the breakdown of various forms of authority. . . . The bureaucracies through which the public sector was administered were said to be dominated by self-serving interests, bureaucrats, professionals and unions, whose main concern was to enlarge their own power. (p. 11)

The Thatcher solution was to install a culture of management in government, modeled on the corporate sector, that would curtail the spending of local governments and the demands of professionals and unions. Professional authority would be subsumed under managerial authority. The norms and mechanisms of the private sector would replace the inefficiencies of the public sector.

In the UK and elsewhere, confidence in the validity and usefulness of professional knowledge faded as evidence of the failures of the state accumulated; demand grew for professionals to be more publicly accountable; professional expansion came to be seen as a cause of the impotence of public sector organisations and, as resource constraint tightened, the tension between traditional and service-oriented professionals and newer management based professionals increased. (Henkel, 1991, p. 15)

In the new scheme, public services were to be accountable to the taxpayers rather than to the users of services, similar to corporate employees being accountable to shareholders rather than to customers. This reformation of local government and professional accountability was to be accomplished through review and control mechanisms such as inspections, reviews, and audits. Henkel studied evaluation in four government endeavors: the Audit Commission to make local and national government efforts more efficient, the Social Services Inspectorate, the Health Advisory Service, and the use of external consultants to conduct evaluations in several departments.

The new Audit Commission began cautiously and then became bolder in exercising its managerial expertise vis-à-vis the professionals and local authorities. As to the use of external consultants, "Reflexiveness between central government and the field gives way to reflexiveness between central government and their consultants, as this form of evaluation takes hold" (Henkel, 1991, p. 232). The Social Services Inspectorate, although proceeding from a professional base, focused on defining performance criteria. The Health Advisory Service resisted the push toward managerial evaluation more than the others and relied on its professional review procedures.

Although evaluation was enacted in different ways, in each enterprise (except the Health Advisory Service) activities converged, with conflicts emerging between professional and managerial orientations. Technical expertise, quantitative analysis, and instrumental (as opposed to substantive) values were favored by the central government. Performance review, including the development of criteria and standards, was an important activity. There was also competition among evaluation groups inside the government, as each sought to increase its influence, power, and resources (Henkel, 1991). The government reinforced the tendency for managers to supersede professionals as the primary authorities. "It [the government] wanted more performance from a reduced public sector" (Henkel, 1991, p. 230).

Performance indicators also have been a government priority (Cave, Kogan, & Smith, 1990). In higher education:

> In many countries there is a move towards an indirectly centralised system in which institutions are increasingly guided to respond to centrally established incentives or to compete for private and public funds through a quasi-competitive process. Thus several countries, including the UK, are moving towards a more market-based framework through a system of competitive contracting for some student places. PI's [performance indicators] play a vital role in this type of system, not only as a way of making institutions accountable and allocations transparent but also as a mechanism for defining the nature of the academic "product" for which contracts are made. (Cave & Hanney, 1990, p. 81)

In health care the development of performance indicators was top-down, and their use has been limited to top managers (Roberts, 1990). In the Audit Commission studies of local authorities, the commission complained of "lack of commitment" to indicators on the part of local personnel (Henderson-Stewart, 1990). These attempts of the central government to install performance indicators resulted in some polarization of professionals and managers, to the surprise of government officials (Burningham, 1990). The private sector approach of directly comparing organizations in terms of ratios based on profitability did not work well in the public sector. For example, the implementation of performance indicators in one local planning department resulted in increases in the outputs measured (number of plans produced), but reductions in other unmeasured activities (informal consultations), and increases in client complaints. Performance indicators replaced peer review as the dominant system of evaluation, resulting in a deterioration of other essential activities.

Even the staunchest advocates of performance measures have recognized problems. In the government with the greatest use of such indicators, the former Soviet Union, "gaming" often reached such proportions as to invalidate the indicators. For example, when nail factories were subjected to weight indicators, they produced such huge, heavy nails as to have a worthless product (Pollitt, 1990). Increasingly complex, specific indicators to avoid such gaming resulted in data too detailed and complex to interpret, and that, in turn, resulted in simplification, more gaming, and the process starting over again. The extensive use of indicators in the former centrally controlled Soviet economy does not encourage optimism. In general, the best advice on the use of cost-effectiveness and cost-benefit procedures is that one should proceed with caution and that the identification and measurement of short-term and long-term effects of social programs are not easy tasks (Levin, 1991).

∂⁀ Government Evaluation in Canada

In Canada, programming, planning, and budgeting initiatives were attempted in the late 1960s, but with little success, the failure being attributed to departmental resistance (Segsworth, 1989-1990, 1990). In 1977, at the instigation of the auditor general, who was concerned about financial management, the Office of the Comptroller General was established to carry out evaluation policies outlined by the Treasury Board: "departments and agencies of the federal government will periodically review their programs to evaluate their effectiveness in meeting their objectives and the efficiency with which they are being administered" (Treasury Board Circular 1977-47, quoted in Segsworth, 1990, p. 23). The Program Evaluation Branch set up a comprehensive review cycle for federal programs.

Whereas the Comptroller General's Office is charged with responsibility for the oversight of evaluation activities, deputy-heads of departments are responsible for organizing evaluations in their areas and are the official clients for the evaluations. Each department has its own evaluation unit that carries out evaluations, with the department bearing the costs. The Treasury Board ties evaluation results to money allocated to programs, and the policy committees of the Cabinet may also request specific evaluations or use findings to shape government actions (Segsworth, 1990).

The process for organizing evaluations is defined in detail in a government guide and set of principles, and ordinarily personnel inside the department conduct the evaluations. Reports are submitted to the deputy-head and sometimes to the Cabinet committees and ministers, and action is expected in response to the evaluation. In the mid-1980s, about 100 reports a year were being produced. The degree to which the reports are accessible to the public is unclear, but it appears that they are not readily available (Segsworth, 1990).

Two main differences exist between Canada and the United States in this regard. First, Canada has a parliamentary system, and evaluation has been tied to the management of programs in a more centralized fashion. Second, less of an applied science tradition exists in Canada, and this difference is reflected in the way evaluations are conducted. Canadian evaluations are focused on value-for-money and the narrower program operations, rather than on broad social issues (Segsworth, 1990).

Rutman and Payne (1985) noted that important differences exist in the evaluation cultures of the United States and Canada. First, large-scale evaluation in the United States originally was tied to major social experiments, and this attempt to use social experiments to guide policy reflected traditional U.S. reluctance to accept government intervention in social problems. Second, the United States has a social science tradition that stresses the "scientific approach," which in the late 1960s and 1970s was interpreted as complex research design and rigorous measurement. Third, the United States has a competitive political process manifested in the separation of powers, which provides numerous forums for experts and others to express their views (Rutman & Payne, 1985, p. 64).

The original purpose of large-scale evaluation in the United States was to determine conclusively what worked before moving ahead, thus neutralizing opposing political forces and building a consensus for action. U.S. evaluation has been conceived as neutral, value-free, a de-politicizing force not appended to any ideological, political, or governmental position (which is not to say that is what it is). Because of its dependence on scientific authority, the U.S. evaluation community has been led by social researchers.

By contrast, Canadians expect government intervention in social problems, and Canadian analysis has relied more on political and ideological debate rather than research methodology. After debate, the government moves ahead without attempting to prove something works, a function of the parliamentary system and the willingness of citizens to follow government leadership. Once a direction is decided, the parliamentary system ensures top-down implementation. Canadian evaluation developed at a time of budget difficulty, and resource allocation has been a primary focus. Evaluation in Canada has become closely integrated with program management (Rutman & Payne, 1985).

The primary evaluation clients are deputy-heads of departments, who focus on program change and accountability. Relevance and practicality are critical concerns, and the timeline for studies is short. The typical evaluation questions are, "Does the program make sense? What are its results? Did it achieve what was expected? Are there better ways of achieving results?" The first and last of these questions are not typically addressed by U.S. evaluators. The evaluation process is centrally guided by the comptroller general, versus little central control in the United States, and the evaluation community is led by government officials rather than researchers.

In general, one would expect that a narrower range of evaluation issues would be addressed and carried out in Canada, that the issues addressed and the results obtained would be more constrained by government policies, and that the findings would be more effectively implemented once formulated. Evaluation in Canada is not conceived as something done by a questioning third party. In the United States, one would expect more conflicting results, more evaluations critical of the government, and less acceptance and use of evaluation findings. In both countries, evaluators are constrained, but in different ways. In Canada, the evaluation is constrained by government policy, which is more fully debated beforehand.[2] In the United States, evaluation is constrained by the prevailing ideology, which is more attuned to market considerations that, in turn, provide a narrower range of policy options to begin with.

‹▲ Government Evaluation in Europe

In Sweden, following a rapid expansion of educational and social services after the World War II, the government has pursued a strong consensus approach to social planning (Franke-Wikberg, 1990; Karlsson, 1992). Large amounts of data are collected, and suggested policies are sent to organized interest groups for comments. By investigating alternatives in advance, policy makers hope to choose the right course of action. Evaluation is a rapidly expanding activity in

Sweden that is coming to play a more central role in political control. As some government activities have been decentralized, evaluation has emerged as a means of controlling these activities. The government is both the sponsor and the consumer of most evaluations.

The most common program evaluations are comparisons between goals and results, employing criteria such as efficiency and economy (Karlsson, 1992). Context evaluations are not common. Evaluation at the central level emphasizes control, with accountability a primary purpose, whereas that at the local level focuses on development. Some critics have argued for a broader approach, such as theory-driven evaluation (Franke-Wikberg, 1990). There are also demands for stakeholder evaluation and a move toward internal evaluation, with new units being created inside government agencies.

In Norway evaluation has been an active but fragmented government activity (Eriksen, 1990). Ministries initiate most evaluation, with the major audience being the parliament. There are no evaluation units within departments, but there are research and development units. Not much evaluation is conducted inside, however. Most is commissioned to research institutions, such as the Norwegian Research Council for Science and the Humanities, an independent research agency that relies on government funding.

Evaluations differ not only with government structures but also with national cultures. Lauglo (1990) has analyzed the culture of Norway, with its special blend of authority strongly influenced by socialist, democratic, and populist traditions that constrain local professional autonomy. Vislie (1990) has suggested ministry control in Norway is limited for similar reasons. Norway also has formulated national evaluation plans to accompany decentralization policies (Granheim, Kogan, & Lundgren, 1990).

One of the most prominent Norwegian studies of the 1980s was the "experiment" on 6-year-old education. Six-year-olds traditionally have received a nursery school education that focuses on child development rather than academics. A large national study was conducted to determine whether 6-year-olds should remain in nursery school or begin an academic kindergarten. Even though the content of the study had little to do with the reform eventually implemented by the government, the "experiment" was used to legitimize and justify the reform, which took the academic alternative (Haug, 1992).

Even within Scandinavia, evaluation differs substantially from country to country. Apparently, there is little demand for evaluation in Denmark, where a broad political consensus exists as to what the government should do and little political conflict occurs (at least until the Danish rejection of the European Community treaty in 1992). Also, there is not a strong social science tradition. Research is carried out in external research institutes, following the general Scandinavian pattern (Albaek, 1989-1990; Albaek & Winter, 1990).

In the Netherlands, a goal specification approach to evaluation was tried in the early 1970s, but it was not successful (Bemelmans-Videc, 1989-1990; Bemelmans-Videc, Elte, & Koolhaus, 1990). In the 1980s, evaluation was closely tied to budget reduction efforts, such as the Reconsideration Procedure, in which evaluations are expected to result in decisions to lower funding for reauthorized programs. In Germany the early evaluation efforts of the 1970s were identified with the reformist programs of the Social Democrats. In the 1980s, the conservative government de-emphasized evaluation and used it as part of deregulation and de-bureaucratization, but not as part of social program curtailment and budget reduction, actions that were taken on political and fiscal grounds without the legitimation of evaluation studies (Derlien, 1990).

In Switzerland there has been little government evaluation, partly because of the historic decentralization, regionalization, and localization of powers in which lower levels of government are free to implement federal policies and in which the federal government is expected to act on social issues only as a last resort (Hober-Papazian & Thevoz, 1990, p. 143). Coalition politics has allowed Switzerland to operate effectively with its pronounced ethnic, language, religious, and cultural differences. Policy is arrived at through extensive consultation and consensus building. The Swiss also are noted for frugality in government expenditures. However, there are increasing demands for evaluation, because the traditional legitimacy of the government is being called into question. "The issue then is the credibility and legitimacy of the public authorities. Given that, politicians may see evaluation as a way of demonstrating their determination to go further towards meeting the electorate's needs and of investing the interventions by public authorities with legitimate authority" (Hober-Papazian & Thevoz, 1990, p. 143).

In examining government evaluation activities across eight countries—the United States, Britain, Canada, Germany, Norway, Denmark, Switzerland, and the Netherlands—Rist (1989-1990, 1990) concluded that differences among them existed along five dimensions. First, there are differences as to how centralized or decentralized the evaluation activities are. Another important difference is whether evaluators report to the executive or legislative units. If evaluators report to executive units, they conduct more management, organizational, and internal process studies. If they report to legislative units, they conduct oversight, budget, and reauthorization studies.

A third difference is the degree of independence of the evaluators, with some having considerable latitude in designing studies and others being under tight control. Fourth is the question of who has access to evaluation reports, which varies from full disclosure to secret reports. The fifth dimension is the manner in which evaluators are connected to auditing, as some evaluation units have evolved with close ties to auditing organizations. In spite of these differences all the countries have established evaluation activities at the federal level, as opposed to decentralizing it in local units or universities, and all governments expect immediate results from evaluation.

Analyzing evaluation in these same countries, Derlien (1990) noted three waves of implementation. First, there were evaluation activities in the United States in the 1960s, which are still the most extensive by far. Sweden, Canada, and Germany followed closely, but evaluation was more fragmented in these countries, with not so many studies. In the late 1970s Britain and Canada re-emphasized evaluation, with Canada locating evaluation in the Comptroller General's Office and Britain propagating managerial evaluation throughout the government. In the 1980s, Norway, Denmark, Switzerland, and the Netherlands emphasized evaluation to increase productivity, often tied to budget processes. Earlier activities had been linked to planning at the program administrator level, whereas later activities were geared to justification of policies and budget processes at the political level, with legislatures the major actors and audiences.

In the economic expansionary period of the 1960s, evaluation was part of the planning of new social programs (Derlien, 1990). In the faltering economies of the 1980s, evaluation was tied to budget cutbacks and the new managerialism, with financial offices becoming prominent sponsors. In the early years reformist governments were in power, but these were replaced by conservative governments. The latter promoted privatization, deregulation, and debureaucratization and often manifested a hostile attitude toward social science, which they saw as linked to social reform. In these conservative regimes business management techniques were imported into government operations and evaluations.

Derlien also contended that the constitutional relationship between executive and legislative branches is important. Where legislative coalitions form against the chief executive, as in the United States, the legislature may develop its own evaluative capacity. A

strong applied social science research tradition also affects evaluation. Such knowledge, training, and tradition are lacking in many
countries. Bureaucrats are often trained in law (France, Germany,
Denmark) or classics (Britain) and do not adjust readily to social
science methods. Nonetheless, in spite of differences, the demand for
evaluation in all these countries has increased in response to the
political and economic forces of the 1980s (Derlien, 1990). Major
proponents have been legislatures and auditing offices.

I would add that evaluation has been largely a North American and
northern European phenomenon until recently. Not much evaluation
has been conducted in Latin countries, South America, or Asia, with the
exception of Australia. Some evaluations have been attempted in
France, Italy, and Spain, but these countries have been less receptive to
the systematic employment of evaluation, in spite of high degrees of
industrialization. These countries also have large, traditional, centralized bureaucracies. This reluctance seems to be fading somewhat now,
as Latin countries move more toward evaluation.

Another important difference is the degree of internal versus
external evaluation, or whether evaluations are organized and conducted inside or outside government agencies. The location is related to the independence of the evaluation. Countries vary greatly
on this dimension, with the Scandinavian countries having more
external evaluations and Canada, Britain, and the United States
having more internally directed ones. Often evaluations are designed inside and contracted out to external organizations to execute
the design, which makes for another set of problems.

ᴥ Conclusions

Evaluation serves important legitimation, information, and control functions for governments in advanced capitalist societies. Noblit
and Eaker (1988) have even argued that different evaluation approaches provide credibility and legitimacy in different ways to
different groups, and that different evaluation strategies are effective, depending on whether the power imbalance among participants is high or low, thus making evaluation itself a political strategy. However, emphasizing the legitimating function of evaluation
does not mean that evaluation is not used for guiding decisions or
that its use is insincere. Evaluation may legitimize, guide, and inform
simultaneously. Without the cultural authority derived from sci-

ence, however, evaluation would not have assumed the role in government operations that it has.

In many countries evaluation has been tied to managerialism, especially in recent years, in attempts to improve economic productivity and the management of government and to control sectors of society, such as the public professional sector, which is closely associated with advocacy of social programs. As economies falter and governments lose legitimacy, evaluation has become a tool for informing and legitimizing the unpopular steps that governments must take, which often means budget cutting. It is easier to slash jobs and curtail popular programs with the support of science.

In performing this role, evaluation has taken various forms in different countries. In Britain, the conservative Thatcher government, concerned with making Britain more competitive economically, imported business techniques wholesale into government operations. On the other hand, the equally conservative Reagan administration in the United States curtailed evaluation. Perhaps the difference lies in the types of evaluation being implemented in both countries: a managerialist evaluation in Britain and a social science evaluation in the United States. Both patterns have occurred in other countries as well.

Underlying these events are conflicts among professionals, bureaucrats, and business managers. On the one hand, there are concerted assaults on professional autonomy. The social programs cut are often programs employing professionals, so that the cuts inflict damage not only on the recipients of the services but also on the professionals supplying the services. And when professionals work in bureaucracies, their autonomy is often challenged. So professional versus bureaucratic interests is a central conflict. This conflict is increasingly manifested in the higher education system, a stronghold of professional knowledge and legitimation. Governments have curtailed funding and increased their control over universities.

The picture is further complicated in that some governments are actively engaged in curtailing government activities and promoting business and free market interests. Evaluations of programs may be based on productivity and efficiency, rather than on the needs of the clients. Clients are sometimes conceived as consumers or shareholders. Often the interests of the citizenry are cast as those of taxpayers who want to restrain spending and maximize personal wealth. The evaluations that professionals want are not always the kind that governments want.

For example, in comparing educational evaluation in Sweden and the United States, Franke-Wikberg (1990) saw attempts in both countries to centralize control of education through establishing new national tests and requiring teachers to teach the content on those tests. Another U.S. project proposed accrediting teachers nationally by proscribing, testing, and certifying their professional knowledge. These projects limit professional autonomy and remove knowledge production and certification from the university, the traditional knowledge base for the professions, and place it in the hands of government.

Where government has a rhetorical commitment to decentralization and local control, as in the United States, philanthropic foundations often take the initiative in centralization processes. Similar trends exist in Sweden, where national tests have been developed by the National Board of Education, and the National Board of Universities and Colleges is developing performance indicators. As in the United States and Britain, the idea of a "core curriculum" has been promoted by the government, with an emphasis on "cultural heritage." Underlying these trends is a drive for economic rationalization, productivity, and efficiency, according to Franke-Wikberg (1990).

It may be that educational systems will tend toward that of the Japanese, which has been test-centered and economically focused for some time and which has a degree of government control, even of ideas, not yet experienced in Western democracies. As a University of Tokyo professor assessed the situation in his country:

> The reorganization of our schools which began in the 1960s following the introduction of unconstrained competition as the major principle of education has had two important consequences. First, it made educational activities totally subservient to economic ones; and secondly, it has prompted the growth of an educational industry in which teaching and learning are transformed from a social enterprise into a money-making one. (Horio, 1988, p. 370)

Professional autonomy is highly constrained in such a system. What has happened in education may be a portent of things to come in all public professions.

On the other hand, Western societies may follow what has been called the "politics of decline," in which governments abandon the Keynesian welfare-state aspiration to include everyone in the largess of the economy and instead employ a politics of exclusion rather than inclusion (Krieger, 1986). Accepting the fact that not everyone can benefit and that there cannot be an ever-expanding economic pie, governments may turn groups against each other in an internally divisive politics, disavowing any obligation toward the poor and disadvantaged (Marquand, 1988). In such a strategy, welfare benefits are reduced, and the government survives by catering to the wealthy and enough of the middle class to maintain itself in power. The Thatcher and Reagan governments are examples of such regimes.

Evaluators themselves are professionals and subject to the same pressures as other professionals working for the government, even though their peculiar task may be to evaluate other professionals. What should evaluators do under these circumstances? To what degree must they follow government policy and to what degree embrace the standards of their own profession? Ultimately, these are matters of professional ethics and social justice.

Notes

1. I owe this insight to Felix Angulo Rasco of the University of Malaga, Spain. Of course, the church still has great cultural authority in Spain, as well.

2. At least the debate is supposed to precede government action. As one Canadian pointed out to me, all too often the government goes ahead without debate, proceeding from the top down.

4

Higher Education: An Example

The split between the demands of political and professional accountability is exemplified by evaluation in higher education. As Western societies have become increasingly industrialized in the past 150 years, the roles of higher education institutions have changed dramatically (Perkin, 1989). Advanced capitalism has created societies in which new educational institutions have been created and old ones transformed. These changes have not been planned systematically, but have evolved as new duties and institutions have been added to old ones.

The increasing division of labor has led to professionalization of the workforce. Professionalism is based on claims of expertise, which is produced through selection by merit and special training. The universities and other institutions of higher education play a central role by acting as gatekeepers to career hierarchies (Larson, 1977). These institutions control access to the professions, establish training programs, and conduct research for them. In former times, apprenticeships served as entry to the original professions of medicine, law, and the clergy. Now higher education institutions of several types prepare large numbers of students for professional specialties that did not exist a century ago. In fact, the primary route to professionalization for an occupation is to establish a higher education training program. University teaching itself became professionalized around the turn of the 20th century.

An earlier version of this chapter was presented as a paper at the National Conference on Evaluation in Higher Education, Hanko, Norway, November 4, 1991. Thanks to Karl Solstad and Mark Dubin for helpful comments.

A related major function that the modern university has assumed is the creation of new knowledge, knowledge that provides the cognitive base for the professions and that is increasingly critical to success in competitive world economic markets. The research university was a German invention of the early 19th century, beginning with the University of Berlin in 1810, conceived by Wilhelm von Humboldt, head of culture and education in the Prussian Ministry of Interior. Von Humboldt saw the university as an ideal community that would develop knowledge independent of the church and state (Bertilsson, 1991). At the time, Prussia was having trouble with government censorship in the universities, which was constraining research and teaching. The free research university, unencumbered by external control, was the answer formulated by von Humboldt. Otto von Bismarck, in his efforts to mold a powerful German state, provided strong government support for research that could be put to industrial and military uses, and German universities soon were highly successful in fields such as chemistry, physics, physiology, and mathematics.

When the United States developed its graduate research schools in the late 1800s, it turned to Germany for its model. Hundreds of Americans attended German universities, and there were strong intellectual ties. Between 1870 and 1900, the number of professors in the United States quadrupled, and the research professor in a large university became the ideal, following the German model (Haber, 1991). However, in contrast to the autonomous personal power of the individual German professor, who possessed a chair, the Americans emphasized peer control, a collegium of equals organized as a department, a significantly different model (Bertilsson, 1991). England, by contrast, was seriously impeded by its rigid social class structure, and the elite universities there maintained the gentleman's education in classics for a long time (Perkin, 1989). France, on the other hand, developed its research academies separate from the universities.

The successes of these disciplined research efforts, especially in the physical and biological sciences, have been dramatic. What is less well understood is that there is a peculiar culture in these institutions that sustains research endeavors. The research disciplines focus on particular and highly specialized problems. Workers in these disciplines ask each other questions, challenge each other's ideas, and test each other's answers, a process of discourse captured by the term *discipline*. Through disciplined inquiry, workers build a body of specific knowledge about limited topics. It is this disciplined mode of inquiry that produces new knowledge. Workers of quite modest intelligence (such as we university professors) occasionally can produce useful and even important results.

This academic culture should not be romanticized. The work that most researchers do is not glamorous. One of my colleagues in agriculture at the University of Illinois spent his entire academic career studying cow udders. The fact is that by applying disciplined intelligence to such focused practical manners, everyone's standard of living can be improved dramatically. Modern societies have become increasingly dependent on such knowledge production and have passed from an age of individual practical inventors to collective science-based invention. So, universities and other institutions of higher learning not only train people for the professions but also create new knowledge, which sometimes has profound and unforeseen effects. I might also note that disciplined inquiry breeds its own pathologies of pedanticism, irrelevance, and pomposity, and the marriage of teaching and research is not entirely compatible (Bertilsson, 1991).

Throughout most of this century, professionalism has expanded, but during the dismal economic conditions of the 1970s and 1980s, a strong backlash has developed. First, professionals have been assailed for their privileges, poor services, and reluctance to reform themselves. Second, government has been attacked as ineffective and inefficient. Politicians such as Reagan and Thatcher have made "big government" a target of their political campaigns. Third, groups, such as labor unions and professional associations, have come under attack as "special interests" (Perkin, 1989).

As professional and technical occupations have multiplied, they have come into conflict with each other as they compete for resources and clients. One major conflict is between public and private professionals. Public professionals, including those in state-supported occupations, such as professors, teachers, bureaucrats, and social workers, favor expanded state services. Private professionals, including managers of corporations and privately supported doctors and lawyers, do not. Private professionals see themselves as producers of wealth and view public professionals as parasitic. These conflicts among professional groups are mediated through the state, with evaluation being one means of adjudication.

Furthermore, as higher education systems have become so large and critical to the economic well-being of modern societies, they also cost much more. Politicians worry about the huge costs and lack of control. The more governments embrace free market economics, the less control they have over industries and businesses, so there is some displacement of attention to sectors over which governments do have control. As a consequence, higher education (as well as primary and secondary education) is blamed for social and economic problems that originate elsewhere, such as in the economic structure itself (House, 1991a).

Since the early 1970s, primary and secondary education have been targets of attack. For example, the first statewide educational accountability scheme appeared in the state of Michigan as long ago as 1973, and the National Education Association, the largest teachers' union, hired three evaluation experts to critique the scheme (House, Rivers, & Stufflebeam, 1974). These accountability pressures have continued with even greater intensity in lower education, and now higher education is being called to account in similar ways. Attacks against higher education have been launched by the media and government officials worldwide (Kogan, 1983).

Many attacks are ideological, inspired by the ideology of the free market and advanced by persons representing business interests. Attacks are directed at the content, as well as the costs, of higher education. One important characteristic of the disciplines and the research universities is their declared independence and autonomy from the ideology of the dominant social groups. Higher education faces another period of ideological critique. The attacks go to the heart of the research enterprise. Like most professionals, professors are shocked, puzzled, and dismayed by these strident assaults. They are afraid that efforts to evaluate could be seriously damaging, and they are justified in their concerns.

ᴥ Higher Education Accountability

As presented earlier, Kogan (1986) contends that there are three models of educational accountability: (a) state or public control, which entails elected representatives, appointed officials, and heads managing schools; (b) professional control, which entails control by teachers, professors, and professional administrators; and (c) consumer control, which can operate either through direct participation of the public or through market mechanisms derived from the private sector. It is my contention that each of these modes of accountability requires different evaluation information and that mixing the different types of evaluations, or using the same data for each, may result in serious problems and inappropriate evaluations. Although it is important to recognize the legitimate claims of the state, the professionals, and consumers, different forms of evaluation are necessary for each.

For example, state authority is exercised through regulating behavior and allocating resources (Weiler, 1990). The principal rationale for centralized regulation in education is the need for standardization of curricula, qualifications, and examinations. Centralized allocation is justified in the name of equity of resources and efficiency. In other words, central state authority is exercised for the purpose of equitable and efficient use of resources. These are purposes different from those of the universities.

In addition to the political authority of the state, there is also the disciplinary authority of the professions, exemplified in the give-and-take discourse within the academic disciplines. This disciplinary authority is not democratic—people do not vote on issues. Nor is it authoritarian—one or two people within the field do not decide issues, although the leading authorities in the field are engaged in key debates. Rather, issues are resolved more or less by consensus based on evidence, deliberation, and persuasion of the other members of the discipline. This authority is cultural, rather than based on power or money, and is difficult for the government and public to understand.

Drawing upon Lundgren's (1990) classification of governance with the central/local dimension on the one hand and the political/professional dimension on the other (see Figure 3.1), an institution can be accountable to the political center or to the professional center, to the local political group or to the local professional group. In U.S. universities, local political governance is exercised through a board of regents or trustees for each institution. This board of laypeople is appointed or elected to its position and oversees the operations of the institution in the same way as a local school board oversees local schools. The board approves personnel appointments, budgets, and operating procedures, usually without interfering in internal academic processes. The information used by the local governing board is local financial and personnel information.

Professional relationships at the central level are handled through individual disciplines and organized interest groups. Each faculty member belongs to a recognized professional discipline, such as physics or psychology, that communicates with members through publications and meetings. Evaluation is exercised through the refereed publications of disciplinary journals, control of presentations at meetings, and the awarding of research and training grants. The disciplinary community is highly influential in guiding the work of the individual professor. The professor's career is dependent on this community (see Chapter 5).

The other two governing domains are the local professional and the central public levels. The local professional level involves evaluation inside the institution itself, which I discuss in detail in this chapter. The central political level involves the relationship between higher education institutions and the central government, which I see as problematic. I discuss accountability to the state later in this chapter.

These multiple functions of higher education and its centrality to society present difficulties for evaluation and accountability. The dilemma is that many methods proposed for accountability violate or seriously impede the conditions necessary for creation of new knowledge in both research and teaching. Without mystifying the creation of new knowledge, the conditions necessary to its production are not well understood, even within the universities themselves. On the other hand, demands for accountability from outside will not disappear and are likely to become much more intense. One response is to create evaluation systems that protect the central functions of higher education and provide relevant information to government and the public.

The basic question, then, is what kind of evaluation will preserve the disciplinary and teaching processes that produce knowledge for faculty and students, while at the same time providing necessary information to the state and public. I deal with the research university here in the expectation that what I say can be applied in amended form to other institutions of higher learning. These institutions are so varied that the same evaluation cannot fit all. (I base these ideas on firsthand experiences of evaluating programs and faculty at the universities of Illinois and Colorado.)

⸙ Evaluating Programs

I describe here typical program review procedures at a research university and suggest how these procedures might be improved. Second, I suggest ways in which higher education institutions might be accountable to the larger society without damaging their own internal operations. In considering evaluation procedures, three criteria are relevant: (a) bias in the evaluation, which might make the evaluation dishonest or inaccurate; (b) how the evaluation might be conducted so as to maximize the usefulness of evaluation results; and (c) ensuring that the evaluation does not damage internal processes of the institution, namely research and teaching.

Within U.S. research universities there are three separate systems of evaluation: one for evaluation of students, one for evaluation of faculty, and one for evaluation of programs.[1] I use the terms *programs* and *units* almost interchangeably. A unit could be an academic department, such as anthropology or physics or business administration, or it could be a large program, such as the black studies program, or a small school, such as the School of Education. What is evaluated is the entire set of activities of the unit—research activities, teaching activities, service activities, and governing activities—in short, pretty much whatever the unit does.

Program evaluation within research universities typically works in the following way. Each program or unit is required to be evaluated at least once every 7 years. A number of faculty, from 9 to 15, are appointed by the vice-chancellor and the faculty senate to serve on the program review panel, which oversees all program evaluations on campus. This panel is chaired by a faculty member or by a university administrator, such as the associate vice-chancellor, who has no vote in the deliberations. The panel also includes one undergraduate and one graduate student, who are selected by student organizations. This program review panel selects the units to be evaluated each year (for details, see Program Review Panel, 1990).

The program review panel, in turn, appoints a special internal self-study committee for each unit being evaluated. The self-study committee consists of faculty and students from within the unit being evaluated and is responsible for preparing a self-study report. This self-study report must address certain predefined topics, such as providing an overview of the unit, its aims and goals, its plans for the next 5 years, its response to recommendations from the previous program review, an assessment of the unit's strengths, its concerns and problems, its comparison to similar units in other universities, how it would use additional resources if available, student opinions about the unit, summaries of individual faculty member vitae, and financial information about the unit. When completed, this self-study report must be reviewed and approved by all faculty members in the unit.

A separate statistical office within the university administration supplies descriptive information on characteristics of students—

numbers, gender, ethnicity, test scores, grade point averages, numbers of degrees awarded—and information on characteristics of faculty—numbers; gender; ethnicity; ages; salaries; comparisons to comparable universities; workloads of faculty; scholarly activities, including numbers of publications and contracts and grants awarded; as well as budget data, such as travel, supply, and equipment expenditures.

When the self-study report is finished, which can take as long as several months or a year, the program review panel appoints an internal review committee, which consists of three faculty and two students from the university, but from outside the unit being evaluated. This committee has special responsibility for the evaluation of the unit. This internal review committee examines the self-study report and conducts its own data collection inside the unit to confirm and supplement the self-study report and to raise issues that may have been overlooked. The internal review committee interviews faculty members and students, with care to record dissenting opinions. This internal review committee then prepares its own short, 10-page report, which summarizes the self-study, appraises the unit, and makes recommendations. This completed report, called the internal review report, is sent to the unit, and the unit has 1 week to respond.

The overall program review panel then appoints an external review committee, which consists of two or three professors from other universities who have prominent reputations in the same discipline. This external review committee reads the self-study and internal review reports. The external review committee visits the unit for a few days; interviews faculty, students, and administrators; and writes its own separate assessment. This external review report discusses the strengths and weaknesses of the unit, the faculty, the leadership of the unit, and the progress toward the unit and university goals. Once this report is finished, the unit has 2 weeks to respond in order to disagree or correct misconceptions.

At this point, there are three reports: the *self-study report* from the unit itself, the *internal review report* from faculty and students internal to the university but outside the unit, and the *external review report* from professors outside the university. All three reports are submitted to the program review panel, which reconciles the three reports and prepares a synthesis, called the *final report*. The final report is about 15 pages in length and must contain a statement about the review process that took place, results of the previous review from years before, important points from the self-study report, a summary of the internal review report, a summary of the external review

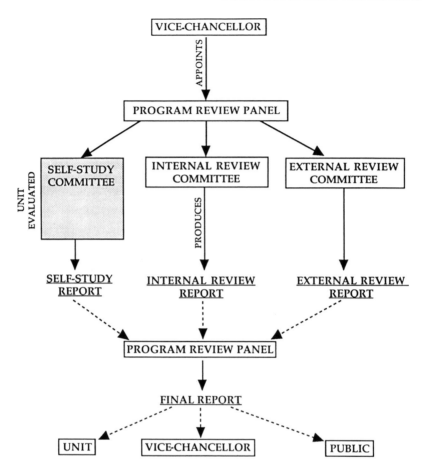

Figure 4.1. University Program Evaluation Scheme

report, conclusions of the program review panel itself after considering all these reports, and recommendations as to what should be done. This final report is shown to the unit for comments and forwarded to the vice-chancellor. The finished Final Report then becomes a public document for anyone inside or outside the university to examine. This whole process is summarized in Figure 4.1.

The vice-chancellor has the authority to make changes in the unit, by providing additional resources, taking resources away, allowing the unit to hire more faculty, insisting that particular kinds of faculty be hired, not allowing new hiring until certain conditions are met, changing student requirements, or eliminating components. These changes are negotiated with the unit based on the final evaluation report. The unit itself is expected to formulate a plan as to how it will build on its strengths and overcome the weaknesses that have been found. The progress of the unit is monitored by the vice-chancellor over the next few years, based on the evaluation reports and recommendations. For the university as a whole, there will be as many of these final reports each year as there are units under evaluation, usually about 15 in a large university.

ᐩ Strengths and Weaknesses of Program Reviews

The strength of this process is that the evaluation is conducted by university faculty, including the unit being evaluated, so it includes serious self-study. The overseeing panel is dominated by faculty whose own criteria for evaluation are those that maintain a supportive work environment, both for teaching and research. The people doing the evaluation, if well chosen, know what good work conditions should be like, and they can recognize these processes when present or absent, as when a unit has serious problems. Panel members convey these findings to the unit and to the university administration. Action is expected. The results of the evaluation are used.

It is often the case that the unit being evaluated knows about problems it has but does nothing about them until they are made public in the evaluation. Solutions for problems often come from within the unit itself, which knows what should be done. The public revelation, under the scrutiny of fellow faculty and the vice-chancellor, sometimes is enough to spur the unit to action. In other cases, the unit is unable to solve its problems, particularly when there is strong factional conflict, and in extreme cases the vice-chancellor may appoint another head of the unit from outside for a period of time. The head of a poorly performing unit may be relieved of his or her administrative duties.

The internal review committee brings the perspective of the university to bear, and the external review committee brings the perspective of the discipline, thus engaging both the local and the central professional interests. Having several different groups examine the unit increases the likelihood of the final report being accurate because each group's findings are checked by other groups. The unit's own self-study report is examined by the internal and external review committees, and all the reports are examined by the program review panel, which checks reports against each other for inconsistencies. At each stage of the process, the unit has opportunities to correct misinformation and misconceptions. Appeal, redress, and participation are available to those evaluated. Finally, because the vice-chancellor reads the evaluation reports and meets with the program review panel, he or she is well informed about the unit. The vice-chancellor and the unit have an agreed-upon report, corroborated and legitimized by the process, on which to base decisions about the unit.

On the negative side, all the committees may be too lenient on the unit being reviewed because faculty members often are personally acquainted with faculty in the unit. The committees may be too generous in their assessments and unwilling to point out problems. Sometimes an administrator, such as the vice-chancellor, has such strong views about a unit that he or she influences the program review panel in writing the final report. This intrusion can bias the evaluation in either a positive or negative direction, resulting in a miscarriage of the process. Also, individual committee members may have favorite ideas that they wish to promote, even when these ideas are not relevant to the unit evaluated. There is also a tendency for units not to be totally honest in revealing their weaknesses, because these deficiencies will be made public. Hence the active pursuit of dissident views within the unit is critical.

Another weakness of the evaluation process is the high cost involved in completing all this work, especially in terms of faculty time. Dozens of faculty are involved in evaluating each unit, and the time expenditure is great, especially for the self-study. There is also a burden on the other committees and the program review panel, which must handle several reports a year. Faculty members are appointed to serve for only a few years on such committees because of the heavy time commitment.

The entire evaluation process reflects the values and goals of faculty and, to a much lesser degree, the students. In these program evaluations (and in the separate system of evaluating individual faculty members for promotion and tenure), research receives highest priority in the research universities. Teaching, particularly undergraduate teaching, is given less attention, though there has been concern about this recently. Teaching is evaluated, but it is not scrutinized as closely as the research. For one thing, there is less variation in teaching performance than in research performance, and the means for discriminating the quality of teaching performances are less well developed. Typically, faculty are required to have students complete rating forms anonymously for each course about how good the teaching has been, and this information is available to the committees. In general, however, the procedures for evaluating teaching are less developed than those for evaluating research.

In summary, I would consider these evaluation procedures to be successful in what they attempt to do. The cost can be mitigated by evaluating programs less frequently. The findings are reasonably unbiased and are used to improve programs. Sometimes the improvement is dramatic. In other cases, the unit could do as well without the evaluation. In general, the evaluation information is useful and used. What is missing is information from clients and consumers, with the exception of limited information from students and graduates. Overall, the evaluations substantially help the university in fulfilling its major functions.

⮞ Public Accountability

Those familiar with the evaluation literature will recognize these procedures as an example of the "professional review" or "accreditation" model of evaluation (House, 1980). This approach has long been employed, particularly in the United States, to accredit secondary and professional schools, such as those for medicine, law, business, engineering, and education. In basic form, there is a self-study by the unit, and then a team of colleagues examines the self-study, writes a report describing the strengths and weaknesses of the unit, and makes recommendations, usually endorsing or accrediting the school. One of the most famous evaluations, Flexner's review of medical schools in the early 20th century, was of this type (Floden, 1983).

Over the past few decades, professional reviews have lost some credibility. Lawyers evaluating lawyers, doctors evaluating doctors, police evaluating police, and professors evaluating professors are viewed with skepticism by outsiders. There are suspicions that professionals are too self-serving and lenient with each other. Few schools are ever discredited, few doctors and lawyers disbarred. Professionals rarely examine each other's work rigorously. (An exception is the evaluation of untenured faculty in research universities, which tends to be fairly rigorous.)

These state-supported professional bureaucracies cost large sums of money. When politicians cut budgets, the largest amounts are often in education or health care or social services. State authorities strive to control these enterprises, and having data about them is one way to do it, or so the state authorities imagine. Professional reviews rarely result in recommendations for reduced funding or provide information that governing agencies want. There is also the recent trend toward discrediting professional services generally.

One idea for public accountability would be to provide outside agencies with the reports produced by the internal professional evaluation process. But I fear the consequences of doing that. Legislators do not understand the internal workings of higher education institutions. They do not understand what conditions must prevail if successful research and teaching are to occur, any more than they could define the proper conditions for performing surgery. If outsiders were to read these internal reports, they might misinterpret them. It does not seem likely that information useful for improving institutions internally will be useful for external accounting.

Those responsible for overseeing higher education are likely to want statistics on enrollments, costs, salaries, expenditures, quality of services, numbers and amounts of research grants, publications, citations, what jobs graduates obtain, and graduates' success in the job market. In general, central ministries want data on productivity that they can compare to other institutions; efficiency and standardization are primary concerns. Cost and productivity studies seem certain in times of financial stringency.

For example, in 1988, the Colorado legislature passed a law requiring all public institutions of higher education in the state to develop accountability plans. Colorado is about two thirds the size of Norway with two thirds the population, most of which is concentrated in the middle of the state, distributed along the eastern edge of the Rocky Mountains. A few people live in ski resorts and mining towns in the high mountains and on cattle ranches and farms on the eastern plains. The state has 10 state-supported universities and 18 two-year community colleges—far too many for the population to support. (There has been a tendency for powerful legislators to enhance the economic prospects of their local communities by establishing higher education institutions there.)

The problem, as seen from the state capital, Denver, is to reduce the costs of this overbuilt higher education system, while at the same time maintaining the economic benefits that accrue from these institutions. As stated in the state accountability mandates, "The overall purpose of the accountability program is to ensure the public that Colorado's state-supported institutions are accountable for providing quality education 'efficiently through the effective use of institutional resources of time, effort and money," (Colorado Commission on Higher Education, 1988). (The quotation within the quotation is from the enabling legislation.)

This legislation designates specific information that must be included in the accountability plans of each institution:

1. A statement of expected student performances as it relates to the goals and objectives of undergraduate education
2. Description of improvements in student knowledge and skills between entrance and graduation
3. Student completion and retention rates
4. Evidence of after-graduation performance, as in employment and professional advancement
5. Student and graduate satisfaction
6. Plans for reporting the information annually
7. A cost description of the accountability plan itself
8. Specific plans as to how minority student data will be disaggregated and reported

The state legislature did not provide additional money for planning or collecting data, but stipulated that if an acceptable plan was not developed, the budget of the institution could be cut by 2%. So far each institution has been allowed to develop its own plan and collect its own data. The Final Reports from the internal program reviews at the University of Colorado are sent to the state, but they are seldom used. What I expect to happen is that the higher education commission will receive 28 different reports and be unable to compare institutions or interpret the information. The state eventually will require exactly the same data from each institution, which will include comparative statistics that emphasize efficiency, productivity, and student knowledge and satisfaction.

Mark Dubin, the associate vice-chancellor in charge of evaluation at the University of Colorado, is more optimistic about the usefulness of the state-mandated outcome information for accountability, though not the use of internal reviews.[2] He believes that the "outcome" data, which typically consist of test or survey data collected by each unit at the university, could be interpreted properly in a ministry of education, provided that ministry officials have the right backgrounds, which they do not have. In his view, central authorities should have two roles: first, to make certain that institutions have a proper evaluation system and, second, to ensure that the system is working properly. Often the state conflates these two roles and tries to micro-manage the institutions. Currently one person at the state level attempts to reduce all the outcome data to a single grade or a score for each institution, but this synthesis has not proved successful.

Fundamentally, the state government has a "value-added" conception of education: What did the institutions add to the students' knowledge, job success, and so on? Did the state get its money's worth? Is the state getting value for its money? Small liberal arts colleges have tried to evaluate in this value-added manner, focusing on outcome measures such as test scores (Mentkowski, 1988; Paskow, 1988; Steele, 1988). Higher education assessment of student learning is a topic in its own right. The large universities have transformed the value-added question into program evaluation. The value-added concept is an economic productivity approach, which results in quantitative indicators, similar to the evaluation fostered by the British government.

The state senator who sponsored the accountability legislation believes the endeavor has not been successful and wants more numbers, although state ministry officials argue that these might misrepresent higher education. Legislators want to be able to compare institutions in terms of productivity, which means numbers, in their view. Although Dubin is optimistic that professional evaluation will prevail through persuading legislators and ministry officials, I am less optimistic, based on the experiences in elementary and secondary education over the past few decades. In my opinion, state authorities will be swept toward quantitative productivity indicators.

The dangers inherent in using such information to make decisions are apparent. One cannot make discoveries in physics more likely by analyzing publication rates, nor improve instruction in undergraduate classes by examining student/faculty ratios. The factors that determine these things are not discernible in information of this kind, but there will be a temptation for state officials to attempt to govern internal processes by reference to the information available to them, without knowledge of the cause and effect processes at work in knowledge production. On the other hand, political authorities do need information to constrain costs and improve efficiency.

If state authorities opt for quantitative measures, I hope that ministries collect data on social outcomes such as equality, social class, and job opportunities, as well as on productivity. Collecting equality data is rarely done, except for information on minorities and women. The State Higher Education Profiles from the National Center for Educational Statistics (National Center for Educational Statistics, 1991) are typical. The profiles include data comparing all 50 states on enrollment, faculty, revenues, degrees, expenditures, and so on, with each state statistic indexed to a national average and ranked against all the other states on each of 25 statistics.

The best one can do is to keep these two systems of evaluation separate. Evaluation to improve the institution internally should not be confused with information for efficiency, and the latter information should not be used to manage institutions internally. Government authorities should allow institutions to conduct their own evaluations for purposes of improvement. The government can insist that higher education institutions have valid evaluation procedures in place without dictating the content of the evaluations or using evaluation results improperly.

What other possibilities exist for public accountability? In addition to creating data systems and ensuring that institutions have their own evaluation, the state might sponsor special studies that examine the workings of the higher education system. This raises the possibility of "theory-oriented" evaluation, as conceived by Franke-Wikberg (1990), Wallin (1990), and others, which attempts to provide an explicit contextual framework for the studies. One of the best sources for such studies is the Swedish higher education research program (Bertilsson, 1991; Bjorklund, 1985, 1989).

There is also the third dimension of accountability and evaluation—the market dimension represented by consumers. Higher education institutions can provide information to consumers, such as students and parents, directly. Self-evaluation has received some attention in elementary and secondary education (e.g., Simons, 1987; Tiller, 1990), and I believe there are possibilities in higher education, although I doubt that self-evaluation reports will satisfy central authorities. There are now information guides for students who are choosing which university or college to attend. Unfortunately, many of these guides are misleading and inaccurate. Large numbers of students use the guides because little information exists to help inform students and parents about such choices. Information for clients and consumers is a potential area for development, especially as the market approach is emphasized.

I conclude by saying that the traditional autonomy that higher education institutions have enjoyed is coming to an end. The question is not whether we should have accountability, but rather what kind of accountability and evaluation we can have that will protect the vital internal processes of research and teaching that are essential to the improvement of society, and that will help protect higher education institutions against the economic and ideological assaults that are certain to come.

Notes

1. There is also a system for evaluating faculty for salaries, which varies across departments, and a system for evaluating staff, such as secretaries, grounds workers, and others. Typically, this second evaluation is run by the state government and consists of supervisors filling out rating forms on the employees, similar to forms used in the armed services and business—hierarchical, supervisory evaluation. It works about as well as it does in the military.

2. Interview with Mark Dubin, Associate Vice-Chancellor, University of Colorado at Boulder, October 25, 1991.

～ 5 ～

Evaluation as a Discipline

*W*hereas a profession is a complementary set of organizations, roles, and people, a discipline is a communal tradition of procedures and techniques for dealing with theoretical or practical problems. Professional history, if written, would be a history of organizations, whereas disciplinary history would be mostly a history of ideas (Toulmin, 1972). In this chapter I explore the nature and structure of evaluation as a discipline and, indeed, whether it can be characterized as such. I consider the nature of disciplines, particularly scientific disciplines; the authority structure of disciplines, or how critical decisions are made within them; and, finally, the future of evaluation as a discipline.

～ Is Evaluation a Discipline?

In the 16th century and for several centuries following, the primary example of a discipline that others tried to emulate was geometry, with its unparalleled logicality and systematicity, and what scholars at the time thought (until the 19th century) was its universal truth. In modern times, the discipline that serves as the standard is physics, with its complex mathematical formulations, counterintuitive insights, and impressive practical implications. Other scientific disciplines have tried to emulate the mathematical approach that geometry and physics have exemplified, the presumption being that the more mathematical a discipline, the more mature it is. Toulmin (1972) defines a discipline this way:

> A collective human enterprise takes the form of a rationally developed "discipline," in those cases where men's [and women's] shared commitment to a sufficiently agreed set of ideals leads to the development of an isolatable and self-defining repertory of procedures; and where those procedures are open to further modification, so as to deal with problems arising from the incomplete fulfillment of those disciplinary ideals. (p. 359)

The ideals of the discipline provide the intellectual framework within which decisions are made regarding what is acceptable. In the scientific disciplines, the primary ideal is explanation. Ideals for a field may be tightly defined, so that the discipline is "compact," as in physics, or less clearly defined, in which the discipline is "diffuse." If little or no agreement exists on ideals, then a field is not a discipline at all. Procedures within a discipline are judged acceptable against the agreed-upon ideals, and without some agreement, there is no common basis for judgment. Disciplines need not be scientific. Law, crafts, and technologies have goals other than explanatory ones—practical or resolution goals—but may also be disciplines (Toulmin, 1972).

Not all fields can become disciplines. The subject matter may be too complex, such as meteorology until recently. Or basic guiding concepts may be lacking, such as physics in the 14th century, or the techniques and methods may be inadequate. When key missing concepts or techniques are discovered, a sudden creative burst of development often occurs in the field. Hence development in the disciplines varies considerably in rate. A mature, compact discipline is one whose conceptual and methodological repertory is exposed at every stage to critical reappraisal and modification by qualified judges in the light of the collective ideals. Activities are organized around a set of agreed ideals, and these ideals impose demands on those committed to the discipline. Discussions revolve around improving the concepts and techniques of the discipline by appeal to the ideals, with the collective ideals also determining the criteria of adequacy. Furthermore, professional forums must exist for these discussions to take place (Toulmin, 1972).

Disciplines fail to achieve compactness through either methodological or institutional deficiencies. Either there are no agreed ideals, criteria, and problems, so that concepts cannot face critical, rational tests, or else there are no suitable professional organizations in which the subject can be explored. Without agreed criteria, theoretical debate becomes largely methodological or philosophical, directed at debating the acceptability of rival approaches or analyzing methodological failures, but without possibility of resolution. The field is splintered into rival factions that do not accept each other's work.

Toulmin, in 1972, took the behavioral sciences, especially psychology, as his primary example of "would-be" disciplines, fields that might become disciplines but are not. In his view, rival schools with little in common (e.g., behaviorism and Gestaltism) and inconsistent conceptions of what constitutes an explanation exemplify lack of agreement in the field. Changes within the discipline are characterized by pendulum swings of fashion, rather than by cumulative development. Journals and organizations reflect rival orientations to the same phenomena, rather than sub-specialties. Toulmin calls psychology a loose confederation of proselytizing sects, each group operating under the dominance of its own high priest, with radical differences in theoretic approaches, and each group claiming sovereign independence, a sign of the undisciplinary character of the field being citations of references only within each sect itself.

Toulmin does not suggest that psychologists simply sit down and agree on basic principles. Such agreement may take centuries, as it did in the physical sciences. However, in his view, there is nothing in the nature of the human sciences that prevents them from becoming disciplines. It may be that the subject matter as now defined is too grand. (Aristotle, after all, wanted to find a general explanation of all change processes.) Or it may be that basic concepts in psychology are inappropriate or unavailable. If physicists had collected empirical data in the 14th century, they would have been unable to make theoretical sense of the data conceptually (Toulmin, 1972). They simply did not have adequate concepts. Within Toulmin's framework, no doubt, evaluation would not be considered a discipline either.

My own view is that Toulmin takes physics as the standard discipline, just as earlier analysts did geometry. His analysis emphasizes agreement within the field too heavily, with not enough emphasis on the social structure of disciplines. I would call psychology a discipline, even while acknowledging that it is diffuse or loose or weak or even unsuccessful, similar to the other human sciences. Few would contend that psychology produces explanations as successful in its domain as biology. Yet psychology does have some common goals, some criteria and standards of agreement, professional forums, and an elaborate disciplinary social structure. The criteria Toulmin employs are matters of degree, rather than kind (Toulmin, 1972).

I would also consider evaluation to be a discipline or almost a discipline, though it does not meet Toulmin's criteria either. My criteria for a discipline would be the degree to which the basic concepts in the field are "joined" and the degree to which the social structure promotes internal critical review. There is a useful contrast here among physics, evaluation, and policy studies. In my opinion, policy science is not a discipline currently because internal criticism is nonexistent, factional, or haphazard compared to that of physics or psychology. When scientists at the University of Utah discovered "cold fusion," it was only a matter of months before their discovery was challenged and discredited (even allowing for the possibility that they may have been correct). The basic issues were joined immediately and decisively.

By contrast, the most influential policy study of the 1980s, Charles Murray's *Losing Ground* (1984), still stands as a credible study, even though it has been attacked in multitudinous ways for its procedures and methodology. There is no definitive way that the findings of policy studies can be disconfirmed within the policy sciences at the current time. Criticisms are dismissed as political or "That's their opinion." Policy science is not a discipline as it currently exists because there is no way of "joining the issues," as there is in physics or nonscientific disciplines such as law. It is not so much whether people in the field agree with one another but whether the issues can be productively discussed and debated.

What about evaluation? It is certainly not as closely "joined" as physics, but it is more closely joined than policy studies because there are ways of deciding the issues in evaluation, albeit sometimes these ways are weak. Sometimes it is possible to critique and invalidate an evaluation study or procedure, even though this is not done regularly. Critiques are conducted ad hoc, if at all, but the degree to which critiques can be definitive is an indicator of the extent to which critical issues can be joined and the extent to which a disciplinary framework exists, in my opinion. What kind of discipline would physics be if no one bothered to investigate or challenge the cold fusion study or, if after all the debate, it still was not clear where the field stood?

The successful critique of studies is an important indicator of the joining of issues that characterizes a discipline. In strong or tight disciplines, issues are joined across the spectrum. The failure to join issues reflects the lack of a cognitive base for doing so, which characterizes the policy sciences. (See Bruner, 1991, for a discussion of the problems of the policy sciences, which are similar to those of evaluation 10 or 15 years ago, i.e., an overreliance on formal quantitative models that do not work very well.)

I would consider evaluation to be a loose or "almost" discipline. We are close to arriving at a fundamental joining of issues, even though possibly we have not done so extensively yet. Equally important, evaluation is close to having a social structure that promotes internal critique and discourse. One must allow the possibility that the human sciences will never be as fully integrated conceptually as the physical ones because of the nature of the subject matter. There may always be more diverse approaches and less integration of concepts in the human sciences. There is no way to tell this in advance of substantive findings themselves. What the human sciences must manage if they are to be disciplines is to have mechanisms of internal critique and a joining of issues and concepts. Evaluation is nearly there, in my opinion.

There are fields of study that are not disciplines. For example, Toulmin calls the fine arts and literature "quasi-disciplines." Artists and writers learn collective techniques, but these techniques are means to the end of personal, individual expression, rather than to collective or communal ends. One can criticize art or literature only in relation to the goals the artist is trying to achieve, according to Toulmin. Yet it seems that at times in history and in other cultures, art has been a communal enterprise subject to collective judgment. When the issues are joined collectively, I would call these enterprises disciplines—easier to see in the crafts, perhaps, than in the Western image of art and literature as personal expression. In my sense of the term, art criticism, music criticism, and literary criticism are disciplines, but not book reviews or movie reviews, because these are individual expressions of the reviewer and are not subject to disciplinary review and control.

Toulmin regards practical problems that call for concrete decisions as incapable of being "disciplinable" because they are not isolatable. In his view, disciplines must have only one set of well-defined goals, such as explanation for science, and be marked off sharply from everyday activities. They must be single-valued. Real world events are too complex, and disciplines must maintain an abstract isolation from the real world. In his example, a politician makes a speech, which may simultaneously honor constituents, give unintended offense to some hearers, make an implicit promise to others, draw public attention to the speaker's oratorical skills, enhance his or her party's chances, accelerate a thrombosis, precipitate a crisis of confidence, and break an assignation with his or her lover

(Toulmin, 1972, p. 402). Because the event can be appraised from many points of view, Toulmin argues, it cannot be subject to disciplinary study. A singular point of view is necessary.

But I think Toulmin's analysis misleads here, for this is just what the evaluator or historian can do within his or her disciplinary framework. A historian with proper background can judge the effects of Antony's peroration for Julius Caesar, in spite of multiple perspectives. He or she can explain and evaluate the speech from several points of view. The historian aims to explain the event and its effects, and the evaluator aims to evaluate, both being isolated from improper biases, such as overweening nationalism or personal interest. Presumably, their respective disciplines provide them with procedures and concepts for achieving this. Proper isolation may be more difficult than in some other enterprises, but it is possible, even when dealing with the practical world.

On the other hand, Toulmin makes an important point about disciplines versus the real world. Disciplines are abstractions, intellectual discourses and frameworks deliberately removed from the world in order to "discipline" the discourse that occurs. Even on its best day, physics cannot account for all the physical events in the world. So disciplines never deal with full world complexity. They only serve as guides to the world. Scientific disciplines provide only partial explanations, and explaining an actual concrete event may require many disciplinary frameworks. Analyzing an event from an economic perspective can never account for the full event because it omits political, psychological, social, physical, and numerous other considerations. There is a tendency, especially among academics, to take single disciplinary explanations as full explanations.

࠮ The Authority Structure of Disciplines

Disciplines are collective, communal enterprises. The ultimate authority is the consent of one's colleagues, but not all colleagues have equal influence. There are both a formal and an informal esteem hierarchy within each field. The formal hierarchy consists of the established positions, the officers, editors, and committees. At the top of the informal hierarchy are those whose ideas are taken most seriously. Toulmin (1972) puts the relationship well: "It is a glorious thing to be President of the Royal Society . . . but what novice will not prefer to win a reputation of brilliance . . . among his [or her] peers, even if this later proves to be a disqualification for worldly office?" (p. 277).

How are scholarly disciplines structured? A discipline is composed of groups and subgroups of scholars linked together through common communication—journals, meetings, associations, informal contacts, e-mail. Imagine a circle with fuzzy boundaries, so that at the boundary lines it is difficult to tell whether someone is inside or outside. The boundaries also overlap with other disciplines, like overlapping Venn diagrams, so that some scholars are in two different disciplines where the circles overlap. At the center are the leading authorities of the discipline, such as Campbell and Cronbach at one time in evaluation, if you will. The discipline changes as people in the field argue and debate new ideas. Those at the center are the gatekeepers who influence the others.

There are two key concepts here: legitimation and validity. Legitimation refers to the process of group acceptance, or whether the group perceives something as legitimate. The major issue for any discipline is how its legitimacy is to be explained and justified. Evaluation is a legitimate discipline because it is accepted by the larger social science community and by the government as a proper field of study. Both the social sciences and government recognize evaluation studies as contributing to public judgments and decisions. There are faculty positions and training programs for evaluators in universities. By contrast, astrology is not considered a legitimate discipline or basis for making decisions, even though most people who practice evaluation read their horoscopes. The government cannot claim to reach judgments legitimately on the basis of astrology, not even Ron and Nancy Reagan.

Legitimation also refers to whether an idea or a method is accepted within the field itself. For example, when I began my career in evaluation, qualitative methods were considered too subjective to be accepted as legitimate. That has changed over the past 20 years. Whether a new idea is accepted depends heavily on the small elite at the center of the field. I remember how joyous we at Illinois were when we received an early outline draft of Cronbach's (1982a) book on evaluation design, which explicitly recognized the legitimacy of qualitative studies. Even though we knew we had many battles ahead, we knew we had won the war for the legitimacy of qualitative approaches.

However, what people within evaluation discuss is not legitimacy, but rather validity. Validity concerns whether inferences from a study are correct. Is the new method valid? Does it produce correct conclusions? How does it compare to other methods? What are the arguments for and against? What is the nature of qualitative studies? In what ways are they similar to or different from quantitative studies? Are there different ways of conducting them? Are there better and worse ways? What techniques would enhance their validity? Exactly what is meant by validity? Should it be redefined? Are the old definitions adequate? Where did the old definitions come from historically? Experts argue with each other back and forth over a period of time, and eventually the issue is resolved within the field.

Note that this authority is not democratic. People do not vote on whether something is valid. Nor is it authoritarian, even though the leading authorities carry on the debate. Rather, the process of decision is one of deliberation and argumentation until a consensus is reached. Even then, some on the losing side never accept the new ideas. Some evaluators will never accept qualitative methods as legitimate, but most in the field do. Those who remain unaccepting retire eventually, and the discipline moves on to another set of critical issues. All concepts in the field are subject to change over a period of time, so no certain foundation of knowledge exists, just the continual debate, dialogue, and argument—the disciplinary discourse. The discourse itself is the center of the discipline. And if it is disciplinary, it must be a discourse in which the issues can be joined.

As part of the process of disciplinary change, the older people, no matter how prominent, have less informal standing in the field eventually, except with peers their own age. Each generation replaces the one before. I remember Ralph Tyler at a meeting on educational indicators at the University of California at Los Angeles (UCLA) in 1990, contesting the idea that the National Assessment of Educational Progress (NAEP), his own creation, should be used to compare states and to hold teachers and schools directly accountable. He argued eloquently, lucidly, and passionately, in spite of his 88 years, that NAEP was meant to help teachers and schools, not to compare them, the same arguments I had heard him use 20 years before to win support for NAEP (Madaus & Stufflebeam, 1989). The people at the meeting listened politely and respectfully, if impatiently, and then turned to the task of how to make teacher, district, and state comparisons, unmoved by Tyler's efforts. Even the most powerful people in the field lose their influence eventually, though not their respect, as has been demonstrated repeatedly in the sciences. (There must be some comfort in knowing that the theorist whose work you detest ultimately will be influential no more.)

This is how evaluation is structured and how most scholarly disciplines are structured. It is a central feature of scholarly fields that the ideas be open to critical review and critique. So we end up with disciplines in which there are theory and practice, with the theorists in the universities producing the theory, which often is irrelevant to the experience of the practitioners. The practitioners encounter problems caused by the social structures in which they operate. Sometimes these problems are addressed by the theorists and sometimes not. Often the theorists can provide no successful resolution because the problems are embedded in worldly social structures that are not amenable to easy intellectual alteration.

ᴥ Disciplinary Change

Novices learn their disciplines by being apprentices to masters, and the progress of a field can be plotted by delineating generations of students, successions of influential teachers, schools of thought, and affiliations of research centers. Underneath these social connections, however, Toulmin contends that the basic intellectual continuity of the discipline is provided by the genealogy of the problems the discipline encounters. Each generation solves certain problems and passes on other problems to the next generation. In addition, the world changes, and new problems emerge, especially in disciplines concerned with social phenomena. In Toulmin's view, a discipline can be defined by the successive sets of problems defined and solved against the disciplinary ideals, which themselves change over time.

In evaluation, Cook and Shadish (1986) and Shadish and Reichardt (1987) have presented a typology of evaluation problems that includes social programming, or the role of social programs in social change; knowledge use, or the use of evaluative information in social programming; valuing, or the role of values in evaluative inquiry; knowledge construction, or how evaluative information should be created; and evaluation practice, or how evaluation ought to be practiced in view of answers provided to the first four problems. In their view, evaluators from education came to the field with the idea of measuring achievement, those from psychology came with the experiment as the solution, those from economics focused on causal modeling techniques, sociologists focused on survey research, and anthropologists focused on case studies. All had to change their original disciplinary conceptions and techniques in the light of problems encountered in the field.

Scientific disciplines attend to ideas internal to the profession based upon expertise, whereas technological disciplines, such as engineering, also must attend to external concerns. External considerations can be weighed differently by different groups, often leading to different schools of thought within the discipline. The key rational consideration is not only the experts' competence in the established concepts and arguments but also their readiness to explore and criticize new concepts and arguments, thus leading to rational development of the discipline. Closely related scientific and technological disciplines, such as those in the field of medicine, interact and influence one another, with the impetus for the science coming as much from the practical technology as the other way around. A much closer symbiotic relationship exists between science and technology than "applied science" would indicate. In fact, some would argue that science consists primarily of abstract or reified technology.

Evaluation is a more practical field than the pure sciences and must attend to both internal and external concerns. Different schools of evaluation have already come into being that developed through different stages, beginning with a disorganized stage in which there was no self-consciousness, progressing to a network stage in which various researchers became interested in a set of ideas, then to a cluster stage in which the school of thought was institutionalized at a university, and giving way to a specialty stage in which prominent students and faculty spread to other places, with the original site being transformed into something else or even going out of existence. Prominent schools of evaluation have included Northwestern University, Stanford University, the University of California at Berkeley, and the University of Illinois (Shadish & Reichardt, 1987).

For example, the social experimentation school was launched by Donald Campbell and Julian Stanley's (1963) *Experimental and Quasi-Experimental Designs for Research,* which attracted a number of interested scholars at Northwestern, including Robert Boruch and Lee Sechrest, and Edward Suchman at the University of Pittsburgh. This was followed by a training program in evaluation at Northwestern, financed by the federal government, which included Campbell, Boruch, Sechrest, Tom Cook, and Paul Wortman. From there prominent faculty and students went to other jobs, including Charles Reichardt, William Shadish, and David Kenny. Replacements were sought, such as Dave Cordray, but the center of the school was transformed. The social experiment group continued in other places and became a specialty within the overall evaluation field, with less coherence and social organization than in the previous stage (Shadish & Reichardt, 1987).

The types of problems encountered by disciplines include the extension of procedures to new phenomena, the improvement of techniques for dealing with familiar phenomena, the integration of techniques within the field, the integration of techniques from other fields, and the resolution of conflicts between the discipline and the external world. Although there is a tendency to systematize ideas inside the field, systematizing is not the most appropriate goal if it excludes too much of the real world that has yet to be touched by the discipline, such as occurred with geometry and formal logic. A sterile over-formalization is too often the result. It is critical that the disciplinary problems chosen be soluble ones, even though the ultimate disciplinary ideals are never achieved (Toulmin, 1972).

Over time, the concepts of a discipline may become quite different from what they were originally, even in fields such as mathematics. There is conceptual change and variation, and it is necessary to have professional forums to generate and discuss the various concepts, to determine how to attack new problems and what new concepts are worth accepting. Without a forum for presentation and discussion of ideas, even brilliant breakthroughs, such as Mendel's studies of plant genetics, have no influence.

In mature scientific disciplines, the evaluations of conceptual variants often take the form of comparisons: not so much, "Is this technique valid or true?" in some absolute sense, but rather, "Does this technique improve our explanatory power?" For evaluators the question might be, "Does this technique improve our evaluative power?" These comparisons necessarily involve local, specific, indisciplinary considerations and informal considerations of particular rival concepts. These comparisons are complex judgments, involving multiple criteria, often with tradeoffs, and are conducted within the local context of the time and place. Disciplinary relevance is decided in context, though later considerations may prove these judgments ill-founded.

The time scale for significant disciplinary change averages 5 years, according to Toulmin, but I am inclined to think that it is a bit longer than this for evaluation. This is the amount of time necessary for one prevailing reference group to be replaced by another. In Toulmin's analysis, a discipline contains a special language, representation techniques, and application methods. It is transmitted through enculturation of the techniques, skills, procedures, and methods of representation. Application skills are essential because novices cannot become proficient without knowing how to use the techniques and procedures. Nonetheless, each generation re-creates the discipline anew. Problems change, and the context changes. New patterns emerge. In scientific disciplines, new techniques last only 2 to 7 years, with few lasting longer than that (Toulmin, 1972).

To take the Illinois school of evaluation as an example of generation change, the founder of the Center for Instructional Research and Evaluation (CIRCE) at the University of Illinois was J. Thomas Hastings, who died in 1992. Hastings studied at the University of Chicago with Ralph Tyler, where he cranked out factor analyses by hand. Contemporary students were Lee J. Cronbach and Benjamin Bloom, with whom Hastings had close personal contacts (Bloom, Hastings, & Madaus, 1971). Hastings arrived at the University of Illinois in 1942 as university examiner, a post similar to that held by Tyler at Ohio State and the University of Chicago. Eventually, Hastings persuaded Cronbach and David Krathwohl, another student of Tyler's, to come to Illinois and founded CIRCE, the major task of which at one time was administration of the state high school achievement testing program. In 1964 Cronbach went to Stanford, where he established an evaluation group, and Krathwohl went to Syracuse University, also continuing the evaluation tradition.

In 1964, Bob Stake came to Illinois, his paper "The Countenance of Educational Evaluation" becoming seminal for the group. CIRCE later added Gene Glass, Jim Wardrop, Terry Denny, Gordon Hoke, and Arden Grotelueschen. I came in 1969, followed by Jim Raths and Bob Linn. There was about 10 years' difference, give or take a few years, between each of these generations. Glass, a student of Julian Stanley's at the University of Wisconsin, went to Colorado to join a research group there that maintained close ties with the Illinois group, and also continued the Stanley experimental design tradition. (Bloom students, such as George Madaus and Malcolm Provus, established their own testing and evaluation units at Boston College and the University of Virginia.)

Each of these generations had somewhat different ideas, often differing quite substantially, as between Tyler's objectives-based and Stake's responsive evaluation. The favorite methodology employed by the CIRCE group changed dramatically from standardized testing to qualitative case studies, in part because of problems encountered in the field doing evaluations. For example, my first evaluation, 1967–1971, was based mostly on quantitative survey and observation techniques, but I realized afterward that we could have obtained similar information in a quarter of the time with a quarter of the budget through interviews, though a qualitative methodology presented problems of legitimacy, as the field then existed. Over the next several years, the school tackled the legitimacy problem in various ways. My monograph *The Logic of Evaluative Argument* (House, 1977) was an attempt to cast evaluation in the larger framework of argumentation, so as to justify qualitative studies.

Yet there were also similarities in the problems all these people addressed with their different ideas, procedures, and methods. Through all these efforts, there was an ideal of making information useful and helpful to practitioners engaged in education—students, teachers, parents, administrators, and the public, whether it meant the state-wide testing program, Tyler's National Assessment of Educational Progress, or Stake's qualitative case study accessible to everyone. Furthermore, and unexpectedly, members of the Illinois school of evaluation emphasized and practiced good writing, not always a goal of evaluators. Good writing was highly valued within the group, commented on, and praised, even though the school's origins were in measurement and testing.

Of course, belonging to a particular school does not exhaust one's ideas. Alkin (1991) has provided a portrait of how a single theorist changes his or her views over the period of his or her career. There are many cross-influences within the discipline, as there should be. I have been strongly influenced by many others outside the Illinois school, as this book indicates. I expect the next group to be about 10 years younger and to have different ideas, albeit ideas derived partially from the preceding generation. The social context and the field of evaluation will be quite different. Also, there is a need for each generation to establish its own identity separate from earlier ones, and this is often done by pursuing different issues.

The social context is important in the development of disciplines. Although the ancient Chinese had exquisite crafts and technologies, they never developed modern sciences, presumably because of their highly conservative social order, to which the sciences would have been threatening. The Western sciences emerged from the unusually inquisitive, open society of ancient Athens. In general, tolerance and support of free conceptual innovation has been rare in history. The amount of innovation in a discipline reflects the social institutional background, with internal disciplinary considerations playing a secondary role. On the other hand, internal considerations are paramount in the content of the discipline (Toulmin, 1972).

Social context is important even to the degree that different countries can have different styles of physical science. For example, French scientific theory has followed the axiomatic mathematical style of René Descartes, whereas British scientific theory has followed

more pragmatic models, even working models, the style of Francis
Bacon. There are different uses and styles of evaluation in different
countries, with some governments using evaluation for program
improvement, whereas others use it for budget control. In the first
case, evaluation is located in program units, and in the second, it is
located in resource allocation units (Johnson, 1991).

A certain amount of isolation is necessary for a discipline to
develop. Without professional autonomy and critical control exercised by internal peer groups, it is difficult to establish and judge
precise claims. Disciplines are concerned internally with rational
judgment and justification. Otherwise, the result is speculative debate or ideology. The isolation provided for evaluation through close
contact with the autonomous social sciences is one reason U.S. evaluation is highly developed. On the other hand, the external environment can be a source of innovative ideas, and this is particularly true,
as well as dangerous, for the social disciplines. The development of
the social sciences in the United States has been both stimulated and
impeded by the social context (see Chapter 6). Conceptual change in
a discipline requires a delicate balance between internal and external
considerations (Toulmin, 1972).

The Future—A Transdiscipline?

The most elaborate vision of how evaluation should develop as a
discipline is that of Michael Scriven (1991). In his view, evaluation is
or should be a "transdiscipline," like logic or statistics—a discipline
in its own right, but one that services other disciplines and is an
integral part of other disciplinary endeavors. In scope it should
embrace not only program evaluation but also product, personnel,
policy, and proposal evaluation. Scriven thinks evaluation falls short
of being a true discipline, but that such an achievement is within
reach.

Evaluation is the process of determining the merit, worth, or
value of things. Its work consists of collecting data, including relevant values and standards; resolving inconsistencies in the values;
clarifying misunderstandings and misrepresentations; rectifying false
facts and factual assumptions; distinguishing between wants and
needs; identifying all relevant dimensions of merit; finding appropriate measures for these dimensions; weighting the dimensions;
validating the standards; and arriving at an evaluative conclusion,

which requires a synthesis of all these considerations. Evaluation requires value judgments, and Scriven is harsh on the doctrine of value-free science.

As a discipline, evaluation is new, but it is an ancient practice, and necessarily so, because few enterprises can exist without it. Scriven provides a hypothetical reconstruction of the evolution of evaluation ideas from practice to methodology to discipline. First, particular scoring or judging rubrics are developed within particular areas. These rubrics are formulated into prescriptive rules for doing evaluations. Next, perhaps, come guidelines that focus on common difficulties, errors, and problems. Then there is a long step to methodology and principles for general investigation and analysis, such as discussions of experimental designs. Methodological discussions in evaluation usually have developed within subfields, such as education, and fall short of being a true disciplinary field, in Scriven's view. Other fields of evaluation, as well as evaluation practices elsewhere, must be included.

A further decisive stage involves discussions defining the boundaries of evaluation; the connections with other disciplines; the reach of methods (metamethodology); the logic of evaluation; what kinds of data and theories are appropriate; economic, political, historical, and anthropological aspects; and theories about the nature of evaluation and where it should go. Most of this third-level discussion Scriven labels "metatheory." Metatheory is close to the self-identity of the discipline itself and essential to distinguishing it from other fields. (Metatheory is what most of this book is about: analyzing the social, political, economic, historical, and cultural influences on evaluation.)

Scriven constructs an elaborate metaphor, "The Country of the Mind," in which disciplines are manifested as feudal country estates. Each disciplinary estate has its own Great House in which a major industry exists. Physics has its house, chemistry its own, and so on, and the ones closely related intellectually are physically together. Each Great House has a ground floor in which applied work is done, a second floor devoted to methods and techniques, a third floor in which theoretical work is done, and an attic that contains the building plans, titles, and records—metatheory. Although the metatheory is unattended and out of sight most of the time, it is embodied in the very way the building is constructed and critical when any serious modifications are attempted.

Sometimes the metatheory is dominated by one metaphor, often identified as a "paradigm," or a dominant model of investigation that strongly influences work in the field. Sometimes there is an entire set of orienting models, analogies, metaphors, methods, standards, and principles. Whatever the form, the metatheory exerts tremendous influence on the field. Other parts of the discipline include theory, possibly methodology, and applications. Applications has the unfortunate connotation of being merely the instantiation of general theories, but, in fact, theoretical work usually is stimulated by the field, generating the need for additional concepts to deal with particular problems.

Development of a new discipline requires the emergence of a consciousness that something new is afoot and a definition of what that something is. Second, it requires an appropriate methodology, a set of procedures for generating results in the field. Third, there must be findings, including reports, facts, and general principles and theories. Fourth, there is the metatheory, which provides a framework for the entire enterprise, both descriptively and prescriptively. The metatheory identifies and defines territory, justifies procedures, and provides an ontology. Disciplinary status ultimately depends on the quality of the metatheory, in Scriven's view.

The Great Houses of the primary disciplines, such as physics and psychology, produce facts about the world, whereas the interdisciplines are smaller houses on overlapping estates. The transdisciplines are the utilities, such as the telephone or electric companies, that supply services to other disciplines. They come into existence to serve the others but develop into autonomous disciplines. They are used every day in other disciplines and have subdisciplines attached to other fields, such as educational evaluation, but also have their own Great Houses.

In Scriven's view, evaluation is an emerging transdiscipline, but one in which the Great House is allegorical at the moment. There is an evaluation estate with several small buildings on it, such as product evaluation, program evaluation, and others, but no Great House as yet. This deficiency costs dearly because evaluation consists of uncoordinated subfields without the help and resources that a dynamic center can bring. Without the Great House, evaluation cannot be a true discipline, in Scriven's opinion, and the establishment of a Great House should be a high priority. In lieu of that, the burden of developing the discipline has fallen on workers in applied fields, as in universities such as Stanford and Illinois, and contract shops such as the University of Western Michigan, Rand Corporation, Boston College, and CIRCE.

Educational evaluators have been particularly productive in contributing key ideas to the metatheory of evaluation, in Scriven's view, because they have had a long history of evaluation in their field in the form of student evaluation, measurement, and testing, and because they were more at home in the radically multidisciplinary array of their own subject area. Social scientists, being bound to traditional social science and its limitations, contributed mostly to metamethodology. However, in spite of seminal developments, evaluation still is deficient in general theory, logic, utilization, and metatheory, the core of the discipline. Although evaluation has been constructed from tools and building blocks from other disciplines, it is not those disciplines, any more than a house is its bricks and tools. "A discipline is an organized intellectual construct, an element in a complex taxonomy; it's not a bag of tricks and bricks. The substance of a discipline is its work; the key to the discipline is the overall concept, the metatheory" (Scriven, 1991, p. 18).

Contrary to a widespread view that the roots of evaluation are in the social sciences, the intellectual skills of evaluation long antedated social science, in Scriven's opinion. The logical roots came from philosophy, and the metatheory from educational researchers. The social sciences contributed methodological roots, along with an implacable resistance to metatheory, this reluctance being based on the value-free doctrine. In Scriven's view the key intellectual problem of evaluation that prevents it from becoming a discipline is its failure so far to validate its own evaluative conclusions, a result of the value-free doctrine. (See Chapter 6 for a detailed discussion of the origins of this issue.)

The separation of evaluation into distinct subareas, such as program evaluation, product evaluation, educational evaluation, medical evaluation, and others, has impeded the development of evaluation theory because similarities across areas are not apparent. Another problem has been the reluctance to provide for the evaluation of evaluations. Scriven's proposals include the establishment of a central discipline linking all subfields of evaluation, separating evaluation from the social sciences, and more attention to meta-evaluation.

This brief sketch of Scriven's metaphor for evaluation barely touches the richness and complexity of his construction. I confess that the "Great House of Evaluation" has an intrinsic appeal for me. In general I think Scriven's analysis is correct, although occasionally overstated. The primary intellectual problem of the field is the validation of evaluative conclusions. We do need to pay more attention to critiquing evaluations within the field, and there is much to be gained by studying evaluation techniques across various areas of endeavor. There is no question that even simple ideas from program evaluation could be applied profitably to other areas, such as to personnel evaluation in the universities, and that product evaluation has been overlooked as a source of ideas, though Scriven himself has used product evaluation as a major source of ideas.

I am less enthusiastic about the prospects of establishing evaluation as a separate discipline, divorced from the social sciences and fields of application, such as education. Both institutional and intellectual problems arise. Institutionally, the universities serve as critical sponsors of the disciplines, and they are quite slow to recognize new disciplines. Few intellectual disciplines exist or are recognized without university backing. Program evaluation has been the spearhead of evaluation in the universities, but it is connected to existing areas. Even statistics has had much difficulty establishing a separate place for itself within the university. Furthermore, the job market has quite an important impact, and the market currently is organized through the subfields.

Intellectually, the problem of separating evaluation from the social sciences is complex. How much of the discipline depends on knowledge of the content being evaluated? Evaluation is not content-free. On the other hand, neither is it totally content-bound. The question of how much content one needs in order to evaluate is an open one. Does one need to have knowledge of educational content to evaluate educational programs? I am certain that one does, but how much knowledge? To what degree can one compensate for lack of knowledge of a field in which the evaluation is being conducted by including content specialists in the evaluation team?

Scriven is correct when he says that the social sciences as currently conceived are not an appropriate basis for evaluation. But perhaps reforming the social sciences is the best way to go. As now conceived, the social sciences are not effective, but they are ripe for radical reform. It might be more appropriate to conceive evaluation within the panoply of the social sciences, rather than trying to separate it altogether. Of course, the value-free doctrine is at the heart of the social science impotence; evaluators—who, it is hoped, know better—are in an advantageous position to advance their own discipline.

❧ 6 ❧

The Legacy of U.S. Social Science

*A*lthough formal evaluation emerges in countries in states of advanced capitalism, it differs in form and content in each country, depending on each country's particular institutions and intellectual heritage. To some degree, each country must invent its own evaluation (though certainly it can learn from others). U.S. evaluation has grown from distinct historical, cultural, and institutional circumstances that make it different from evaluation elsewhere.

U.S. evaluation has been strongly influenced by U.S. social science, which has had a particular history of its own. I would like to take a brief tour of U.S. social science from its inception in the late 19th century to the Great Depression of 1929 to characterize the social science foundation from which U.S. evaluation evolved in part (only in part because evaluation has strong influences from other sources as well). These early years were the formative period of U.S. social science, the time during which it developed its essential shape and content. I am guided here by Dorothy Ross's (1991) excellent history, *The Origins of American Social Science,* as well as by Manicas (1987), Travers (1983), and Bannister (1987).

According to Ross, U.S. social science has been shaped by a deep-seated belief in American exceptionality. Since the beginning of European colonization, America has represented something exceptional, a focus of fantasies and projections, even before the nation of the United States was established. This idea of exceptionality was woven into the national U.S. identity, so that most Americans still think their country is not subject to the same social and historical forces as other countries. Rather, the United States is destined to have a greater and happier future than any other place.

In the early days, this exceptionalist belief was expressed in religious terms: The United States was a land chosen by God with a divine destiny. The secular explanation was that the lack of a hereditary aristocracy, the establishment of a republican form of government, and endless economic opportunities made the United States exceptional. In particular, the United States would not have the mass poverty and social classes so characteristic of other countries. In the U.S. view Europeans were class-bound and class-conscious, whereas the American Revolution was fought against privilege, freeing the country from traditional bondages. Economic plenty and vast resources prevented mass poverty. Furthermore, there was a sense of mission in which the United States, "the last, best hope of mankind," was to transform the world, a millenialism in which material plenty and social harmony would prevail (Robertson, 1980).

In the 19th century this sense of national identity, progress, and destiny merged with the belief in science, stimulated in particular by Charles Darwin's theory of evolution. "For Americans, evolution provided scientific proof, taken from the evidence of the physical universe, of the purpose, mission, and meaning of America. Evolution was proof of progress—unceasing, inevitable progress. And America was and is, as all Americans believe, the living, national embodiment of progress" (Robertson, 1980, p. 288). Science itself was seen as both a sign and an instrument of progress.

During the late 19th and early 20th centuries, the major task of the founding social scientists was to reconcile their exceptionalist beliefs about the United States with the enormous historical changes taking place in the country as a result of industrialism, a monumental transformation from the agrarian yeoman society envisioned by Thomas Jefferson. To accommodate the national ideology and make sense of the actual U.S. experience that was unfolding, the social sciences came to be based on a model of the natural sciences, which gradually evolved into a form of scientism—the view that the inductive methods of the natural sciences are the only source of factual knowledge and that only such methods can yield knowledge about nature and society. In this view, the main purpose of the social sciences is the technocratic manipulation of nature and society for the betterment of humankind, another expression of millenialism.

By the 1920s, for example, the sociology that evolved confined itself to the observable externals of human nature, took experience as the sole source of knowledge, and distinguished between objects accessible to observation and those not accessible. Sociologists had to apply rigorous methods, which cast doubt on the validity of case studies and participant observations. Furthermore, sociologists were supposed to observe strict neutrality in matters of ethics and public policy (Bannister, 1987). This scientism was reflected in all fields of social science and greatly influenced the emerging field of evaluation some decades later.

🔊 U.S. Social Science, 1865-1896

In the early 19th century social science was taught in the liberal arts colleges as part of moral philosophy, heavily influenced by common-sense Scottish philosophy, itself an intermediate step between religious and secular inquiry. Before the Civil War, U.S. social scientists formulated fixed laws of history that would perpetuate the established U.S. institutions. After the Civil War, under the impact of industrialization, it appeared that the United States was developing the same mass poverty and class conflict that was so apparent in Britain and other European countries. In reaction social scientists created social theories that postulated an orderly nature beneath the social turmoil and discord. By 1929 they had established pluralist, behaviorist, statistical models of a social world in flux, but a world in which U.S. forms were re-created, often through social and political processes controlled by technocratic social science. These theories about social change and the role of social science were advanced by professional social scientists (Ross, 1991).

Almost all the first professional U.S. social scientists were trained in Germany. Between 1820 and 1920, 9,000 Americans entered German universities. U.S. universities expanded enormously and adopted the German graduate school as a model. In 1890 there were 154,000 undergraduates and 2,400 graduate students in U.S. universities; by 1930, there were 1,053,000 undergraduates and 47,300 graduate students. The governing system of the universities also changed, with philanthropic capitalists, such as the Vanderbilts, Harrimans, Carnegies, Goulds, and Morgans, becoming influential as benefactors and trustees, and even starting their own universities, as the Rockefellers did the University of Chicago in 1892 (Manicas, 1987).

By the late 19th century the disruptions of laissez-faire capitalism were manifest. The appearance of a permanent working class tied to wage labor and to the vicissitudes of the business cycle was especially difficult to explain within the national exceptionalist ideology. The United States was changing, and it was necessary to explain the changes to differentiate the country from the upheavals in Europe. To explain this disturbing development, U.S. social scientists relied initially on German historicism—German theories of social change— as well as on the liberal positivism of British scholars, such as John Stuart Mill (Ross, 1991).

In 1865 the American Social Science Association was founded. The first U.S. social scientists came from the northeastern gentry, a reflection of the social class structure that formed in the 1870s. As the social scientists became professionalized, they based their authority on science, as well as on their superior class background and education. Many of these social scientists first tried government service in which to apply their new scientific knowledge, but the rapid expansion of the universities provided more secure places of employment. President Charles William Eliot of Harvard University established a position in political economy in 1869 (taking it from moral philosophy) and appointed a free-market newspaper editor sponsored by the local business community (Ross, 1991).

In the 1880s and 1890s the numerous worker and farmer protests were perceived by the upper classes as threatening socialism. Depressions and strikes from 1873 to 1877, followed by the depression of 1885, the Haymarket riot in 1886, and the rising power of the Knights of Labor manifested this socialist threat. The depression of 1893-1897, the Homestead strike in 1892, the Pullman strike in 1894, the march of Coxey's army of unemployed in 1894, and the rise of the Populist party, which nominated William Jennings Bryan for president in 1896, resulted in strong antilabor and antiradical campaigns by the establishment (Goodwyn, 1978; Robertson, 1980).

These social and ideological schisms were reflected in the universities with the purging of radical social scientists from academic ranks. By this time younger social scientists were being recruited from the Protestant middle class, were often the offspring of evangelicals, and were conservative politically, with a few exceptions, such as Thorstein Veblen, descendant of Norwegian farmers, and Edwin Seligman, of German-Jewish parentage. Prejudices against Jews and Catholics, not to mention African-Americans, were quite strong in the universities. Women rarely were admitted to graduate study until the 1890s. Academic social scientists were Anglo-Saxon, middle-class Protestants. However, the failure of English laissez-faire economics to deal with the massive poverty of the laboring classes (and the German training of U.S. scholars) led some U.S. scholars to look toward German historicism, with its tradition of community over individual rights, for arguments against unfettered capitalism (Ross, 1991).

Prominent younger economists, such as John Bates Clark, Henry Carter Adams, and Richard T. Ely, linked the future to progressive (some said socialist) politics, expressed as a cooperative commonwealth with familial values of equality and fraternity. They thought economic equality lacking in U.S. society. In 1885, the American Economic Association was formed with a platform advocating the use of historicist research methods and government regulation of business (though this platform was rescinded a few years later). Government regulation, ownership of industry, and the rights of labor became hotly debated issues among economists throughout the 1880s and 1890s. Ely, for example, argued that economics must be ethical as well as scientific. However, following the Haymarket riot in 1886, which shocked the upper and middle classes, these scholars hastily retreated from their mildly socialist positions (Ross, 1991).

Under political pressure at Johns Hopkins, Ely moved to the University of Wisconsin, but was publicly tried by the regents there. Although exonerated, he moderated his socialist tendencies. Adams was eased out of his professorial position after incurring the ire of a major Cornell University benefactor, Russell Sage, for supporting workers in the Southwestern railroad strike. Clark turned to developing the seminal idea of marginalist economics, which demonstrated how the market automatically achieves social justice by giving to every agent of production the wealth that each agent deserves. In this conception, values are determined by individuals calculating marginal utilities in the interconnected markets of capitalist society. The free market would enable the United States to escape the fate of the Old World (Ross, 1991). By 1890 U.S. economics had thrown off its German influence and was back on the Adam Smith track (Manicas, 1987).

In the 1880s William Graham Sumner (following Herbert Spencer) and Lester Frank Ward (following Auguste Comte) founded U.S. sociology. Sumner made the man-to-land ratio of Thomas Malthus and David Ricardo the center of his "survival of the fittest" sociology. In conditions of underpopulation, he said, one could have yeoman equality, but in overpopulation, brutal competition prevailed. For Ward, the advance of knowledge was the key social dynamic. Society could be shaped and engineered through social knowledge and the discovery of social laws. This was the first statement in U.S. social science that history was subject to social control (Ross, 1991).

Meanwhile, the sociologists were trying to establish a foothold in the universities. The new University of Chicago gave the first chair in sociology to Albion Small, a Baptist minister, in 1892, and 2 years later, Columbia University created a chair for Franklin Giddings, a journalist trained in economics with Clark. Small, drawing on his studies in Germany, turned to historicist approaches, and Giddings turned toward the statistical. In 1896 Small founded the *American Journal of Sociology*, the same year the populist tradition was thoroughly defeated in the rejection of William Jennings Bryan for president (Goodwyn, 1978). Like the economists, the sociologists backed away from action on social issues. Rather, the discovery of solutions to social problems would be done by science, they said, not by direct action. If science could not transform society now, it would do so in the future. Sociology should concentrate on the study of the values held by various groups in society (Ross, 1991).

Political science was the oldest social science but had difficulty defining its subject matter and separating itself from history; the two usually were housed in the same department. One of the first political scientists, John W. Burgess at Columbia, was radically racist and anti-immigrant, even for his day. He advocated the use of violence both at home and abroad to maintain the superiority of the Teutonic nations. Herbert Baxter Adams argued that history is past politics and politics simply present history. In the 1890s political scientists were policy-oriented, concerned about finding principles for government action, and slow to adopt the research methods of the social sciences.

History, the origin of all the social sciences, was not professionalized until the late 19th century. Prior to that time Puritan clergymen or patricians, such as Francis Parkman, Henry Adams, and Theodore Roosevelt, wrote history. In 1884, the year of the founding of the American Historical Association (AHA), there were only 20 full-time history teachers in institutions of higher learning; by 1909, the AHA had 2,700 members (Manicas, 1987). U.S. historians believed in social progress, but disdained "philosophy of history," which was associated with the Germans. They were more in line with the positivist history of Henry Thomas Buckle in England (Buckle, 1857/1970).

In psychology, Americans were especially interested in individual differences. In the 1880s James Cattell studied with Wilhelm Wundt in Germany and constructed mental tests based on sensory processes. Wundt, whose laboratory was established in Leipzig in 1879, put psychology on an experimental basis and distinguished between "experimental" and "social" psychology. Cattell, the first psychology professor in the United States, focused on human variability, which Wundt treated as experimental error. Cattell eventually established the *American Journal of Psychology* and *Psychology Review* (Travers, 1983). By 1882 there were 18 psychology labs in the United States, and by 1917 more psychologists than in Germany, Britain, and France combined (Manicas, 1987). The American Psychology Association was founded in 1892.

Educational research (not a social science but often closely allied to psychology) was strongly influenced by the statistical survey tradition in Europe and also concerned with pupil assessment. In 1845 the first testing survey was conducted in the Boston schools, and researchers (who were educators, administrators, and reformers rather than academics) regularly gave tests of their own construction to students in various school districts, always finding students to be shockingly deficient in their knowledge. Written exams were introduced to the Boston schools by Horace Mann for purposes of interschool comparisons. Educational research focused on data collection, especially test scores, and was local, atheoretical, nonstandardized, and practical in intent. In the 1890s Joseph Rice conducted the first educational program evaluation, on the efficacy of spelling drill, and used quantitative research methods, including comparative experiments (Madaus, Scriven, & Stufflebeam, 1983; Travers, 1983).

Anthropology developed independently from the other disciplines. Early prominent anthropologists, such as E. B. Tylor in England, had a rationalist, positivist view. Through intellectual advancement, cultures and institutions evolve to higher forms that suit the interests of the members, he theorized. Positivist anthropologists believed that societies and institutions could be evaluated on a unilinear scale of rationality. In their view, native societies had not evolved as far as European ones. In fact innate racial characteristics probably accounted for the apparent differences in societal development (Hatch, 1973).

The founder of U.S. anthropology, Franz Boas, however, was not trained in this rationalist, positivist tradition, but was born and educated in Germany. German idealists analyzed events holistically and, through the interpretations of participants, focused on understanding the overall *Geist,* or "spirit," of a time and place. Boas reportedly took a copy of Immanuel Kant's work with him when he studied the Eskimoes. Each culture, Boas contended, was a unique, subjectively perceived whole. In 1896 Boas arrived at Columbia to establish a school of anthropology that dominated U.S. anthropology for decades, and that in some ways was out of step with the rest of U.S. social science.

❧ Progressivism, 1896-1914

With the collapse of the Knights of Labor, the American Federation of Labor became the dominant organized labor group, but composed only 5% of the working class. Violent labor confrontations continued, and socialist Eugene Debs gathered a million votes for president in 1912. A new pluralist, progressive politics emerged, which called for some government regulation of business. However, even when social scientists adopted progressive political positions, they were careful to distinguish themselves from the radicals on the Left. Huge waves of new immigrants fueled nativist and racist reactions in the country, and many social scientists themselves worried about the rise in immigration, the decline in the native birthrate, and whether the new immigrants could be assimilated. Racist theories were widespread in social science and the popular press (Ross, 1991).

In economics, between 1890 and 1910, marginalism became the dominant approach, partly owing to Alfred Marshall's powerful neoclassical synthesis. Mathematical models, comfortably removed from controversial political issues, appealed to economists, who were still likely to be persecuted when expressing unorthodox views. Furthermore, the economists' professional opinions were increasingly solicited by policy makers and government officials. The major intellectual dissenter was Thorstein Veblen, with his iconoclastic, socialist conceptions, but his views (marred by a racist typology characteristic of the time) never captured a large following among economists (Ross, 1991).

In 1905 the American Sociological Association was founded with Lester Ward as president and William Graham Sumner as president-elect.[1] Albion Small worried about the decline of the Protestant standard of values and the multiplicity of ethnic groups, and was careful to balance liberal articles with conservative ones in his journal. In *Folkways*, Sumner (1906/1960) argued that social evolution was determined by industrial processes, but that social mores could be modified somewhat by science. Even when the exceptionalist character of the nation was challenged, as by Edwin Seligman, the United States still was seen as the vanguard of progress, and the existence of social classes was denied (Ross, 1991).

Sociology was led by the competing Chicago and Columbia schools of thought. Small at Chicago defined sociology as the study of the process of association in groups, with pluralistic conflict and accommodation resulting in wider social harmony. Although decrying the inequality in society, he did not see class conflict as inevitable. The Chicago group was strongly influenced by Jane Addams at Hull House and the urban charity movement. Chicago sociologists believed that studying the conditions in which poor people lived would inform public opinion and result in social and political reform.

Giddings at Columbia established a more positivist school, particularly after he read John Stuart Mill's *Logic* and Karl Pearson. Pearson appears repeatedly as perhaps the most influential propagator of positivism during this time. *The Grammar of Science,* first published in 1892, went through numerous editions over the next several decades. Pearson contended that science was description and that theories were merely indirect descriptions. Science was a method of collecting and classifying facts, like placing stones in a great building of knowledge (his analogy). He warned scientists not to probe the real world, but to take a more nominalist approach by using statistics without theory (Bannister, 1987). The unity of science consisted in its method, not its material. Scientists must be objective, abandon metaphysics, and divorce science from values, he contended.

By defining science as description, Pearson thought scientists could avoid metaphysical concepts such as "cause." All that scientists could know were concomitant facts and the reliability of their concomitance, as measured by degrees of probability. Statistics had to be the central tool of social science, he argued. Sociology, as a scientific description of society, would be an empirical and statistical study of the variation and correlation of social facts. Pearson, holding Galton's chair in London, was also a leading statistician and eugenicist, who sought evidence of conformity to racial and social types.

This statistical approach was appealing to Giddings, who was trained in economics, and he looked for indicators of conformity by the new immigrants to U.S. culture. Although Giddings eventually became pessimistic about the polyglot, permissive urban culture developing, he established a powerful quantitative tradition at Columbia, and the more pessimistic he became about U.S. society, the more he urged exact measurement. He embodied the preoccupation of U.S. social scientists to explain the negative changes occurring in their society, though he was not optimistic about the outcome.

Edward A. Ross drew attention to the conflict between social and individual interests and focused on the need for social control of individual feelings, ideas, and behaviors. Being a student of Ely, and having leftist leanings himself, Ross was keenly aware of "unhealthy" social control. He resorted to a biological racial analysis and, like

Veblen, glorified the Teutonic heritage and feared southern Europeans. Liberal political reformers seized Ross's ideas as a rationale for regulating private enterprise. As a result of Ross's work, many sociologists focused on socialization as a key concept, and social psychology and social interaction came to be emphasized as areas of study. Whereas John Stuart Mill first used the term *social control* to argue against it, U.S. sociologists now argued for it (Ross, 1991).

Larger political issues, such as power and the social structure, dissolved in organic metaphors emphasizing the unity of society. Social control was a social rather than a political issue, in this view. Applied social science would help control society. Positivists emphasized prediction and control, though certainly not all social scientists embraced such a technocratic conception. Ross himself argued that new knowledge should be kept esoteric so that not just anyone could use it; knowledge in the wrong hands could be dangerous. Academics stood above the selfish interests of society and could be relied upon to make the proper use of findings, he believed. Social conflict in the United States was not permanent, but merely reflected a transition toward a new, harmonious society.

Although sociologists sometimes challenged the dominance of the economists, and although economists were disdainful of sociologists, these disciplines maintained a truce for the most part. Colleges and universities were receiving strong support from both capitalists and the middle classes, with college enrollments rising rapidly (college enrollment increased from 5% to 15% of the population). The decentralized higher education system enabled new universities and departments to come into being, thus intensifying specialization within departments and separatism among them. In England, by contrast, traditional departments dominated and restricted growth. In Germany and France, university expansion was centrally constrained by the ministries.

Historians and political scientists, such as Frank Goodnow, Frederick Jackson Turner, and Woodrow Wilson, were allied more closely with the establishment, both by background and politics, than were other social scientists. Socialism and leftist politics were hardly a threat among them. Historians emphasized that events had to be understood in terms of particular conditions of the time, not by universal principles or by appeals to human nature. In his history, Turner located U.S. exceptionalism in the conditions faced by the pioneers, the "frontier thesis."

In 1903 the American Political Science Association was formed, with Goodnow as president. Political scientists attempted to provide principles of government that would aid policy makers, usually through studying history. Although Abbot Lawrence Lowell pressed for the study of actual political operations and the collection and classification of statistical data, political scientists and historians did not feel the need for such studies at this time.

In psychology, Alfred Binet in France invented the intelligence test in 1905, but insisted that it be used strictly for identifying students who needed special help. However, the U.S. promoter of the test, H. H. Goddard, director of research at the Vineland Training School for the Feeble-Minded, quickly turned the test to the uses of eugenics and support of a hereditarian theory of fixed intelligence, a concept that has occupied a central position in U.S. psychology ever since. In the hereditarian view, a unilinear scale of fixed intelligence, closely connected to morality, accounted for poverty, crime, and other social ills, as well as for the dilution of the Teutonic race (Gould, 1981; Kamin, 1977; Travers, 1983).

The only way to handle inferior people was to sterilize them or put them in institutions. Goddard administered I.Q. tests to immigrants at Ellis Island and found that 83% of Jews, 80% of Hungarians, 79% of Italians, and 87% of Russians were feeble-minded (Gould, 1981; Kamin, 1977). He taught examining physicians there to use the tests to deport immigrants. The eugenics movement antedated the tests by many years, and testing developed in an already intensely politicized atmosphere. Before long legislators were using the hereditarian arguments as scientific justification for their eugenics policies. Indiana passed the first state sterilization law in 1907, and other states passed similar laws applied to social deviants. Low I.Q., measured by the tests, was often sufficient reason for sterilization.

Lewis M. Terman transformed Binet's test into the Stanford-Binet, the standard for I.Q. tests. Terman, also a eugenicist, called for the removal of defectives from society and promoted his test as the best way to sort people into occupations. The tests could be used to eliminate "an enormous amount of crime, pauperism, and industrial inefficiency" (quoted in Kamin, 1977, p. 47). Terman's primary empirical proof was that I.Q. was strongly correlated with the higher occupations. All these theories were also racist: African-Americans, Hispanics, and American Indians were found to have the lowest I.Q.s. Terman recommended that these groups be segregated in school.

Even though U.S. schools had been major instruments of democratization, the idea that humans differed genetically in their abilities fit the elitist beliefs of the emerging capitalist class and had a strong impact on the schools (Travers, 1983). Many schools emulated the tracking and grouping scheme of the London schools, which was engineered by the first school psychologist, Cyril Burt. Following the emphasis on fixed intelligence and individual differences, U.S. schools became less egalitarian, a pattern not followed in either France or Germany.

Pedagogy as a field of study was a German invention, and U.S. educational researchers visited Wundt's lab. However, the tradition that continued to dominate educational research was the testing survey, and by 1915, 30 or 40 school districts were conducting surveys, usually focused on improving school or teacher efficiency. Joseph Rice and many others used locally constructed tests of the three R's to improve efficiency, standardize instruction, and assimilate immigrants. Standardized tests were not widely available in the schools until after World War I (Madaus, Scriven, & Stufflebeam, 1983).

In 1910 Abraham Flexner conducted an accreditation evaluation of medical schools and an evaluation of the innovative Gary school program in 1911, finding both severely wanting (Floden, 1983; Travers, 1983). In 1915 seven school research directors formed a professional organization called the National Association of Directors of Educational Research, which changed its name to the American Educational Research Association in 1930. Measurement and statistics, particularly testing surveys, were the focus of educational research from the beginning (Travers, 1983).

In anthropology Franz Boas developed his notion of "culture." Like the positivists, he believed there were laws of culture that developed from the human mind, but, unlike the positivists, he believed that these laws could be discovered only from detailed historical investigations and penetration of the subjective understanding of participants, not from the comparative classification of cultures. Boas also rejected the idea of racial types. The presumed superiority of European over other cultures was based on the Europeans' own ethnocentrism and lack of understanding, he contended, a position that distinguished him from most of his colleagues. Differences were cultural rather than innately biological (Hatch, 1973).

Boas also concluded that emotion rather than reason underlay cultures. Customs and institutions form from habit and become emotionally binding. In his subjective approach he emphasized the ideational, rather than the manifest and observable, and in his focus on subjective understanding, he often missed factors such as systems of exchange or population statistics. Cultural diffusion was the dynamic by which he explained most cultural and societal change.

Eventually, he abandoned his earlier belief that cultural laws could be discovered and came to believe that change was accidental and adventitious; customs were the result of myriad influences. Hence, anthropologists should study specific forms because change processes were too complex to unravel separately.

ᨠ World War I Until 1929

The Progressive political movement ended with the outbreak of World War I. By now, many social scientists came from small-town, midwestern backgrounds. Also, the social sciences attracted some students who had majored in physical science and engineering, as well as many more women, especially in sociology (although most of these women were directed into social work). Urbanization had a striking impact on these scholars. Problems of race, ethnicity, and deviance seemed more important than problems of labor and class conflict. Social classes were cast as simply social groups. Pluralism counted more than equality. Methodologically, positivism continued its strong influence. Pearson's *Grammar* (3rd edition by 1911) was a common text, and John Dewey urged the application of the natural science model to human pursuits. During the 1920s, social control was a central theme of the social sciences (Ross, 1991).

The Russian Revolution resulted in the "Red Scare" and rampant suppression of political dissent. Historian Charles Beard published a popular text based on an interest-group analysis in which he held that interest-group conflict resulted in political compromises. Even the Constitution was the compromise of the economic interests of its time, he contended. After an inquisition by trustees, Beard was forced to resign from Columbia, and the Carnegie Foundation refused to fund the New York Bureau of Municipal Research as long as Beard was director. Radical women were also targets. Emily Balch at Wellesley College was forced out, and the social science program there shut down for 10 years. The Wharton School of Business at the University of Pennsylvania purged economics faculty members such as Scott Nearing, who supported child-labor legislation (Ross, 1991).

In economics, Robert F. Hoxie and Wesley Clair Mitchell tried to develop some of Veblen's ideas. Hoxie studied labor unions, their reaction to scientific management, and the absence of class consciousness among workers. He concluded that the reason for lack of class consciousness was that there were no social classes in the

United States. Mitchell studied the business cycle from a historical perspective, as Veblen might do, but employed concepts from marginalist economics. The market needed more planning, he concluded, but essentially was self-correcting and in equilibrium, contrary to Veblen's analysis. By 1924 Mitchell was convinced that collecting social statistics through time was the way to make economics scientific. Others, such as W. H. Hamilton, called for a more realistic and historicist approach to studying economic institutions. J. M. Clark wanted more qualitative research and to expand the concept of overhead to include such things as worker health (Ross, 1991).

However, by 1927, mainstream neoclassicism had prevailed against this institutionalism, and most economists favoring institutional analysis (which they actually did little of) recanted or modified their views. The political atmosphere characterized by the Sacco and Vanzetti trial and nationalist revolts by farmers motivated mainstream economists to enforce their orthodox views. When Hamilton as director of the new Brookings Graduate School issued a report calling for nationalization of the coal industry, the coal industry and government economists forced Hamilton to resign, eliminated the graduate school altogether, and put the Brookings Institute in the hands of a conservative neoclassicist.

Some pieces of Mitchell's and Clark's work were incorporated into the dominant market paradigm, but not the radical parts, such as bringing externalities into the analysis. On the other hand, descriptive economic statistics became a vital resource. In the ensuing Great Depression of the 1930s, everyone was drawn to the Keynesian revision, which called for government intervention in the market. Mathematical, ahistorical, rationalist microeconomic theory, far removed from an analysis of actual institutions, remained dominant.

During these years, Frank Knight laid the groundwork for the Chicago libertarian school of economics, with the concept of rational decision making at its center. Drawing on Karl Pearson's analysis of probability, Knight linked risk and ignorance in practical decisions to estimates of probability. Government interference with the market only distorted the proper outcomes, he contended. It was many decades before these ideas were ascendant, through students such as James M. Buchanan and Gary Becker. History and politics, the countermodes of analysis to ahistorical, rationalist microeconomics, eventually came to be seen as nothing other than the utility-maximizing behavior of individuals (Ross, 1991).

In sociology, Robert Park, another small-town midwesterner, spent 7 years at Tuskegee Institute with Booker T. Washington, where he met William I. Thomas. Both went to Chicago and were enamored of journalism, which was exploring the urban experience. Park was interested in social attitudes and racial and ethnic assimilation. Much of his work focused on the growth of the city. Sociologists should study vocational types, he thought, but not social classes. He postulated stages of the race cycle—contact, competition, accommodation, assimilation. He saw assimilation of African-Americans as taking a very long time and counseled patience. Chicago became a center for African-American sociologists, including Charles S. Johnson and E. Franklin Frazier.

Also at Chicago, Thomas, influenced by Boas's anthropology, sent students into the city to talk with subjects and track down all sorts of evidence, such as church records, handbills, personal letters, and other items. There was much reliance on interpretation of texts. For the most part, however, academics discouraged direct contact with the urban underclasses. Thomas himself was fired by the University of Chicago after he was arrested with a married woman in a downtown hotel, and the University of Chicago Press stopped publication of *The Polish Peasant in Europe and America* (1918, with Florian Znaniecki), the classic study of the period. Social control over deviance was a major concern. Thomas saw his Polish peasant study as a social psychology investigation of attitudes and a search for laws that would explain facts. Poles did not come to the United States as blank slates to be Americanized but formed a new Polish-American society once here. Because attitudes and facts had to be studied in context, the life record or case study was the perfect expression.[2] On the other hand, participant observation, as we know it, was not a major method in these studies. The *Polish Peasant* depended on analysis of documents such as personal letters (Hammersley, 1989).

The Chicago school of sociology established a lasting tradition and became famous for studies of the city, the first of which was Nels Anderson's *The Hobo* (1923/1967), sponsored by the Chicago Committee on Homeless Men. Anderson did not hear the term *participant observer* until after he had done the study, and, "The only instruction from Park was, 'Write down only what you see, hear, and know, like a newspaper reporter' " (N. Anderson, 1923/1967, p. xii). These Chicago studies often were sympathetic to their subjects and critical of the social system:

> This process of personal degradation of the migratory casual worker from independence to pauperism is only an aspect of the play of economic forces in modern industrial society. Seasonal industries,

business cycles, alternate periods of employment and of unemployment, the casualization of industry, have created this great industrial
reserve army of homeless, footless men. (N. Anderson, 1923/1967, p. 57)

Eventually, however, the Columbia school came to dominate
sociology. F. Stuart Chapin promoted quantification and the nomi-
nalism of Karl Pearson, contending that the scientific method consisted of four steps: the formulation of hypotheses, observation,
classification, and generalization. (His *Experimental Designs*, published in 1947, was highly influential following World War II.) William F. Ogburn, a leading proponent of instrumental positivism, was
appointed to Chicago itself in 1927, in spite of the antagonism of
faculty such as Robert E. Park, Louis Wirth, and Herbert Blumer to
the new statistics and "science without concepts" (Bannister, 1987,
p. 176). Ogburn saw society as lagging in response to economic
change, a problem of cultural forms catching up to technology and
industry. He developed measures of social trends. In psychoanalysis
himself, Ogburn saw theory as irrational and emotional in origin.
Self-reports were suspect, and rigorous quantitative methods were
the only antidote to such irrationality.

Thomas's *Polish Peasant* study came under attack for its qualitative methodology (Ross, 1991). Although the Chicago tradition continued, qualitative studies were questioned. Robert and Helen Lynd's
classic Middletown study, published in 1929, did not come from
sociology but from social work and the ministry, strongly influenced
by Veblen and anthropology. Supporters of the Chicago case study
approach eventually rallied in the 1930s with symbolic interactionism (Ross, 1991). Blumer invented the term *symbolic interactionism* in
1937 and called his approach "naturalistic research" (Hammersley,
1989).

Case study came to mean "the collection and presentation of
detailed, relatively unstructured information from a range of sources
about a particular individual, group, or institution, usually including the accounts of subjects themselves" (Hammersley, 1989, p. 93).
The main idea was to try to represent the world in all its complexity.
But at this time qualitative research became a minority practice, and
sociology was set for George Lundberg's quantitative, positivist
sociology (with intersubjective agreement at the center) and Talcott
Parson's ahistorical functionalism (Hammersley, 1989; Manicas, 1987).

For their part, political scientists such as Arthur Bentley defined
society as nothing other than the interest groups that composed it
and denied that social class was a viable category of scientific anal-

ysis. Social class was a workable concept only in caste systems, he contended. There were no social classes in modern societies. Groups freely combined, reformed, dissolved, and recombined incessantly. Various group pressures worked through to an eventual balance of social forces. Bentley's idea of impermanent, open classes proved highly influential.

In the 1920s Charles E. Merriam pushed for a more scientific political science, one more oriented to method and control, which one commentator called "naked positivism" (Manicas, 1987, p. 220). Merriam's earlier optimism about the educability of the public had turned into the need for scientific techniques by which the public could be led. His *New Aspects of Politics* captured the positivist drift of this thinking: "Government is a series of tropisms that are likely to recur in the same order or series as much as in any other part of the domain of nature" (Merriam, 1925, p. 125). These processes must be studied objectively, and here he quoted a 1925 Paul Thurston article that summarized the stages in the solution of a scientific problem (and that might be taken verbatim from some contemporary methodology texts):

1. A felt social need which requires analysis, satisfaction or cure.
2. The phrasing of the need or perhaps a small part of it in the form, "What is the effect of A upon B?"
3. The definition of the variables A and B, preferably in quantitative form.
4. The adoption of a unit of measurement for each variable.
5. The experimental arrangement by which paired observations may be obtained for A and B.
6. The statistical analysis of these observations to determine objectively the degree of the relation between A and B.
7. The interpretation which consists in reading causality into the observed concomitance of the two variables.
8. The formulation of more problems which arise from doubts in the interpretation and from which the cycle repeats itself. (Merriam, 1925, p. 126)

Harold E. Lasswell, Merriam's student, thoroughly debunked the concept of the "will of the people" and argued that social conflicts should be redefined through cultural symbols that rendered such conflicts harmless. Lasswell became father of the behavioral movement in political science, which dominated the 1950s and eventually evolved into the policy sciences (Bruner, 1991). The pluralist-elitist-equilibrium theory of democracy propounded by Joseph Schumpeter (1942) and developed by Robert Dahl (1956) was not far behind.

The first empirical study of political attitudes was undertaken by Floyd A. Allport. Allport encouraged his colleagues to drop the concept of groups altogether and simply measure aggregate individual attitudes and behaviors. These techniques were developed rapidly by psychologists such as L. L. Thurstone. The opinion survey reached new levels of sophistication, even though there were still defenders of the life history approach, which was criticized as unstandardized and diminished in influence as a technique.

During World War I, psychologist Robert M. Yerkes, president of the American Psychological Association, persuaded the army to administer intelligence tests to army draftees, the first massive use of written tests. Although the difficulties in administering the tests would make a good Three Stooges comedy, the results, published by the National Academy of Sciences in 1921, provided much fuel for the eugenics movement by showing that immigrants could be rank ordered by intelligence according to their country of origin, with African-Americans at the bottom. The conclusions were highly questionable, even accepting the numbers at face value (Gould, 1981; Kamin, 1977; Travers, 1983). Yerkes and his colleagues also rounded up prostitutes around army bases, gave them I.Q. tests, and discovered that they were mentally deficient. Publicity from the test results led directly to severe legislative restrictions on immigration in 1924 and to involuntary sterilization of people identified as mentally deficient. By 1931, 31 states had sterilization laws (Travers, 1983). From 1924 to 1972, more than 7,500 people were legally sterilized in Virginia alone (Gould, 1981).

Although Francis Galton, Karl Pearson, and Cyril Burt were also ardent eugenicists, no such sterilization occurred in Britain. The British were more concerned with social class than with race or immigration. They also attributed poverty, crime, and low social class standing to lack of hereditary intelligence. Theoretically, psychologists reified I.Q. as a real entity, mostly on the basis that the test scores could be factor analyzed. If a statistical entity existed, it must represent a real entity in nature, they argued, with psychologists debating whether I.Q. was properly defined by Charles Spearman's g or by Thurstone's primary mental abilities (Gould, 1981). Few doubted that I.Q. was a real, fixed quantity. The major dissenting voices came from anthropologists, sociologists, and some journalists, such as Walter Lippmann (Travers, 1983).

E. L. Thorndike conducted hundreds of studies of transfer and other learning mechanisms based on his associationist psychology, discovering bonds between situations and responses. From his animal experiments, Thorndike conceived the mind as something like a telephone switchboard where connections had to be made by repetition and reinforcement. These findings were applied to classrooms, and B. F. Skinner's later puzzle boxes were derived directly from Thorndike's work. Although operant psychology was Thorndike's major legacy, he also introduced more sophisticated measurement and statistical methods (Travers, 1983).

Meanwhile, John Watson was developing a more radical behaviorism, drawing on Pavlov and the Russian psychologists. Behavior was controlled by external stimuli the organism encountered, not by any internal mechanisms. Behaviorists contended that mental activity was displayed in behavior and should be measured in behavioral terms, that behavior was guided by biological impulses and conditioning, and that behavior could be controlled by science. Although discussed widely in the 1920s, Watson's ideas did not achieve their full impact until the 1930s, when they were combined with concepts such as operational definition, derived from logical positivism. Behaviorism became a powerful influence following World War II, affecting both psychology and education, both in theory and in practical devices such as programmed learning and teaching machines (Travers, 1983).

In educational research, atheoretical testing surveys were still popular, with E. F. Lindquist establishing the Iowa tests and Iowa statewide testing in 1929, which was emulated by many states. Lindquist is also credited with developing the dominant approach to experimental design (Madaus, Stufflebeam, & Scriven, 1983). Also in 1929, Ralph Tyler at Ohio State University developed a method for constructing achievement tests, which he expanded into an approach to curriculum development and evaluation (Tyler, 1983):

1. Identify the objectives of the educational program.
2. Define each objective in terms of behavior and content.
3. Identify situations where objectives are utilized.
4. Devise ways to present situations.
5. Devise ways to obtain a record.
6. Decide on terms to use in appraisal.
7. Devise means to get a representative sample.

During the 1930s, Tyler, called the "father of educational evaluation" by some, directed the 8-Year Study, which led to the objectives-based model of evaluation in the 1950s and the National Assessment of Educational Progress by the 1970s (Madaus, Stufflebeam, & Scriven, 1983). In the post-World War II days, the operationalism of the behaviorists and logical positivists became dominant (Travers, 1983).

Although in his later work anthropologist Franz Boas recognized that environmental factors, such as geography, might influence culture, he clung in his studies to an individualist framework that focused on the interactions of personality and culture, a refrain on the U.S. theme of individual differences. He never developed a theory of politics or interest groups because all human behavior and culture were irrational, in his view, including that of the Western world. Boas's influence and that of his students, including Ruth Benedict, Margaret Mead, A. L. Kroeber, and their students, such as Julian Steward, was immense. They challenged the ideas of unilinear evolution and inherited characteristics (Hatch, 1973).

By the 1920s the U.S. professional social science associations had grown from a few hundred members to 1,000 in sociology, 1,300 in political science, and 2,300 in economics (Ross, 1991). There were increasing numbers of women, although the professional associations were still overwhelmingly male. More philanthropic foundations funded social research. In 1923 the Social Science Research Council was established with Rockefeller money, many of the grants going to the University of Chicago. By contrast, the New School for Social Research, founded in 1918 with a social democratic theme, in spite of association with names such as Dewey, Mitchell, Beard, and Veblen, was never able to secure much foundation funding and had to turn to adult education as a means of support (Ross, 1991).

The social scientists of the 1920s emphasized fluid process, whether as the movement of the business cycle, the social psychology of attitudes, the sociology of urban conflict and assimilation, the balancing of interest groups, or the struggle of economic interests. Society as the product of interacting individuals, forming and reforming as groups, eliminated the need for fixed constraints such as social class, although race survived as an important explanatory concept. In studying these aggregates, statistics and external observation of behavior were the preferred methods. Fluid processes were seen as ultimately resulting in U.S. liberal harmony and progress. What had begun as studies of long-term social evolutionary processes decades before had turned into studies of short-term ahistorical processes (Ross, 1991).

By the beginning of the Great Depression, the crisis in the social sciences generated by the historical transformation of U.S. society, a challenge to the ideology of U.S. exceptionalism, was over. An unexpected result was that social science was defined by method—"scientism." The new social scientific paradigm was one in which quantitative methods were modeled on the physical sciences, and theory was rooted in an ahistorical human nature. Historian Ross concludes:

> What my history shows is that American social science has consistently constructed models of the world that embody the values and follow the logic of the national ideology of American exceptionalism . . . the exceptionalist stance has withal produced remarkable continuities within and across these disciplines. . . . The most striking outcome . . . has been scientism itself. The aim of scientism has been to establish prediction and control of the historical world and perhaps its most conspicuous accomplishment has been a set of quantitative techniques for information gathering and analysis that are used to manipulate such things as the money supply, consumer choices, votes, and remedial social therapies. (Ross, 1991, pp. 471-472)

Later, in the ensuing 1930s, social scientists had to grapple with the Great Depression, and with World War II in the 1940s. The Great Depression gave way to Keynesianism, and World War II resulted in the centralization of power in Washington, with consequent social expectations that the federal government should attend to social problems. A further history of the U.S. social sciences would examine the impact of these events and the effects of influences such as logical positivism and the immigration of foreign scholars, especially German immigrants. Yet, although many significant changes were to come, the broad shape of U.S. social science was set by 1929.

⠎ Conclusions

The founding U.S. social scientists tried to explain the profound changes they were seeing in U.S. society within the framework of the exceptionalist ideology. This framework greatly constrained the explanations available. That is, the social scientists rejected explanations that would portray the United States as having social classes and massive poverty like other countries. The scholars' own social backgrounds also influenced their theories.

Furthermore, the political context and persecution of social scientists for anti-establishment views seriously affected their work. Several prominent scholars lost their jobs because of dissident political and economic views, in particular, views unpopular with the business community and capitalist benefactors, who had achieved considerable influence within the universities. Only small numbers of social scientists were actually persecuted, but it does not take many publicized examples to chill a discipline. Most theories during this time also included strong racist components.

The effect was to make social science politically conservative and in tune with the dominant business ideology. It also led social scientists to establish disciplines based on statistical techniques that claimed to be scientific and value-free, when, in fact, theory was heavily ideological. In both the earlier and later versions of positivism, U.S. social scientists found a philosophical justification for their theories, methods, and social situation. Positivism was not embraced in any other country to nearly the same degree as in the United States. This early form of positivism was blended later with the logical positivism of the Vienna school during the post-World War II period.

Evaluation itself was strongly influenced by the established social sciences. Most evaluators were trained in the social sciences, and in the major impetus to U.S. evaluation, passage of the Elementary and Secondary Education Act of 1965, Senator Robert Kennedy's idea of helping poor, disadvantaged students was transformed by economists in the Department of Health, Education and Welfare into attempts to construct production functions, using standardized achievement test scores as outcome measures—an application of microeconomic theory (McLaughlin, 1975). To the economists' disbelief, the study was a failure. Rather than question their approach, they concluded that the program was designed improperly, which led them to design the Follow Through program as a "planned variation" experiment that would embody the proper research design. The results of Follow Through one decade and $500 million later were similarly disappointing (House, Glass, McLean, & Walker, 1978).

The social scientists could not understand that the model they were employing might be inappropriate for evaluation. As McLaughlin said, the failure "lies in large part in the inconsistency between this particular analytic paradigm and the operational reality of the Title I program" (McLaughlin, 1975, p. 62). The world did not fit the model, to some degree a consequence of the historical development of the social sciences. This kind of failure has been repeated in other evaluations. Evaluators, relying on their social science training, often have applied inappropriate techniques. Social science theory and methods were developed in particular political and social contexts, often with the effect of removing them from real world applicability and of assuring that particular social beliefs went unchallenged.

When Scriven (1983, p. 240) characterized evaluation as plagued by the separatist, positivist, managerial, and relativist ideologies of the "traditional social science model"—of being too scientistic, of being too oriented to the interests of managers, of denying it was taking or could take explicit value positions, and of not wanting to examine itself closely—it is not difficult to understand these biases in a historical perspective. Fortunately, evaluation has changed significantly over the past few decades, and these ideologies are challenged by an enlightened evaluation community. The remedy for such biases is persistent, rigorous, internal critique.

However, one must also recognize the positive side of the social science legacy. Without the social sciences, evaluation would not exist in anything like its current strength. In spite of their deficiencies, the established social sciences provided evaluation with precedents, legitimacy, independence, autonomy, methods, and models of what disciplines should be. Evaluators could look to the established social sciences as bases of operation within the universities, as secure places from which to conduct studies without fear of reprisal. Evaluators could appeal to the social science ideal of independence and autonomy from external control. Evaluators could adopt the research methods of the social sciences and their concern for evidence and reason. Evaluators could present themselves as objective researchers, which was critical to establishing the legitimacy of the field itself.

In summary, it is fair to say that the U.S. evaluation community is the strongest evaluation group in the world, and that one of the primary reasons is that it has had the institutional support, ideas, and research methods provided by the U.S. social sciences, despite the peculiar twists and turns the social sciences themselves have taken over the past many decades. Although U.S. evaluation has been influenced by some of the biases of the social sciences, it also has incorporated their strongest, healthiest qualities as well. U.S. evaluation would not be nearly as effective and powerful as it is without its social science foundation.

Notes

1. Bannister (1987) gives 1903 as the founding date.

2. Pragmatists, such as Dewey and George Herbert Mead, who also were at Chicago, had a strong influence on the Chicago school of sociology, especially in the way that Chicago sociologists conceived society and in methodological issues. Pragmatists believed that inquiry should start with our everyday experience of the world (Hammersley, 1989).

7

Social Justice

$\mathcal{A}$t the end of World War II, the United States achieved a position of unparalleled power, influence, and wealth in the world. To many countries, and certainly to itself, its social, political, and economic system seemed far superior to anything else the world had ever seen, a model for emulation. Americans were united in what one British historian has called "the ideology of the liberal consensus," which included the following beliefs:

1. The American free-enterprise system is different from the old capitalism. It is democratic. It creates abundance. It has a revolutionary potential for social justice.
2. The key to this potential is production: specifically, increased production, or economic growth. This makes it possible to meet people's needs out of incremental resources. Social conflict over resources between classes . . . therefore becomes obsolete. . .
3. Thus, there is a natural harmony of interests in society. American society is getting more equal. It is in the process of abolishing . . . social class.
4. Social problems can be solved like industrial problems: The problem is first identified; programs are designed to solve it by government enlightened by social science; money and other resources . . . are then applied to the problem as "inputs"; the outputs are predictable; the problems will be solved.

Some of these ideas appeared earlier in House, E. R. (1991). Evaluation and social justice: Where are we? In Milbrey McLaughlin & Dennis Phillips (Eds.), *Evaluation and education at quarter century, National Society for the Study of Education Yearbook* (pp. 233-246). Chicago: University of Chicago Press.

5. The main threat to this beneficent system comes from the deluded adherents of Marxism. (Hodgson, 1978, p. 76)

The key to this revolutionary social system was economic growth. Democratic capitalism seemed to work. The massive unemployment and social turmoil of the Great Depression had ended, and everyone was better off. Continued economic expansion provided more for everybody, so there was no need for social class conflict or, indeed, for social classes. Everyone could be middle class. Social problems would be solved with increasing economic resources without taking anything away from anyone.

"Production has eliminated the more acute tensions associated with inequality. Increasing aggregate output is an alternative to redistribution," Galbraith (1958) wrote in *The Affluent Society*. Furthermore, both economic growth and the solutions to social problems could be engineered by the federal government. These ideas guided not only the Truman and Eisenhower administrations, but also those of Kennedy ("In short, our primary challenge is not how to divide the economic pie, but how to enlarge it" [Rowen, 1964, p. 114]) and Johnson ("So long as the economic pie continues to grow, Johnson argued, there will be few disputes about its distributions among labor, business, and other groups" [Kearns, 1976, p. 145]). The size of the economic pie was the critical factor, and new economic indicators, such as the gross national product, were available to measure the size of the pie.

Where did the social sciences and the later emerging field of evaluation fit into this framework? Economists were to determine how to fuel the economy, whereas other social scientists and evaluators were to discover which programs would solve the remaining social problems most effectively. The social science literature of this period reveals supreme confidence in social science's applied capabilities. To put the situation bluntly, "Alternatives were not what the government wanted. It wanted solutions. It expected to get them from men who displayed a maximum of technical ingenuity with a minimum of dissent" (Hodgson, 1978, p. 97). One might label this the liberal technocratic view of democracy.

When Johnson's Great Society ushered in large federal educational programs in 1965, evaluators assessed such things as education for the disadvantaged, Head Start, Follow Through, Job Corps, *Sesame Street*, Community Action, income maintenance, and social welfare. The practice of evaluation fit the dominant public philosophy. As Campbell (1969) said, "[Quasi-experiments and true experiments] . . . stand

together in contrast with a morass of obfuscation and self-deception.
. . . We must provide political stances that permit true experiments,
or good quasi-experiments" (p. 429).

Seminal works presented the basic methodology:

> This chapter is committed to the experiment: as the *only* means for
> settling disputes regarding educational practice, as the *only* way of
> verifying educational improvements, and as the *only* way of establish-
> ing a cumulative tradition in which improvements can be introduced
> without the danger of a faddish discard of old wisdom in favor of
> inferior novelties. (Campbell & Stanley, 1963, p. 171, emphasis added)

And from sociology:

> The most identifying feature of evaluative research is the presence of
> some goal or objective whose measure of attainment constitutes the
> main focus of the research problem. . . . Characterized this way, one
> may formulate an evaluation project in terms of a series of hypotheses
> which state that "Activities A, B, C will produce results X, Y, and Z."
> (Suchman, 1967, pp. 37-38)

This rationale was carried forward in federal policy by government
officials such as Alice Rivlin, former assistant secretary of Health,
Education and Welfare (HEW) and director of the Congressional Budget Office, in her rationale for the Follow Through evaluation:

> In other words, the conditions of scientific experiments should be real-
> ized as nearly as possible . . . individual project leaders have to agree to
> follow the plan and to use common measures of what is done and what
> is accomplished so that the results can be compared. . . . Information
> necessary to improve the effectiveness of social services is impossible to
> obtain any other way . . . effective functioning of the system depends on
> measures of achievement. (Rivlin, 1971, pp. 91, 108, 140)

Despite the hopes of the originators of these ideas that they
promote open democratic processes, these notions hardened into an
orthodoxy, even against the warnings of leading experts (Campbell,
1970). An evaluation practice so formulated led to what Scriven calls
the doctrines of managerialism and positivism (Scriven, 1983). That
is, many studies were conducted for the benefit of managers of
programs, and evaluators acted as value-neutral scientists who relied upon the methods of the social sciences to protect against biases.
In evaluation, these research methods were primarily experimental

or survey, utilizing quantitative outcome measures as befit the demand for maximizing the surrogates of economic growth, such as test scores, years of schooling, and income.

This framework was justified formally by the utilitarian theory of justice. Utilitarianism is a moral theory that holds that policies are morally right when they promote the greatest sum total of good or happiness from among the alternatives. Quantitative measures often serve as surrogates for total happiness in utilitarian calculations, and the logic of many evaluation studies was to find the program or policy that maximized the outcomes. Within this framework, equality is a fundamental notion only insofar as each individual is to count equally in utilitarian calculations. This conception does not entail egalitarianism or even that gross inequality of results be reduced. For example, if it turned out that spending disproportionate sums on education of the advantaged would produce a higher sum total of good for society than spending disproportionate sums on the disadvantaged, then utilitarianism would dictate spending more on the advantaged (House & Howe, 1990).

For utilitarians, justice is a derivative principle. That is, whether reducing unequal shares of wealth and power ought to be attempted depends on whether equal shares contribute to maximizing the good. It usually does make sense to advocate equal opportunity by removing obstacles that stand in the way of developing natural talents, but only to the extent that such policies contribute to the overall good. Utilitarians would be hard pressed to support policies that exacted a cost by reducing the sum total of good. For utilitarians, there is no necessary conflict between equality of persons and unequal shares of goods, such as exist in liberal societies. As long as each person's good is weighed equally and the sum total of all these goods is maximized, the social arrangement is just. Utilitarianism is based on considering individuals, not groups, in utilitarian calculations. Hence, one does not have to deal with social classes or other groups, because it is presumed that the common measures averaging individuals validly represent the common good for all.

⮞ Stakeholders and the Fractured Consensus

Between 1960 and 1972 the liberal consensus came apart. In 1958 Martin Luther King, Jr., began his quest for racial equality as a devout affirmation of the American dream and ended his life in bitter disillusionment and assassination in 1968. The civil rights movement shattered the social harmony and gave way to black power, feminism, gay liberation, and ecology. Students, professors, mothers, and laborers marched in the streets to protest the Vietnam War. Civil disobedience became routine.

The national economy suffered double-digit inflation and decline. The gross national product (GNP) continued to expand but mostly through new workers entering the labor force. Median family income peaked in 1973, decreased 6% by 1984, and became more unequal in distribution (Levy, 1987). Something was wrong, even with the economic pie. Social programs were frozen in place. These social traumas and the emergence of special-interest groups vying for power and advantage did not fit the prevailing ideology. U.S. society needed a new political framework, and social scientists supplied the pluralist-elitist-equilibrium theory of democracy:

> Mainstream current American pluralism . . . disclaims any normative judgements (though they are there, not far below the surface). It is held that the current system of competing parties and pressure groups does perform, as well as is possible, the democratic function of equilibrating the diverse and shifting demands for political goods with the available supply, and producing the set of political decisions most agreeable to, or least disagreeable to, the whole set of individual demands. This empirical pluralism is based on an economic market model: the party leaders are the entrepreneurs, the voters are the consumers. The voters' function is not to decide on policies but merely to choose one set of politicians who are authorized to decide the policies. (MacPherson, 1987, pp. 94-95)

According to this theory, individual demands are fed to group leaders, who articulate these demands to government officials, who adjudicate them as best they can. Hence, the political system is kept in equilibrium by group elites bargaining for their constituencies and government elites reaching accommodations. There is little need for direct participation by individuals other than to express their demands to their leaders. Leaders are made accountable through consumer sovereignty. Unlike the previous utilitarian, technocratic conception, this model of pluralist democracy recognizes the different interests of diverse groups, accounts for social conflict and the lack of social harmony, while still preserving the primary goal of economic growth to satisfy demands.

Among the first evaluators to recognize diverse values and interests were those such as Edwards (1971) and Guttentag (1973), who tried to incorporate these values and interests into a utilitarian calculus using procedures such as multiattribute utility scaling, and those such as Stake and MacDonald, who advocated qualitative methodologies for registering such views directly. Most evaluators continued to practice evaluation based upon the older presumptions, but the changed social context eventually forced these pluralist notions into mainstream evaluation, as evidenced by concepts such as "stakeholders," "contexts of command and accommodation," and the "policy shaping community" (Cronbach & Associates, 1980).

On the surface, this theory allows evaluators to maintain their value neutrality by merely describing the interests of various individuals and groups, who are seen to exist in a plural equilibrium from which legitimate decisions emerge. As Cook and Shadish (1986) state the position:

> Evaluators may also be unwilling to endorse particular prescriptive ethics because few data have been advanced thus far to support particular philosophers' claims that a better society will result if one ethic is followed rather than another and because the American political system has traditionally preferred to foster a pluralism of values. Promoting a single prescriptive ethic is therefore inconsistent with the political context in which evaluation occurs. . . . A descriptive approach to value is better suited to the political context in which evaluators function, since decision making depends more on the values held by relevant legislators, managers, voters, lobbyists, etc., than on any single prescriptive calculus of value. Hence, knowledge of stakeholder values can be used to help select criteria so that no criteria are overlooked that are of crucial importance to particular groups. (p. 210)

Neither the government nor the evaluator is supposed to intervene to support any particular interests but rather should act only to provide information that is interest-neutral and value-neutral. The interests of various groups dissolve into the values of decision makers and stakeholders. This view of democracy, originally advanced by the economist Joseph Schumpeter (1942) and developed by political scientists such as Robert Dahl (1956), is based on a model of the economic marketplace in which interests are registered to work their way out automatically. Sometimes this marketplace derivation is explicit:

> The evaluator engages to produce something—information—that has value to consumers and for which they are willing to pay. Deciding

what product to deliver is an economic decision; both sides of the supply-demand equation contribute to it. The sponsor, as procurer of information, should not have to take sole responsibility for specifying the product. In industry, suppliers perform a part of their economic function by offering options to customers. In a similar way, the sponsor of an evaluation should be a broker for the many interest communities. And, by anticipating the wishes of those who are in the market for social information, the evaluator assists the sponsor (thus increasing in a quite legitimate manner, the demand for the evaluator's services). (Cronbach & Associates, 1980, p. 211)

One result of this new sensibility was that "stakeholders" became a common concept in evaluation. As Weiss (1983a) put it:

The stakeholder concept represents an appreciation that each program affects many groups, which have divergent and even incompatible concerns. It realizes—and legitimizes—the diversity of interests at play in the program world. It recognizes the multiple perspectives that these interests bring to judgment and understanding. . . . Realization of the legitimacy of competing interests and the multiplicity of perspectives and willingness to place evaluation at the service of diverse groups are important intellectual advances. . . . No longer is the federal agency to have a monopoly on control. The concept enfranchises a diverse array of groups, each of which is to have a voice in the planning and conduct of studies. (p. 11)

The National Institute of Education (based partly on the work of many who had criticized earlier technocratic evaluations) developed a stakeholder model of evaluation that focused on the information needs of stakeholders for evaluating two highly visible (and political) programs, Cities-in-Schools and Jesse Jackson's PUSH/Excel program (Gold, 1983). In both cases the evaluations diminished the success of these programs for the disadvantaged because the evaluators did not attend sufficiently to the needs of either the program developers or the program recipients. In truth, the stakeholder model was never implemented (Farrar & House, 1983; House, 1988; Stake, 1986). Charles Murray (1983), the evaluator in both cases, substituted another technocratic model of evaluation and expressed his disdain for the stakeholder concept in his article "Stakeholders as Deck Chairs." In a more considered assessment, Weiss (1983b) concluded that the stakeholder approach holds modest promise for improving the fairness of the evaluation, for marginally improving the range of information collected, for giving more say to local groups, and for democratizing access to information, but that it does not produce harmony or resolve conflicts among diverse groups.

Although the stakeholder concept seems firmly entrenched, there is disagreement about how to implement it. According to Weiss (1983a):

> Many other evaluators simply paid no attention. Their primary commitment was to the canons of social science. Whether they satisfied program people was of secondary concern. They had been trained in proper methodology, and they were not willing to sacrifice their standards in order to satisfy the whims of people who knew little about validity and causality and who cared less. (p. 6)

Some evaluators limited stakeholder involvement to ascertaining participant values, whereas others solicited stakeholders as audiences, and yet others wanted stakeholders actively involved in the conduct of the study. But generally evaluators accepted the pluralist ideas of multiple perspectives, multiple audiences, multiple measures, and multiple methods, and, to some extent, even multiple interests.

⊯ Attempts at Further Reform

Although from the social justice perspective, the stakeholder approach is decidedly superior to the technocratic view that went before, the pluralist-elitist model is no more value-neutral than is the economic marketplace, and the state of methodological grace claimed by some evaluators for themselves does not exist. One problem is that all the relevant group interests are not represented in the planning and negotiations that determine policies, programs, and evaluations. Typically, the powerless and the poor are excluded from bargaining processes, and their interests are ignored. Evaluation agreements negotiated between the sponsor and evaluator consider the powerful interests because of their political potency, but not the powerless. Furthermore, on those rare occasions when powerless groups are included, there is the question of whether their leaders properly represent their interests. For the pluralist-elitist model to work properly, all groups must be included, and the leaders must represent their members interests faithfully.

Another problem is that many critical issues never arise for discussion, study, or evaluation. That is, fundamental issues involving conflicts of interests often do not evolve into public issues because they are not formulated. Powerful groups and ideological screens prevent such issues from arising. In essence, the pluralist model confounds conflicts of interests with conflicts of power. It can balance only those interests that are represented—typically those of the powerful. The pluralist-elitist equilibrium model suffers from the same problems of abuse and inequality that the free market does. Free markets are not usually free for long.

There have been attempts to redress this lack of justice in evaluation. Scriven accepts the marketplace analogy and proposes that evaluators defend the interests of consumers against those of producers, a definite non-neutral stance. For example, he has argued that basing evaluations on program goals biases the studies toward developers, because they define the goals and thus define the content of the evaluation. Scriven's position bewilders evaluators whose practice is based on assessing sponsor goals. Perhaps the issue would be clearer if one thought of the producer and sponsor of an evaluation as being General Motors. Would justice be done if Consumers Union assessed General Motors' goals for its automobiles without taking sides and neutrally allowed the various interests involved to work things out, rather than representing the interests of consumers?

Although advocating stakeholder approaches as a decided improvement, I urged evaluators also to attend to the plight of the disadvantaged and employed Rawls' theory of justice, generally accepted as the major moral theory of the century, as the rationale (House, 1976). Rawls' (1971) theory has two basic principles that supplant the principle of utility: (a) Each person is to have an equal right to the most extensive basic liberty compatible with a similar liberty for others, and (b) social and economic inequalities are to be arranged so that they are both (a) to the greatest benefit to the least advantaged (the difference principle) and (b) attached to offices and positions open to all under conditions of fair equality of opportunity.

The difference principle distinguishes Rawls from both strict egalitarians and utilitarians. Unlike strict egalitarians, Rawls does permit unequal distributions of goods, but is much more restrictive regarding what kinds of inequalities are permissible. Unlike utilitarians, Rawls would distribute educational resources toward the least advantaged and sometimes at the expense of the total good, until the point was reached at which the disadvantaged would receive a greater benefit by more goods being distributed toward the advantaged (e.g., a point might be reached where the disadvantaged could benefit more from expenditures to reduce a shortage of doctors than from expenditures to improve the quality of school facilities for the disadvantaged).

Thus, although Rawls' two principles permit equality of persons and unequal distributions to exist side-by-side, they do so in a way that differs from utilitarianism. His concept of equality is identified with "equal respect" rather than the utilitarian "equal treatment." To treat an individual with equal respect requires responding to needs and thus sometimes requires unequal treatment (e.g., policies that require special educational services for handicapped children). Inequalities in the distribution of goods must meet a strict test. Maximizing the sum total of good is permissible only so long as it does not violate the distributions sanctioned by the "difference principle."

Finally, establishing conditions of "fair equality of opportunity" requires active steps to mitigate the effects of the "natural lottery," and thus levels out class differences to some extent. Individuals do not deserve what it is their good or bad fortune to inherit in the "natural lottery"—levels of intelligence, wealth, social advantages— because they can in no way be credited or blamed for being born with such attributes. Equal opportunity becomes a mechanism for evening out class barriers, instilling in persons a secure sense of self-worth, and empowering them to participate effectively in the democratic process.

I suggested that this conception of justice could be implemented within evaluation by a "fair evaluation agreement" that would include the interests of the disadvantaged, an evaluation agreement having to meet certain conditions to be considered fair (House, 1980). This justice-as-fairness position elicited considerable reaction, both favorable and unfavorable, with critics contending I was biased toward the interests of the disadvantaged. However, it seems to me that making certain the interests of the disadvantaged are represented in the evaluation process is not being biased, but rather is correcting the biases that already exist.

⅔ Social Class

Why is there so much resistance to including the interests of the poor and powerless in evaluations? First, professional and personal ties lead evaluators to believe that the programs being evaluated already incorporate the interests of the poor and powerless, and that it is not the evaluators' job to question this. Evaluators belong to the same professional and social strata as the people who construct and run social programs. These are well-intentioned people with whom evaluators share both careers and friendships. We depend on these people for contracts. Questioning whether their programs incorporate such interests is a potential breach of the relationship, and possibly a dangerous one for the evaluator.

Second, our conceptual models tell us that these interests are included already. The technocratic view assumes that such interests are part of the larger common interests of society, and that these interests are represented adequately in gross outcome measures. The pluralist view assumes that poor and powerless groups already participate in democratic government, demanding and negotiating their interests along with other groups. Is it not the case, for example, that Jesse Jackson was influential enough to obtain funding for his educational program from the Carter administration? And, indeed, sometimes these interests are represented—but not typically.

But I believe there is a deeper resistance that derives from the history of the social sciences in the United States and the ideological background from which Americans conduct evaluations. I believe that we associate the interests of the poor and powerless with the lower social classes and that we are extremely reluctant to recognize social classes as enduring causal entities that influence life chances in U.S. society. The pervasive influences of gender, ethnicity, regionality, and religion have been recognized as more important than social class, which is given no particular emphasis in our studies, except occasionally as a background variable. And, for that matter, only in recent years have race and gender been accorded much importance.

By now most tenets of the postwar ideological consensus have been shattered or seriously weakened, including the idea that social science can provide technocratic solutions to social problems. Japanese capitalism threatens to replace U.S. capitalism as the wonder of the economic world, and fear of Soviet marxism has waned enormously. Yet two steadfast tenets remain: the belief in economic growth and the belief that the United States has eliminated social classes or soon will. Social classes are not recognized as enduring entities like gender and race. Yet they continue to operate as primary causal factors, restricting opportunity for some and enhancing it for others.

And these two beliefs are interconnected. The pluralist-elitist-equilibrium model of democracy depends on

the extreme pluralist assumption that the politically important demands of each individual are diverse, and are shared with varied and shifting combinations of other individuals, none of which combinations can be expected to be a numerical majority of the electorate. . . . Where the economy provides, or promises a share of affluence, class interest will not outrank all other divisions of interest. (MacPherson, 1973, p. 190)

An expanding economy is crucial in preventing individuals from acting politically as members of a social class. To defend the interests of the poor and powerless risks questioning a fundamental tenet of U.S. society. Reluctance to confront the social class structure has shaped much of the content and methodology of U.S. social science for the past 100 years, and this failure has robbed social science of much of its potential.

In evaluation, the reluctance to recognize social class is reflected in assigning failures of educational and social programs to other causes, particularly to traits of individual persons, group subcultures, genetics, lack of knowledge, the intractability of social problems, program management, ambiguous goal statements, unrealistic expectations, lack of coordination, poor planning, inadequate training, not enough time, and other contingencies too numerous to catalogue. Often the topic is simply avoided. For example, the National Assessment of Educational Progress does not even collect social class data such as parents' occupations, though it does collect data on race and parental education. In an examination of articles in four major educational research journals between 1973 and 1983, Grant and Sleeter (1986) found only 71 articles dealing with race, gender, and social class, or 1.775 per journal per year. Of these, 15 dealt primarily with social class, or .375 per major journal per year. These were not evaluation journals but the frequency would not be higher there.

Another way of ignoring conflicting social class interests is to treat matters of conflicting interests as matters of diverse value, as if differences are only matters of personal preference, like religion or life style. Stakeholder approaches to evaluation often ascertain the values of individuals in the program and derive evaluation criteria from these. As important as these values may be, they are not likely to represent the interests of the poor and powerless. An interest is anything conducive to the achievement of an individual's wants, needs, or purposes, and a need is anything necessary to the survival or well-being of an individual. To be free is to know one's interests; to possess the ability and resources, or the power and opportunity, to act toward those interests; and to be disposed to do so (Bhaskar, 1986, p. 170).

Social justice requires that the interests of all individuals and groups in society be served. Whose interests are served and how interests are registered are critical issues for evaluation studies. Whether the social class structure acts as a major impediment to the fulfillment of interests for large groups of people is an empirical question; I believe the evidence is strong that it does. In any case, the influence of social class is an important topic for investigation in evaluations of educational programs if we are to improve the way in which evaluation serves social justice.

≈ Social Justice and Evaluation

Progress on social justice in evaluation is bound to be slow, painful, and controversial, just as it was in securing universal suffrage for males without property, blacks, and women. I interpret the establishment of evaluation as a procedure for arriving at judgments about social programs, policies, and personnel to be a move toward increased democratic control, though evaluation can be anti-democratic as well. Evaluation should be socially just, and it should attend to the interests of everyone in society.

During the past several decades, we have moved from a conception of justice in which it was assumed that increasing the economic productivity of the nation would benefit everyone alike to a conception of justice in which we see that social programs may have differential effects for different groups. During this time, injustices regarding race, gender, and ethnicity have been recognized, though not always remedied. The same cannot be said of inequalities of social class.

Here is a test for evaluation. If this were 1920 and female suffrage were being debated, should evaluators remain neutral, not taking sides, and leave it to the balance of interest groups—legislators, lobbyists, and managers—to work things out? Or should evaluators represent the interests of those ignored, in this case women, in their evaluations? I believe the latter position is morally correct. Evaluators cannot be value-neutral in these matters. Our conceptions, our practices, and even our methodologies are value-laden. Evaluators do not live in a state of methodological grace.

❧ 8 ❧

Methodology and Justice

$\mathcal{N}$o problem is more difficult and complex in the social sciences than that of how values are embedded within the research methodologies that we employ. That values should and must exist in research is no longer denied. In fact, we actively encourage and promote values such as objectivity, impartiality, fairness, and efficiency. Other values, such as partiality, we try to curtail as much as possible, and our failure to do so constitutes bias. Many values, however, remain implicit rather than explicit in our work, hidden in ways not discernible, and though these embedded values may not be harmful or wrong, sometimes they are both. Analyzing research methodology itself presents a particularly difficult problem because we believe that we are protected from bias by our methods. Indeed, that is why we employ those methods.

Social justice is among the important values that we should hope to secure in evaluation studies. The practice of evaluation is part of the authority structure of society, and evaluation as an aid to public decision making involves concepts of democracy and social justice, although often these ideas are implicit. Public evaluation should be an institution for democratizing public decision making, for making decisions, programs, and policies more open to public scrutiny and deliberation. As an institutionalized practice, it should embody the values of a democratic society. Considerations such as justice, impartiality,

Some of these ideas appeared earlier in House, E. R. (1990). Methodology and justice. In K. Sirotnik (Ed.), *New directions for program evaluation: Evaluation and social justice.* Vol. 45 (pp. 23-36). San Francisco: Jossey-Bass. I wish to thank Sandra M. Mathison and Kenneth Howe for making helpful comments on an earlier draft of this chapter.

and equality, though subject to disagreement as to their exact meaning, are neither arbitrary nor relative.

Evaluations should serve the interests not only of the sponsor but
also of the larger society, and of various groups within society,
particularly those most affected by the program under review. Hence,
as a social practice, evaluation entails an inescapable ethic of public
responsibility, and this responsibility extends well beyond the immediate client. Social justice in evaluation concerns the manner in
which various interests are served, and by interests I mean those
things conducive to the achievement of individuals' wants, needs, or
purposes, needs being anything necessary to the survival or well-
being of individuals. To be free is to know one's interests; to possess
the ability and resources, or the power and opportunity, to act
toward those interests; and to be disposed to do so.

Craniometry

The lessons of history suggest that it is not advisable to be too
sanguine about these matters. Grave injustices have been perpetrated by leading scientists operating with what they thought to be
the best research methods of their day. Nineteenth-century craniometry is a dramatic example. Operating from the presumption that
larger brains indicate more intelligence—after all, that relationship
seemed to hold from one species to another among animals—19th-
century scientists developed methods to measure the brain sizes of
humans, with the obvious connection to intelligence that they thought
this entailed. Leading scientists of the day, such as physician Samuel
George Morton of Philadelphia and Paul Broca, professor of surgery
and founder of the Anthropological Society of Paris, developed
rather precise methods for estimating brain size, usually by weigh-
ing the brain or measuring cranial volume (Gould, 1981).

In the volume technique, the skull of the (deceased) subject was
filled with lead shot, following carefully prescribed procedures as to
what type of shot to use, how the shot should be tamped down, what
kind of container the shot should be transferred to, and how it should
be measured. Craniometricians estimated skull capacity with increasing precision and objectivity, carefully recording minute differences among groups of people all over the world. What they found
was that whites had larger brains than other races and that men had
larger brains than women—exactly what they had hypothesized all

along, of course, because whites were more intelligent than other races and men were more intelligent than women, in their opinion. These findings appeared in technical journals and flooded the popular press (Gould, 1981).

Geologist Stephen Jay Gould (1981) examined these 19th-century craniometric methods in detail and concluded in *The Mismeasure of Man* that precision of measurement and objectivity in method could never overcome the inherent racism and sexism implicit in the beginning assumptions, biases the scientists never recognized. Broca, one of the leading scientists of his day, assumed that the human races could be ranked on a linear scale of mental ability and explored any indexes that he thought might yield the proper ranking. The craniometricians asserted the objectivity of their findings on the basis of the careful precision of their measurements and explained away inconsistencies in their findings.

For example, when Germans were found to have larger brains than French, Broca (who was French) eliminated the measured differences by considerations of age and body size, because older and smaller people have smaller brains. But he did not use the same correction for differences between men and women. When it turned out that many prominent men who had donated their brains to these studies had small or average-size brains, Broca reasoned that they were small in stature or had died elderly. At one point he hinted that the work of some was not as eminent as claimed. He did not know that his own brain would prove to be only slightly above average in size. Although craniometry seems ludicrous now, gross injustices were perpetrated on vast numbers of people by this research.

These 19th-century craniometric studies were not evaluations, and I do not mean to imply by this extreme example that we have corresponding problems in the practice of evaluation; I do not believe that we do. In the evaluation examples I wish to explore, even where I disagree with the way the studies were conducted, the evaluations do not approach the crass injustices of craniometry. Fortunately, we start from a higher plateau of moral sensitivity, and the injustices emerging from evaluation methods are far less severe and more subtle. Nonetheless, it is best not to be too serene in these matters.

From Gould's analysis of craniometry, I take two conclusions: First, the complexity and precision of research methods is no guarantee of their impartiality. Second, the intellectual and ideological climate can seriously affect how studies are conducted and what conclusions are drawn, in spite of objective methodology. I focus here on methodological concerns, having dealt with the ideological context in the last chapter. Gross contaminations of our methods, such as coercion, dishonesty, and falsification, I ignore. It is the potential injustice of our best methods I want to explore.

⋙ Two Evaluation Examples

Two examples in evaluation where I think justice was not secured as we might like are the evaluations of Follow Through and PUSH/Excel. In Follow Through, the U.S. Office of Education established different early childhood programs throughout the country with a view to determining which particular approach was best for children from poor families. More than 20 different childhood programs were developed and implemented in sites around the country. About a dozen programs were compared in the final evaluation. Several cohorts of children were followed through 4 years of these programs and their achievement test results compared, mostly in contrast to a comparison site established for each experimental site. The same achievement tests were used across all sites as covariates and outcome measures. The evaluators encountered many technical problems, but finally produced a comparative ranking of the Follow Through programs based on their test outcomes.

Perhaps the most striking thing about the results was that the variance within programs was about as great as the variance across programs, thus making the ranking of programs questionable. That is, a particular program would have several sites, and on some of these sites it would score well and on some it would score badly. Consistency of performance across sites was lacking. For this reason, the evaluators themselves said comparisons of programs could not be made, but having invested so much over such a long period of time, the Office of Education insisted, believing that a ranking of programs was possible (House, Glass, McLean, & Walker, 1978).

The injustice resides in the fact that the interests of large segments of poor students were not properly served by these findings. In fact, if a poor school district wanted to adopt the best Follow Through program, the district would be misled by the evaluation results. For reasons such as these, Cronbach (1982a) advised school administrators interested in adoption of such programs to examine the details of evaluation studies to find the sites that most closely matched their own district and attend to those results. Put another way, the same programs did not produce the same results on different sites, in spite of massive investment ($500 million) in development and control of the programs themselves.

The second example is the evaluation of Jesse Jackson's PUSH/ Excel program (Farrar & House, 1983; House, 1988). Again, PUSH/ Excel was established on several sites around the country. This time the evaluators worked out an elaborate scheme for describing and analyzing the program. The program was conceived as consisting of separate components, each of which could be assessed across sites. Considerable effort was spent documenting activities on each site. By taking criticisms of the program from the ensuing evaluation reports and inverting the criticisms, we reconstructed the evaluators' positive ideal of what the PUSH/Excel program should be: The program should be a coordinated, sequential set of standard activities, with each activity tied to specific outcomes and each activity repeated and sustained. The program had to be specified by detailed, step-by-step concrete procedures and justified by an explicit strategy and rationale. Moreover, it had to be guided and monitored by a central authority that would provide a "how-to" manual for participants.

PUSH/Excel was nothing like this, and when the evaluators looked across sites for standard components they could not find them. Instead, they found different activities at different sites. From this variation, the evaluators concluded that PUSH/Excel did not exist as a program. In the evaluators' judgment, there was no program. A program had to have standard components. Participants on different sites had different activities, local initiative being an initial idea. Jackson's idea of a program was something like what Baptist preachers mean when they say they have a program for their church, by which they mean a set of locally originated activities particular to the setting itself, not organized in a highly sequential manner.

The conclusions of the evaluation appeared on the front pages of newspapers as accusations that Jackson had taken federal money but had not developed a program. The injustice is striking because it helped eliminate an educational program for poor black youths in the inner cities and also was used in later presidential campaigns as evidence that Jackson could not manage large enterprises. What is also striking is that the evaluators conscientiously applied an elaborate evaluation model that had been developed for evaluating rural development projects in Thailand, and that the evaluation included considerable qualitative data, including interviews with students and parents. The conclusions came logically from the presumptions of the evaluation model.

So here are two rather different evaluations, one heavily quantitative with a complex experimental design, and the other with a significant qualitative component and a simple pre/post design, both resulting in serious injustices by damaging the interests of impoverished people. The key element in both cases was the way variations in programs and outcomes were interpreted by the evaluators. The injustices of both evaluations derive from a similar source: from our particular conception of causation and from the way the programs were defined, both ideas being closely connected and embedded deeply in our conceptual structure.

❧ Causation and Methods

Let us turn first to a classic statement of causation in evaluation from Suchman's *Evaluative Research*:

> The most identifying feature of evaluative research is the presence of some goal or objective whose measure of attainment constitutes the main focus of the research problem. . . . Characterized this way, one may formulate an evaluation project in terms of a series of hypotheses which state that "Activities A, B, C will produce results X, Y, and Z." (Suchman, 1967, pp. 37-38)

This formulation, or something quite near it, is repeated in much of the evaluation literature.

Both the Follow Through and PUSH/Excel evaluations subscribed to this notion of cause and effect. In Follow Through, it was expected that programs at different sites would produce similar results. The same programs would produce the same effects, with only minor variations. But, in fact, they did not. In PUSH/Excel, the program was expected by the evaluators to have the same components on all sites, and those components would produce the same results. For example, students signing the "pledge" to join the local PUSH/Excel program were expected to have one of only a few alternative experiences prespecified by the evaluators, and these experiences would lead to prespecified outcomes. The evaluators expected to be able to determine exactly what the result of "signing the pledge" was across all sites, and thereupon inform the program staff as to the effectiveness of this particular component. Hence the program would be built surely and slowly from precise components and their corresponding outcomes.

The analogy in both cases was with physical engineering in which a particular program construction could and would produce a certain outcome, as, for example, in constructing a television set in which one matches certain components. If one constructs an electronic machine, one would expect it to perform consistently under prescribed conditions. In other words, activity A, the program, is followed by activity B, the outcome. Along with this conception of causation is a corresponding notion of the program itself as consisting of engineered components for which one can specify exact outcomes. In this view, a particular definition of program is implied by the overall conception. Social programs are often conceived as machines, assembly lines, and pipelines—industrial metaphors that convey standardized components and totally predictable outcomes. Loosely connected activities or local programs derived from nonstandard sources appear not to be programs at all, according to these conceptions. Hence, the way a program is defined is a major methodology issue.

Furthermore, in such a world of highly regular events, where "Activities A, B, C will produce results X, Y, and Z," formal experimentation makes very good sense. According to Suchman (1967) again: "The ideal evaluation study would follow the classic experimental model. . . . This model represents the ideal experimental design from which all adaptations must be derived. . . the basic logic of proof and verification will be traceable to this model" (pp. 102, 93). The best evaluation design is the pre-test/post-test control group: "The logic of this design is foolproof. Ideally, there is no element of fallibility. Whatever differences are observed between the experimental and control groups, once the above conditions are satisfied, must be attributable to the program being evaluated" (Suchman, 1967, pp. 95-96).

One can determine which activities cause which events by employing the methods of inductive logic developed by John Stuart Mill.

> Mill's most significant contribution—for causal analysis purposes—consists of his work on the methods of agreement, differences, and concomitant variation. . . . The Method of Agreement states that an effect will be present when the cause is present; the Method of Difference states that the effect will be absent when the cause is absent; and the Method of Concomitant Variation implies that when both of the above relationships are observed, causal inference will be all the stronger since certain other interpretations of the covariation between the cause and effect can be ruled out. (Cook & Campbell, 1979, p. 18)

In Mill's own words: "The backward state of the Moral Sciences can only be remedied by applying to them the methods of Physical Science, duly extended and generalized . . . it is by generalizing the methods successfully . . . that we may hope to remove this blot on the face of science" (Mill, 1843/1974, pp. 833-834).

Both the substance and moral fervor of this message were championed in the early days of evaluation. Experimental and quasi-experimental designs became the preferred methods and still are for many evaluators. However, the PUSH/Excel evaluation employed a pre/post design and qualitative methods, which led to equally poor results. Underlying both these evaluations is a particular conception of causation called the Humean or regularity theory of causation. The basic problem is that this underlying conception of causation is incorrect.

This standard conception of causation in the social sciences is incorrect in construing social reality as too simple. In Cronbach's psychometric terminology, there are too many interactions. "Interactions are ubiquitous—that is the 'Achilles heel' of the behavioral sciences" (Cronbach, 1982a, p. 150). In contrast to a standard view of causation such as Suchman's, and following J. L. Mackie's (1974) analysis of causation, Cronbach formulates a causal law this way: "In S, all (ABC or DEF or JKL) are followed by P," where the letters refer to events or situations or to the absence of some objects or events (Cronbach, 1982a, p. 139). Now ABC is sufficient for P to occur but not necessary because P may be preceded by DEF or JKL just as well. In other words, P may occur without ABC. On the other hand, ABC is sufficient for P to occur if all elements—A, B, and C—occur together, but not if only AB or AC or BC occur alone.

Yet the situation may be even more complex than this. J. L. Mackie's (1974) original formulation of causal regularities is, "All F (A . . . B . . . or D . . . H . . . or . . .) are P . . ." (p. 66), where the ellipses indicate missing events or conditions that affect the outcome P, but that are not represented in the law and about which we know little. Such elliptical propositions represent the true state of our knowledge of social causation better than statements of simple regularity, according to J. L. Mackie and Cronbach.

Here is the problem this formulation of causation poses for the evaluator. If event A is the treatment or program, the program is neither necessary nor sufficient for the effect P to occur. The program is only part of a larger package of events that may be followed by P. Furthermore, we are ignorant of what many of these events are, as represented by the ellipses. Hence, specifying the treatment in an experimental design may actually be misleading because it may lead one to believe that the program A is either necessary or sufficient for the outcome to occur when it is not. In other words, an experiment cannot provide a critical test for the effectiveness of a program. With its X and O formulation, traditional experimental design often mistakes the program or treatment for a sufficient condition, one that will produce the outcome by itself, when it is in reality an "inus" (insufficient but nonredundant part of an unnecessary but sufficient) condition.

In a world in which "Activities A, B, C will produce results X, Y, and Z," the program is a sufficient cause and the experiment a critical test of its efficacy. However, that is not the world of social programs and, in general, not the social world at all. The variability experienced in the Follow Through evaluation reflects the fact that Activities A, B, C produced quite different results, depending on other factors. PUSH/Excel, a set of related but loosely integrated activities, was successful in Chattanooga, where certain other factors were in place, such as a determined political power structure, black teachers, southern black students, and strong local advocates, but it did not succeed in other settings. The evaluators interpreted the lack of standardized components as proof of no program, a direct inference from their explicit notion of program and implicit conception of causation. They were misled by their own underlying ideas.

❧ Program Definition

The Humean or regularity theory conceives causation as regular contingent relations between events that one can predict with a high degree of probability, so that the relationship between the program and its outcomes is construed as a relationship between two contingent events, even though one may not know what the program event consisted of. Only the presence or absence of the program event and the presence or absence of the outcomes event is necessary for evaluating the success of the program. And, indeed, one can comparatively evaluate two stereo systems without understanding the nature of their components. But physical analogies are misleading here because a machine can be separated from its environment in ways that a social program cannot.

Social programs are far more complex composites, themselves produced by many factors that interact with one another to produce quite variable outcomes. Determining contingent relations between the program and its outcomes is not as simple as the regularity theory posits.

> Events are the conjunctures of structured processes and are always the outcome of complex causal configurations at the same and at many different levels. If this is the case, then we can also say that causal processes may have surprising effects. They need not, for example, yield the outcomes they usually do. (Manicas & Secord, 1983, p. 399)

A program is not a fixed machine like a stereo system with a simple determined outcome, as physical analogies imply, but rather an event that is caused by several other interacting factors. To use a trivial example, an event such as a cocktail party has a recognizable form but may take different directions depending upon the many factors that produce it. Throwing a cocktail party does not mean it will turn out exactly the same way each time, even if one invites the same people and prepares the same way. Teaching a class is also an event. One can teach the same course exactly the same way, using the same books, and yet have it turn out differently. Understanding such events requires a different conception of causation than that of the standard regularity theory (House, Mathison, & McTaggert, 1989).

How the program is defined seriously affects the evaluation and deserves to be a subject of study. For example, whether the program is conceived metaphorically as a machine or assembly line makes a great difference in the evaluation because criteria appropriate to those domains are applied to the program itself. In much of the evaluation literature, program invariability is either taken for granted, as in Campbell and Stanley (1963), where the program is simply an "X," or variability is treated as a source of error, as in Cook and Campbell (1979), where one is urged to "make the treatment and its implementation as standard as possible across occasions of implementation" (p. 43).

Recently more attention has been paid to how the program is defined. Qualitative evaluators have taken program description as a major focus, and those in the quantitative tradition have begun worrying about the problem as well (Bickman, 1987; Shadish, 1987). For example, Chen and Rossi (1984) have argued against the "black box" approach to program definition that has dominated the experimental literature and have advocated program specification based upon social science theory. "We have argued for a paradigm that accepts experiments and quasi-experiments as dominant research designs, but that emphasizes that these devices should be used in conjunction with a priori knowledge and theory to build models of the treatment process and implementation system" (Chen & Rossi, 1984, p. 354). Whether social science theory is equal to the task remains to be seen, but at least the problem is recognized.

Certainly, program specification based upon social science theory is not what we have had. There is not much scientific about the PUSH/Excel program specification, though it does rest upon a type of means/ends rationality. What seems to be the case is that program definition comes from a number of disparate sources and methods. McClintock (1987) has provided a summary of these "conceptual heuristics," which include metaphors, causal modeling, and concept maps. Program theory is an area worthy of further investigation.

All this is not to say that experiments or quasi-experiments cannot be useful methods of program evaluation. It is to say that the results must be interpreted more carefully and equivocally than in the past and that one should hold more modest expectations as to what these methods might accomplish. They are not the foolproof guides that Suchman envisioned. Methods are no substitute for substance. The social world is far more complex than we have supposed, and a major source of error resides in our standard conception of causation. We need to abandon the Humean/regularity theory and move on to better conceptions.

ꙮ Injustice and Method

How do these methodological problems contribute to injustices? If these methods apply to all programs evaluated, and errors are randomly distributed across populations, then these errors are simply errors of method, not injustices. If injustices exist, it must be that the interests of certain groups of people are systematically abused, as in the case of craniometry. From the craniometry episode, I drew two conclusions: First, the complexity and precision of research methods is no guarantee of their impartiality and, second, the ideological climate of the age can seriously affect how studies are conducted and what conclusions are drawn, despite objective methodology. The 19th-century context was such that scientists believed that women and other races were less intelligent than white males, and elaborate research methods were developed to support those beliefs. The methods followed the substantive beliefs.

The intellectual climate that prevailed during the time that the contemporary practice of evaluation developed was also special. After World War II, the United States reached an unprecedented pinnacle of power, influence, and wealth. Americans were united in the "ideology of the liberal consensus," which included beliefs that the U.S. free enterprise system creates abundance for all, that the system has a revolutionary potential for social justice, that economic growth makes conflict between classes and social classes themselves obsolete, and that social problems could be solved like industrial problems (Hodgson, 1978, p. 76).

These beliefs constituted the ideological background from which post-World War II social science and early evaluation emerged. Social problems such as poverty and racism could be solved piecemeal within the framework of U.S. society; nothing was wrong with the framework itself. Social engineering, guided by social science freed from politics and popular superstition, could eliminate the ugly remnants of a less enlightened age. Only will and resources were needed. Put another way, certain activities would produce certain outcomes and solve certain problems. How did these beliefs affect the interests being served in evaluations?

First, the programs that we evaluate are not randomly drawn from all social programs. They tend to be programs for the poor and disadvantaged. Follow Through is a program for disadvantaged children in grades K to 3. PUSH/Excel was a program for black teenagers in the inner cities. Income maintenance, drug abuse, juvenile crime prevention, and other programs are typically for poor people in trouble. Evaluation as a government mandate began in 1965 to ensure that the education of poor students would be improved. Insofar as our methodology errs, it differentially affects the welfare of the poor and dispossessed.

It is true that evaluation has been extended to a great number of programs not intended to serve the poor and powerless, and there is a sense in which the recipients of program benefits are almost always in a less powerful position than the program providers and evaluators. In that sense there is differential power within every evaluation. The possibility of some injustice exists even when the recipients are teachers or patients or people not particularly disadvantaged. However, the injustice problem is compounded when the recipient group is disadvantaged within the larger society itself.

Second, the criteria of merit are differentially applied. Consider the criteria for success in the PUSH/Excel evaluation: A coherent program should be coordinated, including a sequential set of standard activities, with each activity tied to specific outcomes and each activity repeated and sustained. The program has to be specified by detailed, step-by-step concrete procedures and justified by an explicit strategy and rationale. Moreover, it has to be guided and monitored by a central authority that provides a how-to manual for participants. These criteria seem inappropriate for defining what a program must be, whatever one might think of PUSH/Excel, which did have a multitude of problems. What if this set of criteria were applied to university programs? I dare say that not a university department in the country could stand up to such an examination. But, of course, such criteria are not applied to universities, and if they were, professors would become quite indignant.

One is reminded of how Broca and the craniometricians applied their inappropriate criteria differentially to arrive at their findings, making exceptions for small-brained Frenchmen but not for women. If our evaluation methodology employs inappropriate criteria, it has differential effects because it is most often applied to programs for the poor and powerless. Of course, the reverse is also true, in that when we are correct, we are advancing the cause of social justice because of the programs that we deal with.

Third, there is the possibility that our methodology misguides us as to what is wrong with programs. When these programs are judged to be failures, who and what is blamed? Poor conceptualization and planning on the part of the developers, traits of individual participants and recipients, poor implementation, organizational politics, ambiguous goal statements, unrealistic expectations, lack of coordination, inadequate training, and other contingencies in and around the program itself. The broader societal framework rarely is faulted in the evaluations (Weiss, 1991). Generally, the program is blamed for failure rather than factors in the social structure, such as social class or economic structures or gender reproducing mechanisms. The background ideology itself constrains the available explanations and potential solutions.

Finally, one must wonder whether the standard conception of causation works against the interests of various groups of people. This is a difficult, complex question, but I am inclined to think that it does, at least in the way that it has been employed. In general, the Humean conception implies that experts using the proper methods can ascertain the best programs and approaches for addressing social ills. This delegitimizes knowledge derived from other sources and the views of other people. In other words, the standard view lends itself to a form of scientism—only information derived from certain techniques is true knowledge. In reality, information gathered from other sources—from participants, for example—is critical to understanding social processes. This is not to deny the role of professionals in addressing social ills, but rather to say that they do not have exclusive knowledge.

So the incorrect Humean conception of causation, and the intellectual climate in which the methodology of evaluation developed, both stemming in part from the scientistic tradition of U.S. social science, has resulted in some systematic injustices in the practice of evaluation. Subtle for sure, unintentional perhaps, but real nonetheless.

❧ *9* ❧

Evaluation in
Multicultural Societies

*C*onducting evaluations in multicultural societies, such as Canada and the United States, is one of the most difficult problems evaluators face, and this problem is widespread. In 1990, I spent some time in Spain, where I expected to find bullfighters and flamenco dancers, which I did, but I also found surprising cultural diversity, including several different subcultures and languages, including Basque, Gallego, and Catalan. In fact, a few hundred years ago the Spanish called Spain "Las Españas," the Spains, an indicator of its diversity. During his long dictatorship, Franco sought to eradicate the Basque and Catalan languages—unsuccessfully.[1]

The former Soviet Union is also dramatic testimony to the lasting power of internal cultures and ethnic groups, who vigorously reassert themselves once the overriding central authority is reduced, even to the point of national dissolution. And countries once thought to be homogeneous, such as England, are being transformed into multicultural societies by immigration from former colonies. I also anticipate a time when there is not only a joint Canadian-U.S. economic entity but also Mexico is integrated into a North American common market, thus multiplying the cultural differences between Canada and the United States by those of Mexico, itself a multicultural society.

Based in part on a speech to the Canadian Evaluation Society, Vancouver, British Columbia, May 6, 1991.

141

Even this amalgamation of cultures pales when one considers the coming together of the European Community: dozens of countries each with its own culture, language, traditions, and history, all integrated into one economy and combined under one government in Brussels. And many of these cultures define themselves in opposition to their neighbors and traditional enemies. Sometimes it seems as if there are only multicultural societies and those that are becoming multicultural.

This clash of cultures brings immense governing problems. What should the government do when the Amish will not send their children to school, when Mormons practice polygamy, when Jehovah's Witnesses will not salute the flag, when Barcelonians insist on teaching Catalan in their schools, when the Quebecois will not allow nonanglophone immigrants to be taught in English in their schools, when the Canadian Indians demand vast tracks of land, when Vietnamese boys will not take orders from women teachers, when blacks start Afrocentric schools, or when Hindu men burn their brides because of insufficient dowries? Do we simply say, well, each to his or her own?

Multiculturalism also poses difficult problems for evaluation, because these larger political issues convert easily into program evaluation questions. How should bilingual programs be evaluated? What criteria should one use to evaluate Afrocentric schools? By what criteria should we evaluate social programs in Inuit villages? Should every student be tested on literacy in the majority culture? What happens when different cultural groups involved in an evaluation do not agree on fundamental values and criteria of success? What framework can we have for evaluation in such situations?

There are also cultural conflicts, confusions, and misunderstandings encountered by cross-cultural evaluators working in foreign countries, including problems of data collection, confidentiality, use of data, program definition, sex relationships, politics, values, and social status (Bank, 1985; Cuthbert, 1985; Hoogerwerf, 1985; Merryfield, 1985; Patton, 1985; Seefeldt, 1985). However, I confine myself here to issues within multicultural societies, which do not involve cultural misunderstandings so much as cultural rights. To address the central issues, I explore the nature of nationalism and ethnicity from which these problems derive; second, discuss the particular multiculturalism of Canada and the United States; third, suggest how we might resolve some of these problems; and, finally, apply these ideas to evaluation.

ᵛ Nationalism and Ethnicity

Nationalism and ethnic identity generate such intense feelings that people are willing to die for their nations and ethnic groups. Nationalism has been defined as a principle of political legitimacy specifying that political and national units should be congruent, that ethnic boundaries should not cut across political ones, and that ethnic boundaries within a given state should not separate power-holders from the rest of the populace. An acute violation of this principle is when the rulers of a political unit belong to a nation or ethnicity other than that of the majority of those ruled (Gellner, 1983).

Nationalism is a surprisingly recent phenomenon dating back to only the late 18th century. Apparently, it was generated in part from shared print languages. When cheap books and newspapers became available through new capitalist production and distribution systems, many people could have a local newspaper or book in their native language, and many speakers of the vernacular became readers for the first time (B. Anderson, 1983). Languages became fixed, and certain dialects, such as the king's English, became standardized and propagated from central sources. For the first time, people could imagine a community of which they were a part stretching beyond themselves and their immediate villages, even across time. Nations are imagined communities; one never meets even a small fraction of one's fellow citizens.

The first modern nations emerged from the North and South American colonies that separated from their parent countries. Colonists were second-class citizens, never able to serve in the highest positions in the parent country and often not at home either. For example, prior to 1813, of the 170 viceroys in South America, only four were native-born (B. Anderson, 1983). The native-born were limited in careers to their own capitals and provinces. These American colonies pulled away from their imperial parents in bursts of nationalist sentiments, and new nations were founded along the boundary lines of the old colonial administrative units. Once the colonies had separated, the tables were turned, so that immigrants became the lowest in status rather than the highest. By contrast, the Scots were never denied access to the highest positions in England and the British Empire the way the colonials were, and after the final conquest of Scotland in 1746, the Scots, although having a strong cultural identity, never developed sufficiently strong sentiments to separate, as did the Irish. Access to careers and positions was and is an important dynamic (Hobsbawm, 1990).

Language was not a political issue in these original nationalist outbursts because all the colonies spoke the mother tongue—English, Spanish, French, and Portuguese (B. Anderson, 1983). Rather, perceived common interest against privilege inspired the original revolutions among the higher classes. Nor was language an issue in the French Revolution. In 1789, only 50% of the French spoke French, although after the revolution, speaking French became a requirement for citizenship. Nor did university students play an important role in these revolutions, as they did later (Hobsbawm, 1990).

In the second wave of nationalism, from 1820 to 1920, the empires struck back. The old empires and dynasties created "official nationalisms" in deliberate attempts to prevent popular nationalist movements overseas, and this entailed the establishment of educational and cultural institutions to anglicize or frenchify the native populations and to breed a ruling elite in the colonies loyal to the parent country. When I first saw McGill University, I thought to myself, "What is this fortress-like, English-language university doing in the center of Montreal?" When I saw Protestant Trinity University similarly located in the middle of Catholic Dublin, I had an answer. Official nationalism used the apparatus of the cultural and educational institutions to promote loyalty to the parent country (B. Anderson, 1983).

Since World War I, nationalism has been associated with anti-imperialism, as in Africa, the Middle East, and Southeast Asia. Learning from previous revolutions, modern nationalists invoke strong populist sentiments, a language of state, a nationalist ideology, mass media, education, and all the instruments of official nationalism, turned against the parent country. The schools are always a central element, necessary to break earlier ties, create an indigenous elite, and promote mass loyalty. And although print language provided the original cultural apparatus for nationalism, nations can now be imagined without language communities, as, for example, in Switzerland. Also, bilingual intelligentsia can use new means to propagate national community (B. Anderson, 1983). For example, the mass media promulgate national symbols, such as the British royal family at play or the U.S. president helicoptering to the White House or national athletic events, in ways not dependent on reading (Hobsbawm, 1990).

However, languages are still major instrumentalities of nationalist movements, even when they are semi-artificial constructs such as

Hebrew. Schools are necessary to teach the vernacular language, to inculcate attachment to country, and to prepare citizens for economic roles. Linguistic nationalism revolves around the language of public education and official use, not the private language of the home, because the public language is the medium of jobs and status. The social classes most affected by official uses of the written vernacular are the educated middle strata, who occupy nonmanual jobs requiring schooling, such as journalists, teachers, officials, and university students.

Not surprisingly, nationalist sentiments are strongest in these groups: For example, Irish was made a qualification for entry to all professional jobs in the Irish Republic. Although primary education is vital to literacy and the spread of nationalist sentiments among the populace, secondary education is vital to these middle-tier groups, because language is linked to career and social mobility. Having to be bilingual and operate in an unfamiliar language underlines one's inferior status and fuels linguistic nationalism, as with the Flemish in Belgium or the Quebecois in Canada (Hobsbawm, 1990).

Scholars differ over whether nationalism is economically inspired. Some contend that it is precisely the requirement of having a uniform and standardized industrial workforce that necessitates having one language and one culture within a country (Gellner, 1983; Hirsch, 1987). Otherwise, they say, the country cannot compete successfully, because workers must be interchangeable in modern economies. In addition, they say, a country must have a ruling class that is the same culture as the masses because otherwise civil unrest is endemic, a violation of the nationalist principle (Gellner, 1983). These scholars advocate assimilationist policies that promote one language and culture, such as the cultural literacy and official-English movements in the United States and similar movements in France.

Other scholars see nationalism as a transitory phase of capitalism that is bound to dissolve as nations become economically obsolete and are drawn into larger economic entities, such as common markets (Hobsbawm, 1990). Marxist scholars have never dealt adequately with nationalism, which was supposed to disappear as workers realized their common interests with workers from other nations. Things have not worked out quite that way, as wars between and within socialist countries attest (Avineri, 1990). It does seem to be the case that the world is drifting into larger multinational trading blocs, such as Europe, North America, and East Asia. Nonetheless, the intense sentiments generated by national and ethnic identification seem likely to be with us for a while. People still are willing to die for their countries. Few seem willing to die for the European Economic Community (E.E.C.).

ᵌ Canada and the United States as Multicultural Societies

Multicultural societies are created primarily by conquest, slavery, labor exploitation, and immigration, and these forces have been hard at work in North America. Of course, important cultural differences exist between the United States and Canada. The United States is basically a single-language, nonpartitioned country, whereas Canada is a dual-language, partitioned country, in which the primary cultural groups are segregated by geography (Nickel, 1987). Some prefer to think of Canada as binational, as well as bilingual and bicultural.

Another difference is that Americans are brash nationalists, whereas Canadians tend to be closet nationalists. The national flags symbolize the difference: a battle emblem and a tree leaf. The Canadian sociologist John Porter characterized Canadians (in contrast to Americans) as conservative; authoritarian; more oriented to tradition, hierarchy, and elitism in the sense of showing deference to those in high status; and united in defense of these values against the egalitarianism and aggressiveness of U.S. culture.[2] Canadian literature is suffused with images of personal denial, defeat, and resignation to forces beyond control, perhaps because of climate, terrain, and the aggressive neighbor to the south (Porter, 1987).

One of the most outspoken Canadian nationalists is Peter C. Newman. Two major themes run through Newman's work: fear of being overwhelmed by the United States and a fervent desire to unite the country. "Born out of many defeats," Canadian identity has been shaped by "domination from without, dissension from within" (Newman, 1988, pp. 242, 244). His essays on Pierre Trudeau reveal enrapture with Trudeau's charisma, whom he calls "the magician," then a progressive disenchantment, as Trudeau does not deliver, and, finally, a complete disillusionment, as he sees Trudeau as a technocrat and philosopher/king, to be faulted for his emotional aloofness as much as for his failures (Newman, 1988, pp. 67-104).

Trudeau himself has been less enamored with nationalism:

> To use nationalism as a yard-stick deciding policies and priorities is both sterile and retrograde. Overflowing nationalism distorts one's

vision of reality, prevents one from seeing problems in their true
perspective, falsifies solutions and constitutes a classic diversionary
tactic for politicians caught by the facts. . . . Our comments in this
regard apply equally to Canadian nationalism or to French-Canadian
nationalism. (quoted in Newman, 1988, p. 151)

A technocrat's response, perhaps.[3]

Differences between U.S. and Canadian approaches to multiculturalism are symbolized by the melting pot and mosaic metaphors (Porter, 1987). Both societies experienced immense immigration from 1850 to 1914 and again after World War II. In the decade
from 1980 to 1990, for example, the Hispanic population of the
United States increased by 7.7 million, a 56% increase. Twenty-five
percent of the U.S. population is now minority, up from 20% in 1980,
the largest population change this century (Barringer, 1991). New
immigrants then and now have been greeted with hostility manifested in nativist movements.

Minorities usually have been linked to particular labor force
needs, such as cotton pickers or garment workers or migrant fruit-
pickers, and have been forced into ghetto life. Often they are excluded from the mainstream and band together to protect themselves
against the predations of modern society. Over time, some have
assimilated to the majority culture, such as the Irish, Italians, and
Greeks. Others, such as blacks and Hispanics, have demanded group
access to jobs and schools. Occupational assimilation often has required cultural assimilation and loss of ethnic identity (Porter, 1987).

These minorities differ among themselves in important ways. The
anthropologist John Ogbu (1988a, 1988b) identified three different
types of minority groups. Autonomous minorities, such as Jews and
Mormons, are minority groups who are not subordinated to the
majority. Often, their cultures value schooling, and they are as successful as the majority. Although some immigrant minorities are
assimilated, others, such as the Chinese, alternate back and forth
between their own distinct culture and the mainstream, never being
fully assimilated and never rejecting the majority culture, in fact,
often doing quite well within the majority culture. They do not
abandon their cultural identity, but rather draw on it to accommodate school and job without assimilating.[4] These immigrant minorities develop folk theories of success that emphasize how much better
off they are in the new world compared to where they came from,
thus encouraging themselves and their children to put forth extra
effort.

Involuntary minorities, on the other hand, including blacks, American Indians, native Hawaiians, and Mexican Americans in the Southwest, were originally brought into the United States through slavery, conquest, or labor exploitation, relegated to menial tasks, and denied access to the mainstream. They have evolved an oppositional culture or ambivalent frame of reference, which includes a strong distrust of the dominant group and its institutions. For blacks and American Indians, this deep distrust and pessimism are based on centuries of extremely abusive treatment from the majority.[5] Their special cultural forms enable these groups to cope with subordination and to reject majority behaviors, often developing a sense of identity that includes opposition to the mainstream.[6] They do not have the dual reference system of immigrants, but instead compare themselves to the majority. So the melting pot metaphor has not been entirely accurate in its depiction of minority life in the United States.[7]

The mosaic image of Canada is not quite accurate either. Originally, there was a desire to assimilate immigrants into the mainstream, with the public schools as the main instrument. On the other hand, in the 1870s, there was also a desire to compete with the United States, which was attracting most of the immigrants. Blocks of land were set aside for groups such as Mennonites, Germans, and Hungarians. Unfriendly nativist sentiments greeted newcomers, especially those from southern and eastern Europe, not to mention the treatment of the aboriginal population.[8] Majority Canada has retained its British institutions and preferences well into this century (Porter, 1987).

The Quebecois were no more tolerant of outsiders as they searched for francophone immigrants from abroad. Immigration, as well as language and culture, was always a primary concern of Quebec. The Quebecois have stressed biculturalism, rather than multiculturalism, as the essence of Canadian identity. In 1971, Quebec Premier Robert Bourassa wrote Prime Minister Trudeau, "You will have gathered that Quebec does not accept your government's approach to multiculturalism" (Porter, 1987, p. 155).

At one time the upper levels of the workplace throughout Canada were English-speaking, imposing a bilingual burden on the Quebecois but not on other Canadians, and this limit on upward mobility, even in the home province, was deeply resented. (Ironically, I am told that now anglophones feel their careers are limited in Ottawa because of their poor French, compared to the superior bilingual ability of their Quebec peers.) Of course, whichever side, historically this limitation on career is a primary condition of ethnic-nationalist sentiment and separatism in the upper classes.

Peter Newman (1988) once said of Marcel Chaput, the Quebec separatist leader, "It is somehow typically Canadian that the leader of a movement whose aim it is to destroy the unity of this nation should be, not a hollow-eyed revolutionary in a backstreet basement, but a middle-class civil servant in a dark blue suit" (p. 137). In fact, revolutionaries in suits are typical of most nations torn by ethnic disputes. The civil rights movement in the United States, the Flemish movement in Belgium, and the Catalan movement in Spain were all led by men in business suits. Premier Bourassa of Quebec expressed the basic idea more clinically: "Separatism has at its base economic grievances" (quoted in Newman, 1988, p. 151).

The revival of ethnic nationalism in both the United States and Canada since World War II has come about in response to domestic and foreign events (Porter, 1987). These include decolonization abroad, which resulted in nationalist movements and fierce ethnic hostilities overseas; heavy immigration from people seeking economic betterment, which continues today; and, most important, the existence of large excluded, deprived minorities in both countries who have demanded their rights, the most publicized being the civil rights movement in the United States, the Parti Quebecois in Canada, and American Indian activists in both countries.

More generally, multicultural societies differ from one another in many ways. The dominant culture of a country may be the culture of one of the dominant groups, as in England, or it may be a composite culture, a mixture, as in Brazil (Nickel, 1987). The bonds that hold people together differ. Brazil, surrounded by Spanish-speaking countries, focuses on the Portuguese language for its sense of identity, whereas in Ireland, religion plays an important role (Nickel, 1990). In Argentina, a strong sense of territory bolsters national identity (Dougherty, Eisenhart, & Webley, 1991). In some countries, such as the United States, there is a strong civic culture, a civic religion, that functions as a binding ideology. The public philosophy is that if people embrace the civic culture, they can gain membership in the society (Karst, 1986).

Quite often, the dominant culture demands assimilation of minority groups in order to protect the majority's way of life. For their part, minority groups want equal citizenship, acceptance and recognition by the majority, plus the freedom to shape their own cultural identity (Karst, 1986). A primary cause of separatism is the subordination of minorities to the majority culture, often by excluding them from jobs and public life, a dynamic similar to the early nationalist formation in nations. Because much ethnic pluralism originates in conquest, slavery, and exploitation of foreign labor, subordinated minority groups seem the rule rather than the exception. In fact, minorities often obtain a strong sense of community by being labeled and excluded (Karst, 1986).

ᶻ᷎ Minority Rights

What intellectual and political resources do we have for addressing these multicultural problems? The multicultural countries we live in are liberal democracies. That is, their public philosophy is based on liberalism, which includes a respect for individual equality and the economic marketplace. The liberal multicultural ideal is that different groups will have respect for differing cultural identities and for the common bond that makes them a society. People constitute a nation when they recognize certain mutual rights and duties to each other in virtue of shared membership. Compatriots must have a mutual concern for each other and for the survival of their collectivity. On the other hand, individuals want to be allowed to retain their cultural identity and also to abandon it if they choose (Nickel, 1990).

Although there was interest in recognizing minority rights prior to World War II, during the war the liberal democracies were traumatized by German nationalism and Nazi manipulation of minorities in other countries. Many remembered *volkgeist, lebensraum,* and the horrors perpetrated in the name of a superior culture. The United Nations (UN) chose not to recognize minority rights because minority claims were seen as dangerously threatening to the national stability of nation-states (many of which are in reality "nations-states"). Instead, the UN adopted "color-blind" policies in which individuals were to be regarded as equal and not culturally different. This approach fit the domestic situation in the United States, as blacks fought against segregation. Beginning with the Supreme Court school desegregation decision in 1954, the efforts of U.S. blacks to assimilate became the premier example of ethnic group treatment in the world, and special statuses for minorities were linked to racial segregation.

Many also thought that in majoritarian democracies, minority cultures would inevitably, if regrettably, be overwhelmed and that the sooner this happened the less painful it would be. This assimilationist view has dominated U.S. social science thinking. For example, sociologist Nathan Glazer (1988), a leading ethnicity scholar, construes ethnic membership as an individual, private, voluntary matter, like belonging to a club or choosing one's associates or deciding what college to attend. He treats ethnicity as a matter of personal choice and argues strongly against any notion of group rights. Rights should be strictly limited to individuals.

Nor is this view limited to Americans. Canadian sociologist John Porter said, "The organization of society on the basis of rights or claims that derive from group membership is sharply opposed to the concept of a society based on citizenship. . . . To resort to the group basis of settling claims, if necessary, is regrettable" (Porter, 1987, p. 128). Porter called such an approach regressive in that it bases cultural transmission in the descent group, which is then subject to racism and inequality, because some cultures are always declared inherently inferior to others. Ethnic group values are to be maintained, if at all, only through voluntary association. He saw Canada's future as bilingual, but not bicultural or multicultural. In the long run, he thought the culture of industrial society best for everyone.

Now these are important considerations. Is it possible to have a modern egalitarian society and multiculturalism without spawning subordinated minorities and ethnic stratification? The Canadian philosopher Will Kymlicka (1989) has contended that taking the assimilation of U.S. blacks as the paradigm case for minority rights is a big mistake. Most minorities in the modern world are like the Canadian aboriginals, who try to maintain their culture in the midst of an overwhelming majority culture. Kymlicka argues that cultural minorities such as the American Indians and Inuits need special rights in certain circumstances. Cultural membership, he argues, is a primary good, necessary for self-respect and for carrying out one's life plan. Personal identity and self-respect are bound intimately to cultural membership, and cultural membership cannot be transplanted easily to another culture.

Building on John Rawls' (1971) argument that "the freedom to form and revise our beliefs about value is a critical precondition for pursuing our essential interest in leading a good life," Kymlicka (1989, p. 163) contends that we must start with the ideals and forms of life we have inherited, our culture, which includes the stories, activities, and roles that have shaped our identity. We can make our own judgments only by examining our cultural structure. As liberty is a primary good essential to leading a good life, so is cultural membership. Culture provides the context of individual choice.

Individuals need their cultural structure, including their language, for exploring and evaluating their individual life options.

Without such a cultural framework, especially for children and adolescents, individuals become lost and despondent, as in Inuit communities whose cultural structure is undermined. On the other hand, individuals should be able to opt out of their culture if they want and to change its cultural practices, but first they need to have a cultural structure from which to do this. In other words, one's cultural structure provides a context of choice, even if the individual's choice is to assimilate. Having a cultural heritage is fundamental to one's sense of identity and personal agency, of being able to act effectively in the world.

There is some empirical confirmation of the central importance of cultural membership in Ogbu's studies of minorities. Voluntary minorities such as the Chinese, who are able to maintain their own cultural identity and alternate back and forth, are quite successful and have a strong sense of personal agency. Involuntary minorities, such as U.S. blacks, have managed to maintain self-respect only by adopting an oppositional culture, which mitigates against success in the mainstream. Some have little sense of personal agency. Many government programs require minorities to abandon their identity and self-respect.

Assuming that cultural membership is essential, Kymlicka also argues that minority cultures should sometimes have special rights. Although cultural membership is just as important to majorities as to minorities, minorities have particular disadvantages maintaining their cultural identity when they are part of a much larger majority culture. Minorities may be outbid or outvoted on issues critical to the survival of their culture. For example, in southern Canada, where American Indian land is scarce, the stability of Indian communities is maintained by denying non-Indians the right to purchase or reside on Indian land without special permission. In the north, which is threatened by temporary workers who might overwhelm the aboriginal culture, multiyear residency requirements for local voting have been recommended, again to protect the aboriginal community. The most common way for whites to break open aboriginal communities has been to force them to cede the land to individuals and then buy the land, thus destroying the community itself (Kymlicka, 1989). In addition, nonaboriginals with a vote might be able to force the teaching of English in aboriginal communities.

A 2-year-old Inuit girl without special protection may have her cultural community undermined by the time she is 18, no matter what she does, whereas a majority Canadian boy does not face this problem, no matter what he does. Hence, simply to maintain their culture in place requires an extra expenditure of resources for Inuits. Majority cultures get for free what minority cultures must struggle for: the security of their native community, which gives meaning and self-respect to their lives. The conflict is that in order to maintain the culture, the citizenship rights of some must be restricted and unequally distributed in certain circumstances—a conflict between the cultural and political communities.

Why not simply have the Inuit girl move to English Canada and adopt its language and culture? Because cultural membership is an integral part of one's personal identity, and to do so would denigrate the girl's identity, sense of personal agency, and meaning of life. Although she may choose to make such a move later in life, she will always interpret the world somewhat differently. Cultural membership is not easily transferable, as the failure of assimilationist policies around the world demonstrates.

Hence when their basic cultural structure is threatened with destruction, in order to maintain their culture and personal identity, minorities are entitled to special considerations. Sometimes they must be given special political rights. In these circumstances the very existence of the minority culture is at stake, and maintaining the culture is vital to its members. Kymlicka endorses the correctness of the Canadian constitution's guarantee of aboriginal rights. "The system of aboriginal rights in Canada can be seen as an attempt to distribute fairly the costs that arise from our recognition of the value of cultural membership" (Kymlicka, 1989, p. 200). By contrast, U.S. law and policy treat aboriginal privileges as gifts that can be revoked, not rights.[9]

On the other hand, when the existence of the culture is not at issue, or when no inequalities are present, then special minority rights are not necessary. Only when the minority culture is actually threatened are special rights justified. There should be inequalities to be redressed, and the policies chosen to do so must address the inequality. When the minority culture is not at risk, then minority claims should be considered along with the claims from other groups. Members of the majority also have a right to their cultural membership.

It is crucial to understand that the argument for minority rights is based on the welfare of the individual, not the welfare of the group.[10] The basis of the argument is that individuals have a right to cultural membership. The group itself does not have the right, as in forms of communitarianism. Group members are still citizens entitled to rights we ascribe to individuals in liberal democracies. Minority groups cannot do anything they want to members of their group. Such a framework would outlaw many practices.

For example, the burning of one's bride for insufficient dowry is not permissible because it infringes on individual rights, no matter how ingrained the practice might be in East Indian culture. Nor is the subordination of women condoned, as in Vietnamese or Arabic societies, for similar reasons of individual equality. In rare cases, the community might justifiably restrict individual rights to preserve the culture, as when certain liberties would threaten the community's existence, as in prohibiting alcohol in communities unable to deal with its impact. However, these instances restricting liberties should be seen as temporary and transitional restrictions.

Freedom of religious choice also is ordinarily guaranteed, even in theocratic communities. Individuals are entitled to a cultural structure but are free to interpret that culture as a citizen of a liberal democracy, as long as the existence of the culture is not threatened. The point is to prevent disintegration of the culture from the outside, but protect freedom of the individual to choose inside. Mere changes in group beliefs, such as an individual becoming a Christian in an Indian theocracy, would not seem to threaten the existence of the group. Nor, in Kymlicka's view, do most changes in norms, values, and life styles threaten group existence. Quebecois are still Quebecois after the "Quiet Revolution," even if some are atheists and others Catholics.

Whether Mormons should practice polygamy depends on whether such a practice treats women unequally and whether the practice is essential to the maintenance of the Mormon culture. On first glance, it would seem that the practice is not essential to the existence of Mormon culture and that it denies individual rights to women. On the other hand, the refusal of Jehovah's Witnesses to salute the flag is hardly a threat to the majority culture of the United States or a violation of individual rights. Presumably, there are circumstances where the existence of the majority culture might be threatened. The size of the minority in question has some bearing on the preservation of the majority culture, which also has a right to maintain its cultural identity.

Quebec is a difficult case, and how the minority rights principle can be applied depends on specific policies. It would seem that the French language is necessary to maintain the culture of Quebec. Within Canada itself, the survival of Quebecois culture would seem assured (though not all Quebecois would see it this way), partly because of existing policies of governmental autonomy and constitutional guarantees. Similar provincial autonomy exists in Spain. The extent of provincial powers, if not justified by threat to the disintegration of the culture, is open to political negotiation. (Kymlicka himself seems somewhat ambivalent about Quebec and treats Canada as having two majority cultures.)

What about language rights? Certainly, the Quebecois have a right to their own language, as do the American Indians. Do they have the right to deny publicly funded English-language instruction to non-English-speaking immigrants to Quebec on the basis of this minority principle? If the culture is being seriously undermined (and it is arguable as to whether it is), such restrictions might be necessary to preserve the community. If the existence of the majority culture is not seriously threatened, then there would seem to be no "right" to deny immigrants such instruction. In a community where minority members can receive their education in the language of their own cultural community (French), the principle of minority rights would not justify denying others access to publicly funded instruction in English. But it is not clear why such immigrants should have a right to publicly funded education in a particular language other than that of the local community, in this case French. This particular issue may elude the minority rights principle and be a matter for negotiation, not for rights.

On the other hand, occupying the same continent with the United States is a complicating factor. The Quebecois have reason to be worried about their long-term future, when a North American common market is established, and when Quebec of necessity enters a community of 250 million Americans and 70 million Mexicans. It is not paranoid to be concerned about the existence of Quebecois culture in such a situation, and, indeed, majority Canadians should be concerned as well. If I were in this situation, I would calculate my prospects of negotiating as part of a larger Canada, as opposed to going it alone, and I would support the principle of minority rights. The guarantee of minority rights that I have been advocating as a morally enlightened principle is not a U.S. idea, and perhaps Canadians should think about these issues not only from the stance of a majority culture vis-à-vis minority cultures, but also from the position of a minority culture vis-à-vis perhaps the most influential culture in the world.

ᴥ Stakeholder Evaluation

How do these considerations affect evaluation? In general, the politics of evaluation reflect the prevailing political theory of democracy, the pluralist-elitist-equilibrium theory explicated earlier (Chapter 7). According to this theory, individual demands are fed into groups, and group leaders articulate these demands to government officials who adjudicate them. Hence, the entire system is kept in equilibrium by group elites bargaining for their constituencies and government elites reaching accommodations. This model of pluralist democracy recognizes the different interests of diverse groups and accounts for social conflict among groups, while preserving the national goal of economic growth to satisfy demands.

This political model is manifested in the concept of stakeholder evaluation, which means that groups having a stake in the program should be represented in the evaluation. On the surface, the stakeholder concept allows evaluators to maintain their value neutrality by merely describing the interests of various individuals and groups, who are seen to exist in a plural equilibrium from which legitimate decisions emerge. Neither the government nor the evaluator is supposed to intervene to support any particular interests, but rather only to provide information that is interest-neutral. The interests of the various groups dissolve into the values of stakeholders. This view of democracy is based on the metaphor of the marketplace, in which the various interests are registered to work their way out automatically.

Although I helped develop the stakeholder approach, I also have criticized it as being sometimes unjust. Once one has recognized the various stakeholder groups, how does one combine, organize, and prioritize the divergent and often conflicting views and interests of the different groups? The interests of the poor and the powerless often are neglected or overridden, just as they are in the larger society, whereas those of the powerful are given priority. The views and interests of the poor and powerless should be given at least equal priority in the evaluation.

What about minority culture groups? The usual way of dealing with these groups is to treat them like other groups, if they are treated at all. But they are not like other groups. Following Kymlicka's analysis, I would say that there is an obligation to recognize the views and interests of these groups, and in circumstances where the basic issue is the maintenance of the minority group culture, to give priority to these groups in the evaluation, even to the degree of invoking minority group rights to override other considerations. If the maintenance of the minority group culture is not an issue, minority groups should be treated like other groups. If minority groups violate individual rights, that also is a legitimate concern.

What does this mean for the evaluator's task? It means the evaluator should deliberately search out and define the views and interests of these minority cultures if they are stakeholders in the program being evaluated. Of course, in many cases their interests will not be an issue, but if they are, then the evaluator has an obligation to give them special consideration. In other words not all group interests should be weighted equally in all circumstances. (I would also argue that the interests of the poor and disadvantaged and women should also receive special consideration for other reasons.)

After consideration, the evaluator may determine that minority interests are not at issue in the way specified, that there is no inequality operating, or that there is inequality but it has no relationship to the program being evaluated, or that the minority culture is not threatened. Minority interests should receive special consideration only in certain circumstances. Of course, it is often the case that the minority groups are also the poor and powerless, and then the obligation to address the issue is especially acute.

Contrast this position to the regular stakeholder orientation. In that framework, minority groups would receive no special consideration. There would be no effort to search out their views and interests and no obligation to treat them differently. In the relativist evaluation approach advocated by Guba and Lincoln (1989), minorities would have the right to present their views along with anyone else, but minority views and interests would be treated like any others. Differing views would be negotiated face-to-face by representatives of the various groups. In my judgment, this procedure would result in the majority culture dominating the evaluation, even in cases where the minority culture is threatened.

This special consideration of minority group interests requires a different role for the evaluator. It is not a neutral role, but then I would contend that the neutral role is not neutral either; it only appears neutral. The neutral role allows the most powerful players and the majority culture to dominate under the guise of fairness. In majoritarian democracies, one would expect the majority to prevail most of the time, but not always and not on all matters. Finer sensitivity to the special circumstances of minorities does not make a society any less democratic, any more than does a Bill of Rights guaranteeing certain liberties for individuals.

Let me work through an example of a program evaluation in which this principle would apply. In the United States, cultural literacy advocates such as E. D. Hirsch (1987) and Diane Ravitch (1990) have argued that the public schools should teach the common

U.S. culture, and that self-esteem for individuals is a matter of what individual students are able to do and accomplish through their own individual efforts, not a matter of knowing what their ethnic ancestors did. For cultural literacy advocates, the purposes of the public school are to teach children the skills and knowledge they need to succeed in society and to create a national community by teaching the common culture. Hirsch claims that becoming culturally literate in U.S. culture is both necessary and sufficient for minority groups to advance in society and for the country to become politically unified.

According to these advocates, the evaluation of such programs should consist of achievement tests over the common cultural content. For example, Ravitch and Finn (1987) have conducted national assessments of history and literature through the National Assessment of Educational Progress. The content of what every American should know was defined by a small committee, and then multiple-choice tests were constructed and administered by the Educational Testing Service. Ravitch has advocated administering such tests to every student as a priority of national educational reform. Minorities would be treated like the majority and held to the knowledge and standards of the majority culture.

How would minority groups react to this assimilationist position? Autonomous minorities such as the Amish likely would do what is necessary to get by. Immigrant minorities such as the Chinese would play their dual roles, alternating back and forth between minority and majority demands, probably doing well on the national tests. Involuntary minorities such as blacks, American Indians, and Mexican-Americans would feel that this curriculum and its evaluation were new forms of exclusion and domination and would react negatively in opposition. They would continue to be rejected at school, partly by their own doing, and be eliminated from the job market, thus increasing unemployment, crime, and dependency. For them to succeed, they would have to "act white" and reject their own ethnic identity.

The folk-theory of success developed by these involuntary minority groups stresses job limitations imposed by the majority, and these beliefs preclude them from doing well in school because they believe that they will not advance occupationally, even if they follow the rules of the majority culture and do well in school. Such perceived exclusion results in withdrawal, as happens in dropping out of school, and if physical withdrawal is impossible, they attempt other means, such as participating in oppositional behavior. Although the assimilationist approach was successful in assimilating voluntary minorities in the past, it has not been successful with involuntary minorities.

Howe (1991), among others, has presented a position opposing the assimilationist viewpoint. Following Kymlicka, Howe argues that to ignore the student's cultural background is not to treat the student as an equal. Cultural membership is an integral part of one's personal identity and self-respect, and to rob people of their cultural identity is to deny them self-respect. Providing educational opportunity requires recognizing (a) that education should be enabling and that early education leads to later opportunities, (b) that equal educational opportunity is best applied to careers rather than isolated situations, and (c) that children are not in a position to exercise freedom and choice until they gain the ability to effectively deliberate, which requires prior education. To deny minorities their cultural structure is to deny them the opportunity to deliberate effectively. In this view, the curriculum should be negotiated to incorporate elements of the minority culture, so that there is genuine participation and self-definition by minorities. The curriculum should not negate the minority identity.

If I were evaluating programs in schools with large minority populations, I would seek out the views of these minority groups and ascertain how well the school recognized the value of their culture, whether the school negotiated the curriculum to protect the minority culture, and whether it attended to minority self-definition. By allowing minority students their cultural heritage, I would expect to see more participation from them and better student achievement. In assessing student achievement, I would not rely exclusively on a test of majority culture. Rather I would seek indicators of achievement and accomplishment that reflected the minority culture itself, and indicators of attendance, participation, and enthusiasm. I would be especially concerned about the effect of school practices on the students' self-esteem and sense of personal agency.

⁕ Conclusion

Looking ahead to a North American entity, Canadians might find themselves a minority culture, just as most Europeans will find themselves minorities in the new European Community. Rutman and Payne (1985) have noted that important differences exist in the evaluation cultures of the United States and Canada, as discussed earlier (Chapter 3). Large-scale evaluation in the United States was tied originally to major social experiments, reflecting U.S. reluctance to accept government intervention in social problems. The purpose was to determine what worked, thus building a consensus for action. The United States also has a social science tradition that stresses the scientific approach. U.S. evaluation has been conceived as neutral, value-free, and de-politicized. Finally, the United States has a competitive political process that provides forums for experts and others to express their views (Rutman and Payne, 1985, p. 64).

By contrast, Canadians expect government intervention and rely more on political, ideological debate. After debate, the government moves ahead without attempting to prove something works, a function of the parliamentary system and the willingness of citizens to follow government leadership. The evaluation process is centrally guided, and the evaluation community is led by government officials rather than researchers. In general, one would expect that a narrower range of evaluation issues would be addressed in Canada, that the issues and results would be more constrained by government policies, and that the findings would be more effectively implemented once formulated. Evaluation is not conceived as something done by a questioning third party. In the United States, one would expect conflict over results, evaluations critical of the government, and less acceptance of evaluation findings.

In both countries, evaluators are constrained, but in different ways. In Canada, the evaluation is constrained by government policy, which is more fully debated beforehand.[11] In the United States, evaluation is constrained by the prevailing ideology, which is more attuned to market considerations. For example, although U.S. medical care is a disaster by any standard, U.S. policy makers cannot formulate solutions, primarily because they are bound to physicians' control of the medical market under the banner of consumer choice, a position supported by the powerful private insurance industry.

On the other hand, once the Canadian government decided to act on medical care, evaluators could address issues of program success and change. Acid rain is a similar issue. So, as similar as the majority cultures of the United States and Canada are, there are important differences, which can result in different evaluations. In conclusion, my message is simple and not very original: Treat minority cultures as you would be treated. Sooner or later, everyone may be a minority.

Notes

1. In fact, Catalan has been under assault since the Castilians came to dominate Catalonia in 1716. However, at the 1992 Olympics in Barcelona, the official languages were English, French, Spanish, and Catalan, the first minority language recognized by the European Community (M. Simons, 1991).

2. I especially like the Canadian characterization of Americans by Ian Pearson (1991) in *The Globe and Mail* (p. E-8). Reviewing English journalist Jonathan Raban's book about traveling around the United States as a new immigrant looking for a place to settle down, Pearson quotes Raban, who looks at himself in the mirror: "With his bloodshot eyes and patchy, greying stubble, he looked criminalized. He had green teeth. He was still a long way short of being mistaken for a cocaine or marijuana runner, but he had the air of a man who might make his living by stealing things from unlocked cars." To which Canadian Pearson adds, "In short, he has affected enough savagery to pass as American, and his quest is successful."

3. This is a 1964 statement from the Montreal Committee for Political Realism, to which Trudeau belonged. Now, at age 71, Trudeau is more popular than ever: 55% of Canadians say they would vote Liberal if he headed the party, an approval rating that beats every other party leader. Paul Schratz (1991), in an article entitled "Pierre the Popular: Western Canada's Love Affair with the King of Fuddle-Duddle," says that Canadians wanted to hear from someone with a vision, "even an arrogant one" (p. 33). Trudeau holds to strong centralist views, against devolution of powers to the provinces. The magical leader calls Prime Minister Brian Mulroney "the sorcerer's apprentice" for having revived separatism, in his view. For Americans, Trudeau remains the quintessential Canadian, and none would be surprised if he suddenly appeared on television in a Mountie outfit.

4. Immediately after I presented an early version of this paper as a speech in Vancouver, a Chinese immigrant in the audience took me aside to explain in detail that this interplay was exactly how he managed to adjust to his new country, a cultural identity that includes the obligation of personally helping the new Chinese immigrants entering Canada.

5. See, for example, what happened with black education in the South after slavery in James D. Anderson (1988), *The Education of Blacks in the South, 1860-1935*. After all that has been inflicted on blacks, only a rabid optimist or a saint could still trust the majority.

6. A black professorial colleague raised in a segregated community in the South, who raised his four children in an entirely white university community, lamented the fact that his children did not have a sense of black identity. He said, "No matter how much my wife and I tell them that they cannot trust what white people say, they nod their heads yes, but they just don't understand emotionally." In his mind, distrust is a fundamental part of being black in the United States.

7. The first blacks who landed in the American colonies were 20 slaves purchased from a Dutch warship at Jamestown, Virginia, in 1619. That's a pretty slow meltdown.

8. I am reminded here of the first teaching job of Art McBeath of Saskatchewan, an old friend from graduate school. His first teaching assignment was in a remote Indian school in the far north. He landed in a pontoon plane along with a Mountie, and when they got out of the plane, the villagers all rushed enthusiastically to greet them. The Mountie pulled up his rifle and shot down several of the dogs running ahead

of the people, saying, "That'll teach the sons-of-bitches who's boss." Which, at least, was a succinct statement of government policy at the time.

9. It has been brought to my attention that legal safeguards may be enacted in different ways. American Indians do have autonomous control over their territory in many cases, and Canadian Indians often have less control than their U.S. counterparts, even though they are constitutionally guaranteed such rights.

10. Kymlicka bases his theoretical position on an extension of John Rawls' (1971) theory of justice. Rawls contends that all individuals have a right to self-respect as a primary good, and Kymlicka extends this argument to include cultural membership as a primary good. Self-respect is tied inextricably to one's cultural membership, and both are necessary to pursue one's life plan. Kymlicka maintains that Rawls and Dworkin have simply assumed that there is one culture and that the political community and cultural community are congruent, which is not the case.

11. At least the debate is supposed to precede government action. As one Canadian pointed out to me, all too often the government goes ahead without debate, proceeding from the top down.

❧ *10* ❧

Professional Ethics

*E*thics are the rules of right conduct or practice, especially the ethical standards of a profession. What particular ethical problems do evaluators face? What ethical standards have been proposed? What general principles underlie these standards? Are the standards and principles sufficient to ensure ethical practice? What violations of ethics are most likely to occur? Although ethical questions sometimes seem academic, when evaluators assemble, such questions are often the focus of attention. Alkin (1990), for example, has captured the reflections of ten evaluators discussing the uses of evaluation among themselves. Ethical concerns occupied a good portion of their discussion, even though it was not the designated topic.

❧ Definition

The ethics of evaluation are a subset of ethics or morality in general, but ethics applied to professional problems. According to Sieber (1980):

> If there were a field of applied ethics for program evaluation, that field would study how to choose morally right actions and maximize the

Some of these ideas are also discussed in House, E. R. (1993). Ethics in evaluation studies. In *International encyclopedia of educational research* (2nd ed). Pergamon Press: Oxford, England. Felix Angulo Rasco of the University of Malaga, Spain, was very helpful in providing feedback on this chapter.

163

value of one's work in program evaluation. It would examine the kinds
of dilemmas that arise in program evaluation; it would establish guidelines for anticipating and resolving certain ethical problems and encom-
pass a subarea of scientific methodology for performing evaluation that
satisfies both scientific and ethical requirements; and it would consider
ways to promote ethical character in program evaluators. (p. 52)

Some ethical problems in evaluation are the same as those in social
research generally. Conner (1980) has identified four basic problems
with research techniques: withholding the nature of the evaluation
research from the participants in the study, exposing participants to
acts that would harm them, invading the privacy of participants, and
withholding benefits from participants. Two issues involving use of
control groups are denying a valuable service to eligible clients who
might not be chosen for the beneficial treatment and equitably allocating scarce resources to a large group of eligible recipients. For example,
a study of the efficacy of aspirin for preventing heart attacks was
abandoned when interim results showed that the treatment was so
effective that the researchers could not ethically deny treatment to the
control group. Acceptance of clients as equals and multiple treatment
groups are ways of dealing with these problems. (See Sieber, 1982, on
general ethical problems in social research.)

What special ethical problems do evaluators face? First, evaluators
exercise special powers over people that can injure self-esteem, damage
reputations, and stunt careers. In education and social services, often
these people are children, who are not able to defend or state their own
interests. On the other hand, evaluators are engaged in contractual
situations in which they themselves are vulnerable to people awarding
future work. Some people whom evaluators deal with are powerful
within the evaluators' career realm. Also, evaluators come from the
same social classes and educational backgrounds as those who sponsor
evaluations and whose programs are evaluated. In addition, many
evaluation studies are conducted by contractors, with the work designed by one group being conducted by another (Carter, 1982; Rossi,
1982). All these factors increase ethical dangers.

૨ Codes of Conduct

Two major codes of ethics have been proposed for dealing with
problems in program evaluation (ERS Standards Committee, 1982;

Joint Committee, 1981), plus one for personnel evaluation (Joint Committee, 1988). In the educational evaluation program standards, there are four areas of concern: utility, accuracy, feasibility, and propriety. Although most of the standards deal with methodology, the propriety section includes formal obligations, conflicts of interest, full and frank disclosure, the public's right to know, rights of human subjects, human interactions, balanced reporting, and fiscal responsibility. These standards relate to privacy, protection of subjects, and freedom of information. In the 1982 standards of the Evaluation Research Society, ethical standards are not set aside in a special section, but are included in the general list.

In these sets of standards, evaluators are urged to forge a written contract with the sponsor and adhere to that contract, being aware of how conflicts of interest, especially the evaluators' own personal interests, may be involved. Openness, full disclosure, and release of information are the suggested ways of dealing with ethical problems. The rights of subjects are understood to limit full disclosure. Informed consent of subjects must be obtained. Prior mutual agreement among evaluators, sponsors, and subjects is emphasized. Overall the standards do a good job of addressing issues of professional ethics, although some reviewers have reservations (Berk, 1982; Cordray, 1982; Cronbach, 1982b).

In reflecting on the educational evaluation standards, Stufflebeam (1982, 1991), the person responsible for their development, has pointed out that the standards are appropriate only for the United States, not for other countries. He sees the standards as useful for dealing with ethical problems, but not sufficient by themselves to ensure ethical conduct. Other professional safeguards might include ethical training, examinations, licensing, review boards, sanctions for malpractice, and de-certification for unethical conduct. None of these standards is enforced; compliance is strictly voluntary.

For the most part, the ethical standards focus on infringements of personal rights. The codes assume that there are inherent individual rights prior to the conduct of evaluation, that the participants must be accorded these rights, and that individuals must voluntarily agree to participate in evaluation studies. The codes require that evaluators enter into contractual agreements with sponsors and adhere to the agreement as a matter of ethics. Not adhering to the agreement is considered unfair and unethical. People are obligated to uphold their part of the agreement when they have voluntarily accepted the benefits of the arrangement or taken advantage of its opportunities.

Not just any evaluation agreement is binding, however. House and Care (1979) have suggested that a binding evaluation agreement must meet certain conditions. For example, parties to the agreement cannot be coerced into signing, and all parties must be rational, well informed, and have a say in the agreement. Those not party to the agreement, but who are affected by it, also have certain personal rights, such as the right to be informed about the study and the right to volunteer.

The fundamental notion is that of contractual ethics, the establishment of an implicit or explicit voluntary contract as the basis for conduct. Contractual ethics is entailed by viewing society as a collection of individuals. "The essence of liberalism . . . is the vision of society as made up of independent, autonomous units who cooperate only when the terms of cooperation are such as to further the ends of the parties" (Barry, 1973, p. 166). Consent of participants is essential to ethical conduct within this framework, and intrusions on people without their consent is considered unethical. Individual autonomy is a first principle, reflected in establishing agreements, informing participants, and requesting consent.

?• Principles

Ethics are best discussed in specific, concrete situations because there are a thousand factors that can make a difference in particular situations. Although prescribing normative action for all situations is impossible, however, there are some considerations that arise repeatedly, even though their resolution may be different each time, depending on circumstances. Some ethical principles are worth attending to, even though they do not exhaust ethical concerns. One aim of ethical theory is to explicate and systematize standards of ethical deliberation that may be used to evaluate ethical choices, even though these considerations may not be complete (Howe & Miramontes, 1991).

The National Commission for the Protection of Human Subjects of Biomedical and Behavioral Research identified three underlying principles for social research: beneficence, respect, and justice (Bradburn, 1982; Campbell & Cecil, 1982; House, 1982; Sieber, 1980). Beneficence means avoiding unnecessary harm and maximizing good outcomes. This principle is served by the research being valid, by researchers being competent, by the participants being informed, by the results being disseminated, and by the research being weighed along with other evidence. Respect means respecting the autonomy of others by reducing the power differential between the researcher and participants, having participants volunteer, informing participants, and giving participants a choice in matters affecting them. Justice, in the commission's view, means equitable treatment and representation of subgroups in society. It is defined by equitable design and measurement, and access to data for re-analysis.

Perloff and Perloff (1980) consolidated ethical rules under four issues: withholding the nature of the evaluation research from participants or involving them without their knowledge; exposing participants to physical stress, anxiety, or acts that would diminish their self-respect; invading the privacy of participants; and withholding benefits. House (1990b) suggested three principles: mutual respect, noncoercion and nonmanipulation, and support for democratic values and institutions. The mutual respect principle is stated by John Rawls (1971):

> Mutual respect is shown in several ways: in our willingness to see the situation of others from their point of view, from the perspective of their conception of the good; and in our being prepared to give reasons for our actions whenever the interests of others are materially affected. . . . Thus to respect another as a moral person is to try to understand his [or her] aims and interests from his [or her] standpoint and to present him [or her] with considerations that enable him [or her] to accept the constraints on his [or her] conduct. (pp. 337-338)

The second principle is that of noncoercion and nonmanipulation. Coercion, the application of force or threats to secure compliance, is clearly forbidden. Coercion is not a common problem in evaluation studies, although whether compliance is gained through legitimate consent rather than through illegitimate access is sometimes difficult to determine. Nonmanipulation is more difficult to ascertain. Both coercion and manipulation are relevant when people are cooperating in a study contrary to their own interests. That is, there may be a conflict of interests such that participants may be damaging themselves through cooperation and should not be forced to comply. Manipulation is more insidious because participants do not realize that their interests are at risk. Sometimes the researcher convinces participants to cooperate when the researcher knows the participants may be in jeopardy, which would be unethical, according to this principle.

The third principle is the duty to uphold democratic values and institutions. We live in democratic societies and have an obligation to support the democratic values of those societies. Foremost among these are equality and liberty. The liberal theory of justice has several variations—utilitarianism, pluralism, justice-as-fairness, libertarianism, communitarianism—each of which emphasizes somewhat different ethical actions, while at the same time agreeing on other aspects, such as the protection of human rights. Which particular conception of justice should prevail is unresolved among evaluators, but nearly all would embrace liberal values in their work.

Finally, there is the formidable problem of applying ethical principles to the actual conduct of evaluation. Ethical principles are abstract, and it is not always obvious how they should be applied in given situations. Concrete examples and guidelines are useful if evaluators are to guide their behavior by ethical principles. Even when people endorse the same principles, however, there can be reasonable disagreement as to how principles apply. Some of the most intractable ethical problems arise from conflicts among principles and the necessity of trading off one against another. The balancing of such principles in concrete situations is the ultimate ethical act. Knowledge of how to do this resides within the craft and practical knowledge of evaluators, born from many experiences in complex evaluation situations.

ᴥ Ethical Fallacies

Several ethical mistakes occur so frequently in evaluation that they deserve the label of ethical fallacies. These include clientism, contractualism, managerialism, methodologicalism, relativism, and pluralism/elitism.

Clientism is the claim that doing whatever the client wants, or whatever is to the benefit of the client, is ethically correct. The analogy is with the doctor-client relationship. To take an extreme example, what if the client is Adolph Eichmann, and he wants the evaluator to study the efficiency of his concentration camps? Evaluators must recognize responsibilities beyond duty to the client, as medical doctors do. If a doctor determined that a client with a dangerous virus would be best off if allowed to move freely in society, but that the virus was highly contagious and would infect other people, the doctor's duty would be to the health of the community as a whole. The same is true for evaluators. Service to the client, though highly desirable, is insufficient as the entire ethical basis.

Managerialism takes managers of programs as the sole beneficiaries of the evaluation. This tendency is particularly salient in evaluation inside government. The negative case is stated forcefully by Bertram S. Brown, former director of the National Institute of Mental Health, who said, "It was my contention, harsh and clear, that internal evaluation was next to impossible, and that internal evaluation would always serve the needs not of the supposed client group studied, but of the organization" (quoted in Salasin, 1980, p. 5). Internal evaluation entails new ethical problems that evaluators have not been able to solve so far and that deserve serious study.

Another fallacy is contractualism, which holds that the evaluator must follow the written contract absolutely, whatever the situation. This is a fallacy because situations arise that cannot be foreseen, and sometimes it is necessary to act beyond the contract or even in contradiction to the contract. For example, what if the evaluator discovers a serious human rights abuse, but such a contingency was not part of the contract? The lack of contractual authority does not alleviate moral responsibility. Following the agreement is the correct thing for the evaluator to do most of the time, but not always. There must be considerations beyond the contract, although these must be assessed with caution. As currently conceived, professional ethics in program evaluation is a contractual ethics predicated on an agreement. This is not the case in product evaluation, where organizations such as Consumers Union evaluate products in the interests of the consumer without agreements between the producer and evaluator. Eventually, evaluation ethics must have a broader rationale than contractual obligations.

Some evaluators hold to methodologicalism, in which following acceptable research methods is believed to be sufficient for ethical performance. This position is a return to a time when facts and values were conceived as totally separate. The social scientist's responsibility was to produce value-free facts, thus avoiding ethical problems altogether. This position has been refuted in theory, but practitioners sometimes resort to the value/fact distinction when placed in difficult ethical situations. In fact, ethical considerations extend beyond proper research methodology, and the evaluator is not relieved of ethical duty by following methodological prescriptions.

With relativism, another fallacy, it is believed that the evaluator's responsibility is to collect data from participants in the study and accept everyone's opinions equally. Knowledge and judgments are strictly relative, in this view. Again, what if Adolph Eichmann is a member of the group? Are we to accept his opinions equally with everyone else's and accord his views full ethical validity? Obviously not. Ethical considerations beyond individual and group opinions must come into play. There is a sense in which everyone deserves to be listened to and to express his or her interests, but this does not mean that those expressions are to be judged morally equal. The racist does not rate equally with the victim of racism.

Pluralism/elitism is similar to relativism in that the evaluator collects the opinions and values of various participants in the program, such as decision makers, administrators, legislators, and participants, and puts these opinions and values together in some unspecified way. How these values and opinions are adjudicated is not clear. This is probably the most common position in evaluation, but one also burdened with ethical problems. Often, the result of such an approach is to give the powerful a priority voice in the evaluation, because it is mostly they whose opinions and criteria have been solicited and used. Evaluators must adopt a more democratic stand than this. They must solicit the opinions and criteria of those not powerful and make sure that these are included as well. There is an ethical obligation to include the interests of all.

‱ Ethics and Justice

Professional ethics inevitably involve issues of social justice, social justice being the moral concern about the entire social structure, and not just one's role within that structure. As one moral philosopher has said:

> There can be no ethics without politics. A theory of how individuals should act requires a theory—an ethical theory, not just an empirical one—of the institutions under which they should live: institutions which substantially determine their starting point, the choices they can make, the consequences of what they do, and their relations to one another. (Nagel, 1986, p. 188)

Professional ethics are enacted within the framework of these larger institutions. For example, both Sjoberg (1975) and Weiss (1991) contend that evaluation studies usually take for granted the structural and ideological constraints of society. Evaluations are used for purposes of effectiveness, efficiency, and accountability within the dominant bureaucratic hierarchies and political ideologies, without questioning the overall social structure. The evaluative categories used by evaluators are ordinarily those of the status quo, and the measures employed are allied to the power structure.

The balancing and resolution of the various interests, opinions, values, and criteria within an evaluation, as manifested in the stakeholder model, remains one of the most difficult and unresolved problems of ethics and social justice in evaluation. This is because a full theory of making value judgments in evaluation has yet to be developed within the discipline, a residue of the value-free tradition. Perhaps this is the most critical part of evaluation theory now missing. How to balance and adjudicate various interests is a critical problem for the society as a whole as well. It may be that the direction of such a resolution lies along the lines suggested for women, social classes, and minority cultures.

Another critical issue is how far to carry the increasingly dominant criterion of efficiency, which now is promoted by so many governments in their efforts to increase economic productivity.

> To say that costs and benefits, in welfare terms, are all that morally count in making a public decision, is to say that any ethical variable that is not directly translatable into a monetary equivalent is of consequentially less importance to the outcome. To treat individuals strictly as consumers (rather than citizens, for example) limits the evaluation system to questions of consumption, when the real moral concern might demand that the obligation be considered from the angle of obligation or protection. (Gillroy, 1992, p. 100)

The market, of course, is only one way to regulate society (Wolfe, 1989).

At its best, evaluation should be a method for democratizing public decisions in society, although it is not always used this way. Other social forces sometimes distort the process or turn evaluation to the ends of special groups, without regard for the public interest. When evaluation goes awry, it is worse than no evaluation at all. Ideally, all relevant interests should be represented in an evaluation, and the evaluation should inform deliberation processes that benefit everyone. The basic idea of legitimacy is that the use of power is capable of being authorized by everyone through acceptance of principles, institutions, and procedures that determine how that power will be used (Beetham, 1991; Nagel, 1991). Legitimation is not arbitrary.

In conclusion, evaluation is a powerful social force that has evolved only recently in advanced capitalist societies, a new institution that promises to be a major influence over the long term. Its influence can be both good and bad. In either case, society before formal evaluation is not the same as society afterward. Exactly what shape the practice, institution, profession, and discipline will take in the future is impossible to predict. What is clear is that its fate will be bound to the government and the economic structure and determined in part by its own history and traditions. Some of its destiny lies within the control of the evaluators themselves; some does not.

ও

References

Albaek, E. (1989-1990). Policy evaluation: Design and utilization. *Knowledge in Society*, 2(4), 6-19.

Albaek, E., & Winter, S. (1990). Evaluation in Denmark: The state of the art. In R. C. Rist (Ed.), *Program evaluation and the management of government* (pp. 95-103). New Brunswick, NJ: Transaction Books.

Alkin, M. C. (1990). *Debates on evaluation*. Newbury Park, CA: Sage.

Alkin, M. C. (1991). Evaluation theory development. In M. W. McLaughlin & D. C. Phillips (Eds.), *Evaluation and education: At quarter century* (pp. 91-112). Chicago: Published by the University of Chicago Press for the National Society for the Study of Education.

American Evaluation Association. (1990, October). *Membership survey: Preliminary summary* (Mimeo).

Anderson, B. (1983). *Imagined communities: Reflections on the origin and spread of nationalism*. London: Verso.

Anderson, J. D. (1988). *The education of blacks in the South, 1860-1935*. Chapel Hill: University of North Carolina Press.

Anderson, N. (1967). *The hobo*. Chicago: University of Chicago Press. (Original work published 1923)

Avineri, S. (1990). Toward a socialist theory of nationalism. *Dissent*, 37(7), 447-457.

Bank, A. (1985). Evaluation in Israel: A conversation with Ariah Levy. In M. Q. Patton (Ed.), *New directions for program evaluation: Vol. 25. Culture and evaluation* (pp. 79-92). San Francisco: Jossey-Bass.

Bannister, R. C. (1987). *Sociology and scientism: The American quest for objectivity, 1880-1940*. Chapel Hill: University of North Carolina Press.

Barringer, F. (1991, March 11). Census shows profound change in racial makeup of the nation. *New York Times*, pp. A1, A12.

Barry, B. (1973). *The liberal theory of justice*. Oxford, UK: Clarendon Press.

Beetham, D. (1991). *The legitimation of power*. London: Macmillan Education.

Bemelmans-Videc, M. L. (1989-1990). Dutch experience with evaluation research. *Knowledge in Society*, 2(4), 31-48.

Bemelmans-Videc, M. L., Elte, R., & Koolhaus, E. (1990). Policy evaluation in the Netherlands: Institutional context and state of affairs. In R. C. Rist (Ed.), *Program evaluation and the management of government* (pp. 105-118). New Brunswick, NJ: Transaction Books.

Bergmann, B. R. (1986). *The economic emergence of women.* New York: Basic Books.

Berk, R. A. (1982). Where angels fear to tread and why. In P. H. Rossi (Ed.), *New directions for program evaluation: Vol. 15. Standards for evaluation practice* (pp. 59-66). San Francisco: Jossey-Bass.

Bertilsson, M. (1991). From university to comprehensive higher education. *Studies of higher education and research* (Mimeo paper series). Stockholm: Council for Studies of Higher Education.

Bhaskar, R. (1986). *Scientific realism and human emancipation.* London: Verso.

Bickman, L. (Ed). (1987). *New directions for program evaluation: Vol. 33. Using program theory in evaluation.* San Francisco: Jossey-Bass.

Bjorklund, E. (1985). The Research on Higher Education program: An overview. *Studies of higher education and research* (Mimeo paper series). Stockholm: National Board of Universities and Colleges.

Bjorklund, E. (1989). Two decades of Swedish research on higher education. *Studies of higher education and research* (Mimeo paper series). Stockholm: National Board of Universities and Colleges.

Bloom, B. S., Hastings, J. T., & Madaus, G. F. (1971). *Handbook on formative and summative evaluation of student learning.* New York: McGraw-Hill.

Boruch, R. F., & Riecken, W. H. (Eds.). (1975). *Experimental testing of public policy.* Boulder, CO: Westview.

Bradburn, N. M. (1982). Critique of Campbell and Cecil's proposal: Don't throw out the baby with the bathwater. In J. E. Sieber (Ed.), *The ethics of social research: Fieldwork, regulation, and publication* (pp. 125-130). New York: Springer-Verlag.

Braudel, F. (1972, 1974). *The Mediterranean and the Mediterranean world in the age of Philip II.* 2 vols. New York: Harper & Row.

Braudel, F. (1980). *On history.* Chicago: University of Chicago Press. (Original work published 1958)

Braudel, F. (1981). *Civilization and capitalism: 15th-18th century: Vol. 1. The structures of everyday life: The limits of the possible.* New York: Harper & Row.

Braudel, F. (1982). *Civilization and capitalism: 15th-18th century: Vol. 2. The wheels of commerce.* New York: Harper & Row.

Braudel, F. (1984). *Civilization and capitalism: 15th-18th century: Vol. 3. The perspective of the world.* New York: Harper & Row.

Bruner, R. D. (1991). The policy movement as a policy problem. *Policy Sciences, 24*(1), 65-93.

Buckle, H. T. (1970). *On Scotland and the Scotch intellect.* Chicago: University of Chicago Press. (Original work published 1857)

Bullock, A., Stallybrass, O., & Trombley, S. (Eds.). (1988). *The Harper dictionary of modern thought* (rev. ed.). New York: Harper & Row.

Burningham, D. (1990). Performance indicators and the management of professionals in local government. In M. Cave, M. Kogan, & R. Smith (Eds.), *Output and performance measurement in government* (pp. 124-142). London: Jessica Kingsley.

Callahan, R. E. (1962). *Education and the [cult ? I couldn't read the fax well] of efficiency.* Chicago: University of Chicago Press.

Campbell, D. T. (1969). Reforms as experiments. *American Psychologist, 24,* 409-429.

Campbell, D. T. (1970). Considering the case against the experimental evaluations. *Administrative Quarterly, 1,* 1094-1115.

Campbell, D. T., & Cecil, J. S. (1982). A proposed system of regulation for the protection of participants in low-risk areas of applied social research. In J. E. Sieber (Ed.), *The ethics of social research: Fieldwork, regulation, and publication* (pp. 97-121). New York: Springer-Verlag.

Campbell, D. T., & Stanley, J. C. (1962). Experimental and quasi-experimental designs for research on teaching. In N. L. Gage (Ed.), *Handbook of research on teaching* (pp. 171-246). Chicago: Rand McNally.

Campbell, D. T., & Stanley, J. C. (1963). *Experimental and quasi-experimental designs for research.* Chicago: Rand McNally.

Carter, L. F. (1982). The standards for evaluation and the large for-profit social science research and evaluation companies. In P. H. Rossi (Ed.), *New directions for program evaluation: Vol. 15. Standards for evaluation practice* (pp. 37-48). San Francisco: Jossey-Bass.

Cave, M., & Hanney, H. (1990). Performance indicators for higher education and research. In M. Cave, M. Kogan, & R. Smith (Eds.), *Output and performance measurement in government* (pp. 59-85). London: Jessica Kingsley.

Cave, M., Kogan, M., & Smith, R. (Eds.). (1990). *Output and performance measurement in government.* London: Jessica Kingsley.

Chelimsky, E. (1987). The politics of program evaluation. *Society, 25*(1), 24-32.

Chelimsky, E. (1990). Expanding GAO's capabilities in program evaluation. *The GAO Journal, 8,* 43-52.

Chelimsky, E. (1991). On the social science contribution to governmental decision-making. *Science, 254,* 226-231.

Chen, H. T., & Rossi, P. H. (1984). Evaluating with sense: The theory-driven approach. In R. F. Conner (Ed.), *Evaluation studies review annual* (Vol. 9, pp. 337-356). Beverly Hills, CA: Sage.

Clark, S. (1985). The Annales historians. In Q. Skinner (Ed.), *The return of grand theory in the human sciences* (pp. 179-198). New York: Cambridge University Press.

Colorado Commission on Higher Education. (1988). *Policies and general procedures for the development of accountability programs by state-supported institutions of higher education as required by 23-13-101.* Denver: Colorado Commission on Higher Education.

Comte, A. (1957). *A general view of positivism.* New York: Robert Spiller. (Original work published 1857)

Conner, R. F. (1980). Ethical issues in the use of control groups. In R. Perloff & E. Perloff (Eds.), *New directions in program evaluation: Vol. 7. Values, ethics, and standards in evaluation* (pp. 63-75). San Francisco: Jossey-Bass.

Cook, T. D., & Campbell, D. T. (1979). *Quasi-experimentation: Design and analysis issues for field studies.* Boston: Houghton Mifflin.

Cook, T. D., & Shadish, W. S., Jr. (1986). Progam evaluation: The worldly science. *American Review of Psychology, 37,* 210.

Cordray, D. S. (1982). An assessment of the utility of the ERS standards. In P. H. Rossi (Ed.), *New directions for program evaluation: Vol. 15. Standards for evaluation practice* (pp. 67-81). San Francisco: Jossey-Bass.

Cronbach, L. J. (1982a). *Designing evaluations of educational and social programs.* San Francisco: Jossey-Bass.

Cronbach, L. J. (1982b). In praise of uncertainty. In P. H. Rossi (Ed.), *New directions for program evaluation: Vol. 15. Standards for evaluation practice* (pp. 49-58). San Francisco: Jossey-Bass.

Cronbach, L. J., and Associates. (1980). *Toward reform of program evaluation.* San Francisco: Jossey-Bass.

Cuthbert, M. (1985). Evaluation encounters in third world settings: A Caribbean perspective. In M. Q. Patton (Ed.), *New directions for program evaluation: Vol. 25. Culture and evaluation* (pp. 29-36). San Francisco: Jossey-Bass.

Dahl, R. A. (1956). *A preface to democratic theory.* Chicago: University of Chicago Press.

Derlien, H.-G. (1990). Genesis and structure of evaluation efforts in comparative perspective. In R. C. Rist (Ed.), *Program evaluation and the management of government* (pp. 147-175). New Brunswick, NJ: Transaction Books.

Dougherty, K. M., Eisenhart, M., & Webley, P. (1991). *National identity in context* (Mimeo). Boulder: University of Colorado, School of Education.

Edelman, M. (1964). *The symbolic uses of politics.* Urbana: University of Illinois Press.

Edelman, M. (1988). *Constructing the political spectacle.* Chicago: University of Chicago Press.

Edwards, W. (1971). Social utilities. *The Engineering Economist, 6,* 66-80.

Eisner, E. W. (1979). *The educational imagination.* New York: Macmillan.

Eriksen, B. (1990). Institutional aspects of evaluation in Norway. In R. C. Rist (Ed.), *Program evaluation and the management of government* (pp. 119-131). New Brunswick, NJ: Transaction Books.

ERS Standards Committee. (1982). Evaluation research society standards for program evaluation. In P. H. Rossi (Ed.), *New directions for program evaluation: Vol. 15. Standards for evaluation practice* (pp. 7-19). San Francisco: Jossey-Bass.

Farrar, E., & House, E. R. (1983). The evaluation of PUSH/Excel: A case study. In A. Bryk (Ed.), *New directions for program evaluation: Vol. 17. Stakeholder-based evaluation* (pp. 31-57). San Francisco: Jossey-Bass.

Floden, R. E. (1983). Flexner, accreditation, and evaluation. In G. F. Madaus, D. L. Stufflebeam, & M. Scriven (Eds.), *Evaluation models* (pp. 261-277). Boston: Kluwer-Nijhoff.

Franke-Wikberg, S. (1990). The American research on educational evaluation and the national evaluation in Sweden. In M. Granheim, M. Kogan, & U. Lundgren (Eds.), *Evaluation as policymaking: Introducing evaluation into a national decentralised educational system* (pp. 155-171). London: Jessica Kingsley.

Galbraith, J. K. (1958). *The affluent society.* Boston: Houghton Mifflin.

Gellner, E. (1983). *Nations and nationalism.* Oxford, UK: Blackwell.

Gerson, K. (1985). *Hard choices: How women decide about work, career, and motherhood.* Berkeley and Los Angeles: University of California Press.

Gillroy, J. M. (1992). The ethical poverty of cost-benefit methods: Autonomy, efficiency, and public policy choice. *Policy Sciences, 25,* 83-102.

Gilpin, R. (1987). *The political economy of international relations.* Princeton, NJ: Princeton University Press.

Glazer, N. (1988). The affirmative action stalemate. *The Public Interest, 90,* 99-114.

Gold, N. (1983). Stakeholder and program evaluation: Characterizations and reflections. In A. Bryk (Ed.), *New directions for program evaluation: Vol. 17. Stakeholder-based evaluation* (pp. 63-72). San Francisco: Jossey-Bass.

Goodwyn, L. (1978). *The populist moment.* Oxford, UK: Oxford University Press.

Gould, S. J. (1981). *The mismeasure of man.* New York: Norton.

Granheim, M., Kogan, M., & Lundgren, U. (Eds.). (1990). *Evaluation as policymaking: Introducing evaluation into a national decentralised educational system.* London: Jessica Kingsley.

Grant, C. A., & Sleeter, C. E. (1986). Race, class, gender in education research: An argument for integrative analysis. *Review of Educational Research, 56*(2), 195-211.

Guba, E. G., & Lincoln, Y. S. (1989). *Fourth generation evaluation,* Newbury Park, CA: Sage.

Guttentag, M. (1973). Subjectivity and its use in evaluation research. *Evaluation, 1*(2), 60-65.

Haber, S. (1991). *The quest for authority and honor in the American professions, 1759-1900.* Chicago: University of Chicago Press.

Habermas, J. (1975). *Legitimation crisis.* Boston: Beacon.

Hammersley, M. (1989). *The dilemma of qualitative method: Herbert Blumer and the Chicago tradition.* London: Routledge.

Hatch, E. (1973). *Theories of man and culture.* New York: Columbia University Press.

Haug, P. (1992). *Educational reform by experiment.* Stockholm: HLS Forlag.

Held, D. (1984). *Political theory and the modern state.* Cambridge, UK: Polity.

Henderson-Stewart, D. (1990). Performance management and review in local government performance indicators for higher education and research. In M. Cave, M. Kogan, & R. Smith (Eds.), *Output and performance measurement in government* (pp. 106-123). London: Jessica Kingsley.

Henkel, M. (1991). *Government, evaluation, and change.* London: Jessica Kingsley.

Hirsch, E. D., Jr. (1987). *Cultural literacy: What every American needs to know.* New York: Houghton Mifflin.

Hober-Papazian, K., & Thevoz, L. (1990). Switzerland: Moving towards evaluation. In R. C. Rist (Ed.), *Program evaluation and the management of government* (pp. 133-143). New Brunswick, NJ: Transaction Books.

Hobsbawm, E. J. (1990). *Nations and nationalism since 1780.* Cambridge, UK: Cambridge University Press.

Hodgson, G. (1978). *America in our time.* New York: Vintage.

Hoogerwerf, A. (1985). The anatomy of collective failure in the Netherlands. In M. Q. Patton (Ed.), *New directions for program evaluation: Vol. 25. Culture and evaluation* (pp. 47-60). San Francisco: Jossey-Bass.

Horio, T. (1988). *Educational thought and ideology in modern Japan: State authority and intellectual freedom.* Tokyo: University of Tokyo Press.

House, E. R. (1976). Justice in evaluation. In G. V. Glass (Ed.), *Evaluation studies review annual* (Vol. 1, pp. 75-100). Beverly Hills, CA: Sage.

House, E. R. (1977). *The logic of evaluative argument* (Monograph No. 7). Los Angeles: University of California at Los Angeles, Center for the Study of Evaluation.

House, E. R. (1978). Evaluation as scientific management in United States school reform. *Comparative Education Review, 28*(3), 388-401.

House, E. R. (1980). *Evaluating with validity.* Beverly Hills, CA: Sage.

House, E. R. (1982). Critique of Campbell and Cecil's proposal: Subjects need more protection. In J. E. Sieber (Ed.), *The ethics of social research: Fieldwork, regulation, and publication* (pp. 122-125). New York: Springer-Verlag.

House, E. R. (1988). *Jesse Jackson and the politics of charisma: The rise and fall of the PUSH/Excel program.* Boulder, CO: Westview.

House, E. R. (1990a). Decentralised evaluation for Norway. In M. Granheim, M. Kogan, & U. Lundgren (Eds.), *Evaluation as policymaking: Introducing evaluation into a national decentralised educational system* (pp. 211-218). London: Jessica Kingsley.

House, E. R. (1990b). An ethics of qualitative field studies. In E. G. Guba (Ed.), *The paradigm dialog* (pp. 158-164). Newbury Park, CA: Sage.

House, E. R. (1991a). Big policy, little policy. *Educational Researcher, 20*(5), 21-26.

House, E. R. (1991b). Evaluation and social justice: Where are we? In M. W. McLaughlin & D. C. Phillips (Eds.), *Evaluation and education: At quarter century* (pp. 233-247). Chicago: University of Chicago Press.

House, E. R. (1991c). Realism in research. *Educational Researcher, 20*(6), 2-9.

House, E. R., & Care, N. (1979). Fair evaluation agreement. *Educational Theory, 29*, 159-169.

House, E. R., Glass, G. V., McLean, L. D., & Walker, D. (1978). No simple answer: Critique of the follow through evaluation. *Harvard Educational Review, 48*(2), 128-160.

House, E. R., & Howe, K. (1990). Second chance as education policy. In D. Inbar (Ed.), *Second chance in education* (pp. 45-65). London: Falmer.

House, E. R., Mathison, S., & McTaggert, R. (1989). Validity and teacher inference. *Educational Research, 18*(7), pp. 11-15.

House, E. R., Rivers, W., & Stufflebeam, D. L. (1974). An assessment of the Michigan accountability system. *Phi Delta Kappan, 55*(10), 663-669.

Howe, K. R. (1991). Liberal democracy, equal educational opportunity, and the challenge of multi-culturalism. *American Educational Research Journal, 29*(3), 455-470.

Howe, K. R., & Eisenhart, M. (1990). Standards in qualitative research: A prologomenon. *Educational Researcher, 19*(4), 2-9.

Howe, K. R., & Miramontes, O. B. (1991). A framework for ethical deliberation in special education. *Journal of Special Education, 25*(1), 7-25.

Jenkins, B., & Gray, A. (1990). Policy evaluation in British government: From idealism to realism? In R. C. Rist (Ed.), *Program evaluation and the management of government* (pp. 53-70). New Brunswick, NJ: Transaction Books.

Johnson, P. L. (1991). Ray Rist talks about the IIAS working group on policy and program evaluation. *Evaluation Practice, 12*(1), 45-53.

Joint Committee on Standards for Educational Evaluation. (1981). *Standards for evaluations of educational programs, projects, and materials.* New York: McGraw-Hill.

Joint Committee on Standards for Educational Evaluation. (1988). *Personnel evaluation standards.* Newbury Park, CA: Sage.

Kamin, L. J. (1977). The politics of I. Q. In P. L. Houts (Ed.), *The myth of measurability* (pp. 45-65). New York: Hart.

Karlsson, O. (1992). *Evaluation in the Swedish context: An introduction* (Mimeo). Stockholm: University of Stockholm, School of Education.

Karst, K. L. (1986). Paths to belonging: The Constitution and cultural identity. *North Carolina Law Review, 64*, 305-377.

Kearns, D. (1976). *LBJ and the American dream.* New York: Harper & Row.

Kennedy, P. (1987). *The rise and fall of the great powers.* New York: Random House.

Kogan, M. (1983). *The attack on higher education.* London: Kogan Page.

Kogan, M. (1986). *Education accountability.* London: Hutchinson.

Krieger, J. (1986). *Reagan, Thatcher, and the politics of decline.* New York: Oxford University Press.

Kymlicka, W. (1989). *Liberalism, community, and culture.* New York: Oxford University Press.

Larson, M. S. (1977). *The rise of professionalism: A sociological analysis.* Berkeley: University of California Press.

Lauglo, J. (1990). A comparative perspective with special reference to Norway. In M. Granheim, M. Kogan, & U. Lundgren (Eds.), *Evaluation as policymaking: Introducing evaluation into a national decentralised educational system* (pp. 66-88). London: Jessica Kingsley.

Levin, H. M. (1983). *Cost-effectiveness: A primer.* Beverly Hills, CA: Sage.

Levin, H. M. (1991). Cost-effectiveness at quarter century. In M. W. McLaughlin & D. C. Phillips (Eds.), *Evaluation and education: At quarter century* (pp. 189-209). Chicago: National Society for the Study of Education.

Levitan, S. A. (1992). *Evaluation of federal social programs: An uncertain impact.* Washington, DC: George Washington University, Center for Social Policy Studies.

Levy, F. (1987). *Dollars and dreams: The changing American income distribution.* New York: Russell Sage.

Lloyd, C. (1986). *Explanation in social history.* Oxford, UK: Blackwell.

Lundgren, U. (1990). Educational policymaking, decentralisation and evaluation. In M. Granheim, M. Kogan, & U. Lundgren (Eds.), *Evaluation as policymaking: Introducing evaluation into a national decentralised educational system* (pp. 23-41). London: Jessica Kingsley.

MacDonald, B. (1977). A political classification of evaluation studies. In D. Hamilton (Ed.), *Beyond the numbers game* (pp. 224-227). London: Macmillan.

Mackie, J. L. (1974). *The cement of the universe: A study of causation.* Oxford, UK: Oxford University Press.

MacPherson, C. B. (1973). *Democratic theory: Essays in retrieval.* Oxford, UK: Oxford University Press.

MacPherson, C. B. (1987). *The rise and fall of economic justice.* Oxford, UK: Oxford University Press.

Madaus, G. F., Scriven, M., & Stufflebeam, D. L. (1983). Program evaluation: An historical overview. In G. F. Madaus, M. Scriven, & D. L. Stufflebeam (Eds.), *Evaluation models* (pp. 3-22). Boston: Kluwer-Nijhoff.

Madaus, G. F., & Stufflebeam, D. L. (1989). *Educational evaluation: Classic works of Ralph W. Tyler.* Boston: Kluwer Academic.

Madaus, G. F., Stufflebeam, D. L., & Scriven, M. (Eds.). (1983). *Evaluation models.* Boston: Kluwer-Nijhoff.

Manicas, P. T. (1987). *A history and philosophy of the social sciences.* Oxford, UK: Blackwell.

Manicas, P. T., & Secord, P. F. (1983). Implications for psychology of the new philosophy of science. *American Psychologist, 38,* 399-413.

Marquand, D. (1988). *The unprincipled society.* London: Fontana.

McClintock, C. (1987). Conceptual and action heuristics: Tools for the evaluator. In L. Bickman (Ed.), *New directions for program evaluation: Vol. 33. Using program theory in evaluation* (pp. 43-57). San Francisco: Jossey-Bass.

McLaughlin, M. W. (1975). *Evaluation and reform: The elementary and secondary education act of 1965.* Cambrige, MA: Ballinger.

Mentkowski, M. (1988, October). *Faculty and student involvement in institutional assessment.* Paper presented at the meeting of the American Evaluation Association, New Orleans, LA.

Merriam, C. E. (1925). *New aspects of politics.* Chicago: University of Chicago Press.

Merryfield, M. M. (1985). The challenge of cross-cultural evaluation: Some views from the field. In M. Q. Patton (Ed.), *New directions for program evaluation: Vol 25. Culture and evaluation* (pp. 3-18). San Francisco: Jossey-Bass.

Mill, J. S. (1974). *A system of logic: Ratiocinative and inductive.* Toronto: University of Toronto Press. (Original work published 1843)

Morell, J. A. (1990). Evaluation: Status of a loose coalition. *Evaluation Practice, 11*(3), 213-219.

Morell, J. A. (1991, November). *Industrial productivity: New perspectives for a traditionally trained evaluator.* Paper presented at the meeting of the American Evaluation Association, Chicago.

Morell, J. A., & Flaherty, E. W. (1978). The development of evaluation as a profession: Current status and some predictions. *Evaluation and Program Planning, 11*(3), 213-219.

Murray, C. A. (1983). Stakeholders as deck chairs. In A. Bryk (Ed.), *New directions for program evaluation: Vol. 17. Stakeholder-based evaluation* (pp. 58-61). San Francisco: Jossey-Bass.

Murray, C. A. (1984). *Losing ground: American social policy, 1950-1980.* New York: Basic Books.

Nagel, T. (1986). *The view from nowhere.* Oxford, UK: Oxford University Press.

Nagel, T. (1991). *Equality and partiality.* Oxford, UK: Oxford University Press.

National Center for Educational Statistics. (1991). *State higher education profiles* (3rd ed.). Washington, DC: U.S. Department of Education.

Newman, P. C. (1988). *Home country: People, places, and power politics.* Toronto: McClelland and Stewart.

Nickel, J. W. (1987). Equal opportunity in a pluralistic society. *Social Philosophy and Policy, 5,* 104-119.

Nickel, J. W. (1990). *Liberal pluralism and community* (Mimeo). Boulder: University of Colorado, Department of Philosophy.

Noblit, G. W., & Eaker, D. J. (1988). Evaluation designs as political strategies. In J. Hanneway & R. Crowson (Eds.), *The politics of reforming school administration* (pp. 127-138). New York: Falmer.

Norris, N. (1990). *Understanding educational evaluation.* New York: St. Martin's.

Ogbu, J. U. (1988a). Cultural boundaries and minority youth orientation toward work preparation. In D. Stern & D. Eichorn (Eds.), *Adolescence and work: Influences of social structure, labor market, and culture.* Hillsdale, NJ: Lawrence Erlbaum.

Ogbu, J. U. (1988b). Diversity and equity in public education: Community forces and minority school adjustment and performance. In R. Haskins & D. MacRae (Eds.), *Policies for America's public schools: Teachers, equity, and indicators* (pp. 127-170). Norwood, NJ: Ablex.

Paskow, J. (Ed.). (1988). *Assessment programs and projects: A directory.* Washington, DC: American Association for Higher Education.

Patton, M. Q. (Ed.). (1985). *New directions for program evaluation: Vol. 25. Culture and evaluation.* San Francisco: Jossey-Bass.

Patton, M. Q. (1988). The evaluator's responsibility for utilization. *Evaluation Practice, 9*(2), 5-24.

Pearson, C. (1892). *The grammar of science.* London: Walter Scott.

Pearson, I. (1991, May 4). A bard's-eye view of America. *The Globe and Mail* [Toronto, Ontario], p. E-8.

Perkin, H. (1989). *The rise of professional society: England since 1880.* London and New York: Routledge.

Perloff, R., & Perloff, E. (1980). Ethics in practice. In R. Perloff & E. Perloff (Eds.), *New directions for program evaluation: Vol. 7. Values, ethics, and standards in evaluation* (pp. 77-83). San Francisco: Jossey-Bass.

Pollitt, C. (1990). Performance indicators, root and branch. In M. Cave, M. Kogan, & R. Smith (Eds.), *Output and performance measurement in government* (pp. 167-178). London: Jessica Kingsley.

Porter, J. (1987). *The measure of Canadian society: Education, equality, and opportunity.* Ottawa: Carleton University Press.

Program Review Panel. (1990). *Program review procedures.* Boulder: University of Colorado, Office of Academic Affairs.

Ravitch, D. (1990). Multiculturalism. *American Scholar, 59*(3), 337-354.

Ravitch, D., & Finn, C. E., Jr. (1987). *What do our 17-year-olds know?* New York: Harper & Row.

Rawls, J. (1971). *A theory of justice.* Cambridge, MA: Belknap.

Rist, R. C. (1989-1990). On the application of program evaluation designs: Sorting out their use and abuse. *Knowledge in Society, 2*(4), 74-96.

Rist, R. C. (Ed.). (1990). *Program evaluation and the management of government.* New Brunswick, NJ: Transaction Books.

Rivlin, A. (1971). *Systematic thinking for social action.* Washington, DC: Brookings Institution.

Roberts, H. (1990). Performance and outcome measures in the health service. In M. Cave, M. Kogan, & R. Smith (Eds.), *Output and performance measurement in government* (pp. 86-105). London: Jessica Kingsley.

Robertson, J. O. (1980). *American myth, American reality.* New York: Hill and Wang.

Ross, D. (1991). *The origins of American social science.* Cambridge, UK: Cambridge University Press.

Rossi, P. H. (Ed.). (1982). *New directions for program evaluation: Vol. 15. Standards for evaluation practice.* San Francisco: Jossey-Bass.

Rowen, H. (1964). *The free enterprisers, Kennedy, Johnson and the business establishment.* New York: Putnam.

Rutman, L., & Payne, J. (1985). Institutionalization of evaluation in Canada: The federal level. In M. Q. Patton (Ed.), *New directions for program evaluation: Vol. 25. Culture and evaluation* (pp. 61-68). San Francisco: Jossey-Bass.

Salasin, S. (1980). The evaluator as an agent of change. In R. Perloff & E. Perloff (Eds.), *New directions for program evaluation: Vol. 7. Values, ethics, and standards in evaluation* (pp. 1-9). San Francisco: Jossey-Bass.

Schratz, P. (1991, May 5). Pierre the popular: Western Canada's love affair with the king of fuddle-duddle. *The Province* [Vancouver, British Columbia], p. 33.

Schumpeter, J. A. (1942). *Capitalism, socialism and democracy.* New York: Harper & Row.

Scriven, M. S. (1980). *The logic of evaluation.* Inverness, CA: Edgepress.

Scriven, M. S. (1983). Evaluation ideologies. In G. F. Madaus, M. S. Scriven, & D. L. Stufflebeam (Eds.), *Evaluation models* (pp. 229-260). Boston: Kluwer-Nijhoff.

Scriven, M. S. (1991). *Evaluation thesaurus* (4th ed.). Newbury Park, CA: Sage.

Seefeldt, F. M. (1985). Cultural considerations for evaluation: Consulting in the Egyptian context. In M. Q. Patton (Ed.), *New directions for program evaluation: Vol. 25. Culture and evaluation* (pp. 69-78). San Francisco: Jossey-Bass.

Segsworth, R. V. (1989-1990). Freedom of information laws and evaluation research. *Knowledge in Society, 2*(4), 49-61.

Segsworth, R. V. (1990). Policy and program evaluation in the government of Canada. In R. C. Rist (Ed.), *Program evaluation and the management of government* (pp. 21-36). New Brunswick, NJ: Transaction Books.

Shadish, W. R., Jr. (1987). Program micro- and macrotheories: A guide for social change. In L. Bickman (Ed.), *New directions for program evaluation: Vol. 33. Using program theory in evaluation* (pp. 93-109). San Francisco: Jossey-Bass.

Shadish, W. R., Jr., & Reichardt, C. S. (1987). The intellectual foundations of social program evaluation. In W. R. Shadish, Jr., & C. S. Reichardt (Eds.), *Evaluation studies review annual* (Vol. 6, pp. 13-30). Newbury Park, CA: Sage.

Sieber, J. E. (1980). Being ethical? Professional and personal decisions in program evaluation. In R. Perloff & E. Perloff (Eds.), *New directions for program evaluation: Vol. 7. Values, ethics, and standards in evaluation* (pp. 51-61). San Francisco: Jossey-Bass.

Sieber, J. E. (1982). *The ethics of social research.* 2 vols. New York: Springer-Verlag.

Simons, H. (1987). *Getting to know schools in a democracy.* London: Falmer.

Simons, M. (1991, April 6). Catalan is spoken here (Do you hear, Madrid?). *New York Times*, p. A6.

Sjoberg, G. (1975). Politics, ethics, and evaluation research. In M. Guttentag & E. Struening (Eds.), *Handbook of evaluation research* (Vol. 2, pp. 50-75). Beverly Hills, CA: Sage.

Smith, J. K. (1983). Quantitative versus interpretive: The problem of conducting social inquiry. In E. R. House (Ed.), *New directions for program evaluation: Vol. 19. Philosophy of evaluation* (pp. 27-51). San Francisco: Jossey-Bass.

Smith, N. L. (1989). The Weiss-Patton debate: Illumination of the fundamental concerns. *Evaluation Practice, 10*(1), 5-13.

Stake, R. E. (1986). *Quieting reform: Social science and social action in an urban youth reform.* Champaign: University of Illinois Press.

Starr, P. (1982). *The social transformation of American medicine.* New York: Basic Books.

Steele, J. (1988, May). *Using measures of student outcomes and growth to improve college programs.* Paper presented at the National Forum of the Association for Institutional Research, Phoenix, AZ.

Stufflebeam, D. L. (1982). A next step: Discussion to consider unifying the ERS and Joint Committee standards. In P. H. Rossi (Ed.), *New directions for program evaluation: Vol. 15. Standards for evaluation practice* (pp. 27-36). San Francisco: Jossey-Bass.

Stufflebeam, D. L. (1991). Professional standards and ethics for evaluators. In M. W. McLaughlin & D. C. Phillips (Eds.), *Evaluation and education: At quarter century* (pp. 249-282). Chicago: University of Chicago Press.

Suchman, E. A. (1967). *Evaluative research.* New York: Russell Sage.

Sumner, W. G. (1960). *Folkways.* New York: Mentor. (Original work published 1906)

Thomas, W. I., & Znariecki, F. (1918, 1927). *The Polish peasant in Europe and America* (Vol. I and II). New York: Alfred Knopf.

Tiller, T. (1990). Evaluation in a decentralised school system: Where do we stand? Where are we headed? In M. Granheim, M. Kogan, & U. Lundgren (Eds.), *Evaluation as policymaking: Introducing evaluation into a national decentralised educational system* (pp. 219-233). London: Jessica Kingsley.

Toulmin, S. (1972). *Human understanding.* Princeton, NJ: Princeton University Press.

Travers, R. M. W. (1983). *How research has changed American schools: A history from 1840 to the present.* Kalamazoo, MI: Mythos Press.

Tyler, R. (1983). A rationale for program evaluation. In G. F. Madaus, M. Scriven, & D. L. Stufflebeam (Eds.), *Evaluation models* (pp. 67-78). Boston: Kluwer-Nijhoff.

Veblen, T. (1957). *The higher learning in America.* New York: Sagamore Press. (Original work published 1918)

Vislie, L. (1990). Evaluation and political governing in a decentralised educational system. In M. Granheim, M. Kogan, & U. Lundgren (Eds.), *Evaluation as policymaking: Introducing evaluation into a national decentralised educational system* (pp. 197-210). London: Jessica Kingsley.

Wallin, E. (1990). Some notes on a Norwegian evaluation programme. In M. Granheim, M. Kogan, & U. Lundgren (Eds.), *Evaluation as policymaking: Introducing evaluation into a national decentralised educational system* (pp. 172-178). London: Jessica Kingsley.

Weiler, H. (1990). Decentralised evaluation in educational governance: An exercise in contradiction? In M. Granheim, M. Kogan, & U. Lundgren (Eds.), *Evaluation as policymaking: Introducing evaluation into a national decentralised educational system* (pp. 42-68). London: Jessica Kingsley.

Weiss, C. H. (1983a). The stakeholder approach to evaluation: Origins and promise. In A. Bryk (Ed.), *Stakeholder-based evaluation* (pp. 3-14). San Francisco: Jossey-Bass.

Weiss, C. H. (1983b). Toward the future of stakeholder approaches in evaluation. In A. Bryk (Ed.), *Stakeholder-based evaluation* (pp. 83-96). San Francisco: Jossey-Bass.

Weiss, C. H. (1988). Evaluation for decisions: Is anybody there? Does anybody care? *Evaluation Practice, 9*(1), 5-19.

Weiss, C. H. (1991). Evaluation research in the political context. In M. W. McLaughlin & D. C. Phillips (Eds.), *Evaluation and education: At quarter century* (pp. 211-231). Chicago: University of Chicago Press.

Williams, J. E. (1989). *A numerical taxonomy of evaluation theory and practice* (Mimeo). Los Angeles: University of California at Los Angeles, Graduate School of Education.

Wills, G. (1990). *Under God: Religion and American politics.* New York: Simon & Schuster.

Wolfe, A. (1989). *Whose keeper? Social science and moral obligation.* Berkeley and Los Angeles: University of California Press.

Index

About the Author

Ernest R. House is a Professor in the School of Education at the University of Colorado at Boulder. His primary interests are evaluation, innovation, and policy. He has been a visiting scholar at the University of California at Los Angeles; Harvard University; the University of New Mexico; and in England, Spain, and Sweden. His books include *The Politics of Educational Innovation, Survival in the Classroom* (with S. Lapan), *Evaluating with Validity,* and *Jesse Jackson and the Politics of Charisma.* He is the 1989 recipient (with W. Madura) of the Harold E. Lasswell Prize for the article contributing most to the theory and practice of the policy sciences and the 1990 recipient of the Lazarsfeld Award for Evaluation Theory, presented by the American Evaluation Association.